HIP

SPANISH-ENGLISH
ENGLISH-SPANISH

(Latin American)

HIPPOCRENE COMPACT DICTIONARY

SPANISH-ENGLISH
ENGLISH-SPANISH
(Latin American)

Ila Warner

HIPPOCRENE BOOKS
New York

Third Printing, 1999.

For information, address:
HIPPOCRENE BOOKS, INC.
171 Madison Avenue
New York, NY 10016

ISBN 0-7818-0497-3

Printed in the United States of America.

CONTENTS

ACKNOWLEDGMENTS

The very best way to guarantee authenticity of language usage is to consult the people who actually speak the language in the manner of their respective countries. Thus, the people who have been consulted in the elaboration of this dictionary include students, housewives, soccer players and ambassadors from the Spanish-speaking countries of this hemisphere.

For their help with both language usage and information about cuisine I would specifically like to thank the following:

Juan Pedro Amestoy, Uruguayan Ambassador to Mexico; Alberto Cazorla Talleri, Peruvian Ambassador to Mexico; General (Ret.) Nelson Herrera, Ecuadoran Ambassador to Mexico; Professor Abelardo Rodas Barrios, Press Secretary of the Embassy of Guatemala in Mexico; Embassy of the Dominican Republic in Mexico; Embassy of Panama in Mexico; Embassy of Nicaragua in Mexico; Consulate of Cuba in Veracruz; Lili McAvoy, of Puerto Rico; Nelda Aguirre de Wong, of Cuban descent; Jorge Aquino Sánchez, of Cuba; Carlos Alberto Poblete Jofre, of Chile; Dennisa A. Ramírez Quiroga, of Bolivia; Sully Mata of Venezuela; Oscar

Valenzuela, of Argentina; Winston Hyde, of Honduras; Angela Amaya de Vigil, of El Salvador.

And finally, I owe a heartfelt "gracias" to Professor Ricardo Pérez Corro, Rosario Mármol de Kieszenia, Xóchitl Ortíz Martínez and Rogelio Juárez Zenteno for their excellent help with revision and word processing.

ABOUT THIS DICTIONARY

In my book, *Hippocrene's Language and Travel Guide to Mexico*, I include a section entitled "The Dictionary: Friend or Foe?" In it, I point out that dictionaries typically provide long and complicated entries full of grammatical and idiomatic detail which are only meaningful to those who already have a knowledge of the language. This dictionary, on the other hand, presents only the most essential information and in the simplest manner possible.

The following brief explanation of how the dictionary is organized should help maximize its usefulness.

Selection of Words

Words were selected with three areas in mind:

1) Common words in general

2) Words important to travelers

3) Words useful to the person traveling on business

For ease in locating these words and phrases, every useful variation is listed as a separate entry. Such idioms as "be hungry" and such common phrases as "good morning" will be found under B for "be" and G for "good."

Pronunciation

Pronunciation is presented here in a purely phonetic manner making it unnecessary for the user to be acquainted with any type of system of symbols. The accent marks indicate the syllable on which the stress falls.

In the Spanish-speaking world, just as in the English-speaking world, there are variations in pronunciation from one region to another. The pronunciation found in this dictionary is what is generally considered to be "standard."

Grammar

Fine points of grammar have been studiously avoided. Gender of nouns, for example, has not been included on the assumption that most users will not be overly concerned about the agreement of adjectives and nouns.

Parts of speech, however, are included as they seriously affect the meanings of words. For example, as a noun the word *strike* means a "work stoppage," while as a verb it means "to hit."

Spanish verbs that appear with the word se at the end are reflexive, i.e. reflect the action back on the speaker. This grammar detail, of necessity, has been included as it is often essential to meaning. No attempt, however, has been made to explain the complexities of its forms.

Meanings of Words

Meanings of words have been limited to the commonest ones. For example, the meaning given for *caballero*, is "gentleman" and is a valuable entry for those seeking the men's room. That the word also means "knight" is quite useless information for most people passing through Latin America.

Whenever possible the first meaning in each entry is a standard word understood in most parts of Latin America. Common usages specific to a particular country or region follow and are labeled by geographic area. A list of the abbreviations used is found on page 17.

No attempt has been made to label words as standard, colloquial, slang, etc. For example, a number of words appear, without label, that are in common usage in Argentina and come from a type of underworld slang known as *Lunfardo*. The only rule of thumb in selecting the meanings to be included was that the words reflect *what people say*.

As a final comment I would like to point out that regional usage is extremely varied in Latin America, often differing from one part of the same country to another. So the user of this dictionary should in no way consider this work as exhaustive in this regard.

-The author

Sobre la pronunciación del inglés

El sistema de sonido del idioma inglés es complejo y difícil en comparación con el del español. Es por eso que mucha gente de habla española se quejan, con justificación, de que el inglés se escribe en una manera y se pronuncia en otra.

El *alfabeto* inglés tiene veintiseis letras, pero el *dioma* inglés consiste de 40 a 50 diferentes unidades de sonidos representadas por letras solas o por combinaciones de las 26 letras del abecedario.

Igual que el español, las letras del alfabeto inglés están divididas en dos tipos: Las consonantes y las vocales. Un buen número de consonantes en inglés se asemejan a las de español y no causan problema serio de pronunciación. La pronunciación de las vocales, sin embargo, es mucho más variada y sutil.

Aquí hay algunos de los sonidos más comunes en inglés:

Las vocales

A Como la A española. Ejem. far /far/ lejos
La A breve. Ejem. have /jav/ tener
Como EI. Ejem. say /sei/ decir

E Como la E española. Ejem. pencil /pén-sl/ lápiz
La E corta. Ejem. men /men/ hombres
Como la I española. Ejem. he /ji/ él
La E al final de las palabras normalmente es muda.

I Como en español. Ejem. fix /fiks/ arreglar
Una I más larga. Ejem. clinic /klí-nik/ clínica
El sonido AI. Ejem. ivory /ái-vor-i/ marfil

O Como la O española. Ejem. come /kom/ venir
El sonido OA. Ejem. or /oar/ o

U Como una O breve. Ejem. tub /tob/ bañera
Como el diptongo IU en español. Ejem. union /iú-nion/ unión.
Como la E española. Ejem. purse/pers/ bolsa

Las consonantes

B Más fuerte que en español. Es muda cuando se encuentra después de la M o antes de la T Ejem. comb /koum/ peine; debt /det/ deuda

C Como la K. Ejem. come /kom/ venir
A veces como S. Ejem. city /sít-i/ ciudad
Siempre como la S en la terminación *ice*. Ejem. service /sér-vis/ servicio

D Más fuerte que en español.
Como T en la forma del tiempo pasado que termina en *ed*.

F Más fuerte que en español.

G A veces igual que en español. Ejem. gift /guift/ regalo
A veces parecido a la Y en español. Ejem. general /yén-er-al/ general.

GH Al final de una palabra se pronuncia como F. Ejem. cough /kof/ tos

H A veces como J en español. Ejem. he /ji/ él
A veces es muda como en español. Ejem. honest /ón-est/ honesto

J Como la Y en español. Ejem. just /yost/ justo

K Es fuerte en la mayoría de palabras. Ejem. key /ki/ llave
Es muda antes de la N. Ejem. know /nou/ saber

PH Como la F en español. Ejem. photograph /fóu-to-graf/ fotógrafo

W Como UA. Ejem. water /uá-tr/ agua

Y Como la Y en *ya*. Ejem. yes /yes/ sí

Z Suena más fuerte que la S. Ejem. zipper /dzi-per/ cierre

La pronunciación de las consonantes L, M, N, P, Q, R, S, T y V se asemeja mucho a la del español.

Desafortunadamente hay sonidos en inglés que sencillamente no existen en español y, por eso, no se puede imitarlos usando sílabas españolas. Existen varios sistemas para presentar la pronunciación del inglés en forma figurada, por ejemplo, el sistema Merriam-Webster y el Alfabeto Fonético Internacional. Estos sistemas tienen la ventaja de poder representar los sonidos con bastante exactitud, pero tienen la desventaja de que la persona que usa el diccionario forzosamente tiene que aprender el sistema primero.

Este diccionario presenta la pronunciación del inglés en una forma figurada que no recurre al uso de símbolos. Esta transcripción fonética le ayudará al usuario a conseguir una pronunciación aproximada, aunque no exacta, de los sonidos.

Para dominar el sistema de sonido del inglés, es esencial oír y practicar intensamente el idioma hablado. Pero siguiendo cuidadosamente las transcripciones en este diccionario, dando atención especial a las consonantes finales de las palabras, el usuario debe poder aproximarse a la pronunciación correcta y ser entendido relativamente bien.

Brief Guide to Pronouncing Spanish

The sound system of the Spanish language is relatively simple. For example, with limited exceptions, each vowel has a single sound as follows:

Vowels

A The sound of a in "father"
E The sound of a in "date"
I The sound of e in "even"
O The sound of o in the exclamation "Oh!"
U The sound of oo in "pool"

Consonants

Many Spanish consonants are similar to those in English. Those that call for further explanation are as follows:

B and V Both are pronounced alike, but they each have two different pronunciations depending on where they fall in a word or sentence. B or V at the beginning of a sentence or phrase sounds like the B in "bird." B or V between vowels has a soft sound.

C Sounds like S before E and I. Sounds like K before A, O and U. **G** Sounds like the English H before E and I. Sounds like G in "go" before A, O and U.

H Always silent. No exceptions.

J Approximately like the English H

LL Like the Y in "yes."

Ñ Like the NY in "canyon."

Q Q is always followed by a U in Spanish and is pronounced like the English K.

X Before a consonant it sounds like the English S. Before a vowel, like the English word "eggs."

Z Like the English S.

W and K These letters are not part of the Spanish alphabet. They are only found in foreign words such as "whisky" and "kilo."

Stress

In words bearing a written accent, the accent indicates the syllable to be stressed. The stress falls naturally on the next-to-last syllable in unaccented words ending in a vowel, n or s. If a word ends in a consonant other than n or s, the stress falls on the last syllable.

The phonetic pronunciation presented in this dictionary is for what is considered standard Spanish. The English-speaker traveling through Latin America, however, will encounter many variations in pronunciation. In most cases this should raise no serious obstacle to communication.

Parts of Speech / Partes de la Oración

adjective	*adj.*	adjetivo
adverb	*adv.*	adverbio
article	*art.*	artículo
conjunction	*conj.*	conjunción
imperative	*imper.*	imperativo
interjection	*interj.*	interjección
interrogative	*interj.*	interrogativo
noun	*n.*	nombre
preposition	*prep.*	preposición
pronoun	*pron.*	pronombre
verb	*v.*	verbo

Countries and Regions / Países y Regiones

Andes	*Andes*	Andes
Argentina	*Arg.*	Argentina
Bolivia	*Bol.*	Bolivia
Caribbean	*Carib.*	Caribe
Central America	*CA*	Centroamérica
Chile	*Chi.*	Chile

Colombia	*Col.*	Colombia
Costa Rica	*CR*	Costa Rica
Cuba	*Cuba*	Cuba
Dominican Republic	*Dom.*	República Dominicana
Ecuador	*Ec.*	Ecuador
Guatemala	*Gua.*	Guatemala
Honduras	*Hon.*	Honduras
Latin America	*LA*	Latinoamérica
Mexico	*Mex.*	Méjioco
Nicaragua	*Nic.*	Nicaragua
Panama	*Pan.*	Panamá
Peru	*Pe.*	Perú
Puerto Rico	*PR*	Puerto Rico
River Plate	*RP*	Río Plata
South America	*SA*	Sudamérica
Uruguay	*Uru.*	Uruguay
Venezuela	*Ven.*	Venezuela

Other Abbreviations / Otras abreviaturas

commercial	*com.* comercial
electrical	*elec.* eléctrico
grammatical	*gram.* gramatical
legal	*leg.* legal
medical	*med.* médico
military	*mil.* militar
political	*pol.* político
religious	*rel.* religioso
zoological	*zool.* zoológico

The Cuisines of Hispanic America

One of the pleasures of traveling in the Hispanic countries is sampling their various cuisines. And although there tend to be similarities in the dishes of the Spanish-speaking countries, there are also many important differences.

The following pages aim to provide the traveler with the names in Spanish, the phonetic pronunciation and the description of the most typical dishes in the various Spanish-speaking countries of this hemisphere.

ARGENTINA

Bife a caballo (bée-fay ah cah-báh-yoh) - Steak with fried eggs and potatoes.
Parrillado (pah-ree-yá-doh) - Mixed grill of steak, organ meat and various types of sausages.
Chorizo (choh-rée-soh) - Sirloin steak.

Popular seafoods include:
merluza (mayr-lóo-sah) hake
cholgas (chóhl-gahs), large clams
calamaretes (cah-lah-mah-ráy-tays), fried squid

BOLIVIA

Empanada salteña (aym-pah-náh-dah sahl-táy-nyah) - Mixture of ground meat or chicken, olives, raisins, potatoes and hot sauce baked in dough.

Lomo montado (lóh-moh mohn-táh-doh) - Steak topped with fried eggs.

Picante de pollo (pee-cán-tay day póh-yoh) - Fried chicken with potatoes, rice and a salad containing hot peppers.

Lechón al horno (lay-chóhn ahl óhr-noh) - Roast suckling pig, served on special occasions.

CHILE

Cazuela de ave (cah-soo-áy-lah day áh-vay) - Chicken stew with broth.

Empanadas de carne (ehm-pah-náh-dahs day cáhr-nay) - Meat pies. filled with chopped meat, fried onions and spices, or spiced cheeses.

Pastel de choclo (pahs-táyl day chóh-cloh) - Casserole of corn, ground beef, chicken, raisins, onions and hard-boiled eggs.

Flan (flahn) - The ubiquitous dessert of the Spanish-speaking world, an egg custard usually topped with a burnt sugar sauce.

Tortas de milhojas (tóhr-tahs day meel-óh-hahs)- Cakes made of dough flavored with the yarrow herb.

The above excellent dishes are much enhanced

when accompanied with a fine Chilean wine. Highly recommended are the Santa Carolina and the Casillero del Diablo.

COLOMBIA

Peto (páy-toh) - Corn and milk soup.

Ajiaco con pollo (ah-hee-áh-coh cohn póh-yoh) - Chicken and potato soup.

Bandeja paisa (bahn-dáy-hah páh-ee-sah) - Beans, rice, fried pork rinds, corn cakes, fried plantains, fried eggs and shredded beef.

Guarapo (gwah-ráh-poh) - Fermented cane juice.

COSTA RICA

Gallo pinto (gáh-yoh péen-toh) - Black beans and rice.

Arroz con pollo (ah-róhs cohn póh-yoh) - Chicken and rice.

Casado (cah-sáh-doh) - Stew made of chicken, beef or pork with vegetables such as green bananas or squash.

Pejibayes (pay-hee-báh-yays) - Palm fruit, boiled and served with mayonnaise.

Guaro (gwáh-roh) - National alcoholic drink made of sugar cane.

CUBA

Potaje de... garbanzos, colorados, judías (poh-táh-hay day... gahr-báhn-sohs, coh-loh-ráh-dohs, hoo-dée-ahs) - Thick chickpea or bean soups, Spanish-style.

Arroz con pollo (ah-róhs cohn póh-yoh) - Chicken in yellow rice.

Moros y cristianos (móh-rohs ee crees-tee-áhn-nohs) - Black beans and white rice.

Congrí oriental (cohn-grée oh-ree-ayn-táhl) - Black or red beans mixed with rice.

Lechón asado (lay-chóhn ah-sáh-doh) - Suckling pig roasted over a pit, a holiday specialty.

Mojito (moh-hée-toh) - Favorite summer drink made with rum, lime and fresh mint, a sort of rum julep.

DOMINICAN REPUBLIC

Bandeja dominicana (bahn-dáy-hah doh-mee-nee -cáh-nah) - Rice, beans and meat platter.

Sancocho (sahn-cóh-choh) - Stew made with yucca, plantains and seven different kinds of meat.

Manjú (mahn-hóo) - Purée of plantain.

ECUADOR

Locro (lóh-croh) - Cheese and potato soup.

Humitas (oo-mée-tahs) - Com tamales.

Llapingachos (yah-peen-gáh-chohs) - A mashed potato and cheese dish.

Paico (páh-ee-coh) - Local drink made of lemon and aguardiente, a cane licquor.

Pilsener and Cerveza Andina (sayr-váy-sah ahn-dée -nah) - Excellent local beers.

EL SALVADOR

Sopa de res (sóh-pah day rays) - Beef vegetable soup.

Pupusas (poo-póo-sahs) - Thick fried tortillas stuffed with ground pork.

Yuca cocida (yóo-cah coh-sée-dah) - Boiled yucca fried with pork rind.

Plátanos maduros fritos con crema (pláh-tah-nohs mah-dóo-rohs frée-tohs cohn cráy-mah) - Fried ripe bananas with cream.

GUATEMALA

Tamales (tah-máh-lays) - All types, ranging from meat or cheese to sweet. Large, wrapped in the local pasham leaves.

Jocom (hoh-cóhm) - Sauce made of pureed vegetables (lettuce, celery, coriander, etc.) and thickened with corn flour.

Fiambre (fee-áhm-bray) - Dish for special occasions containing various types of sausage, bacon, shrimp, sardines and salmon. Served with pickled vegetables.

Rellenitos de plátano (ray-yay-née-tohs day pláh-tah -noh) - Croquette-style dessert made of plantain pureed with sugar, cinnamon and bread crumbs. Stuffed with sweetened black beans, fried and topped with cream sauce.

Boj (bohj) - Native drink made of fermented corn.

HONDURAS

Tapado (tah-páh-doh) - A fish, salt beef or conch stew made of plantain, sweet potato, pumpkin, yucca, yam and arum in a coconut milk gravy. Of African origin.

Agua de... nance, jobo, tamarindo (áh-gwah day..náhn-say, hóh-boh, tah-mah-réen-doh) - Popular drinks made of local fruits and water.

Pastel de... yuca, camote, plátanos maduros (pahs-táyl day.. yóo-cah, cah-móh-tay, pláh-tah-nohs mah-dóo-rohs) - Heavy pot cake made with grated yucca, sweet potatoes, ripe bananas or mangoes.

MEXICO

Tortillas (tohr-tée-yahs) - Flat, thin pancakes, made of flour in the north and of corn in the south. Are the basis for:

Tacos (táh-cohs) - Soft tortillas stuffed with meat or

chicken.

Tostadas (tohs-táh-dahs) - Fried tortillas topped with meat, beans, cheese, tomato and lettuce.

Quesadillas (kay-sah-dée-yahs) - Tortillas stuffed with cheese, then fried.

Chilaquiles (chee-lah-kéy-lays) - Strips of corn tortilla baked with chilli sauce and cheese.

Tamales (tah-máh-lays) - Cornmeal or flour dough filled with chicken or meat, wrapped in corn husks or banana leaves and steamed. Sometimes made with sweet fillings.

Regional favorites include:

From Jalisco, **pozole** (poh-sóh-lay) - Hominy and pork soup garnished with tortilla chips, lettuce, onions and hot sauce.

From Puebla, **mole poblano** (móh-lay poh bláh-noh) - Turkey or chicken in a sauce of bitter chocolate, chilies and spices. Sprinkled with sesame seeds.

From the Yucatán, **pollo pibil** (póh-yoh pee-béel) or **cochinito pibil** (coh-chee-née-toh pee-béel) - Chicken or pork in a sauce of orange juice, garlic and the regional spice **achiote**, wrapped in banana leaves and baked in a pit.

From Veracruz, **huachinango a la veracruzana** (ooah-chee-náhn-goh' ah lah vay-rah-croo-sáh-nah) - Grilled red snapper in a sauce of onions, chili, olives and capers.

Tequila (tay-kéy-lah) and **mezcal** (mays-cáhl) - Hard licquors, both made from the sap of the maguey plant.

NICARAGUA

Vijorón (vee-hoh-róhn) - Pork rind with yucca.

Nacatemal (nah-cah-tay-máhl) - Meat tamales with salad on top. Also sweet tamales.

Mondongo (mohn-dóhn-goh) - Tripe soup.

Chicha de maíz (chée-chah day mah-ées) - Soft drink made of corn.

PANAMA

Cebiche (say-vée-chay) - Fish marinated in lime, onions and chili.

Sancocho (sahn-cóh-choh) - Chicken or meat stew with vegetables.

Carimañolas (cah-ree-mah-nyóh-lahs) - Meat, chicken or cheese turnovers.

Palacones de plátano (pah-lah-cóh-nays day pláh-tah-noh) - Friedgreen plantains.

PARAGUAY

Sopa paraguaya (sóh-pah pah-rah-gwáy-yah) - Mashed corn soup with cheese, milk, eggs and onion.

Soo-yosopy (soo-yoh-sóh-pee) - Hamburger and cornmeal soup.
Chipa (chée-pah) - Cheese cornbread.
Parrillada (pah-ree-yáh-dah) - Mixed grill.

PERU

Cebiche (say-vée-chay) - Fish marinated in lime juice, onions, chili and other condiments.
Lomo saltado (lóh-moh sahl-táh-doh) - Stir-fried sirloin, grilled onions and tomatoes, served with rice or french fries.
Tallarín saltado (tal-yah-réen sahl-táh-doh) - Noodles with various kinds of meat.
Cau cau (cáh-oo cáh-oo) - Tripe stew with diced potatoes, peas, coriander, turmeric and hot sauce.
Chicha (chée-chah) - The most popular alcoholic beverage of Peru, usually made of fermented corn, but sometimes of peanuts or manioc.

PUERTO RICO

Arroz con pollo (ah-róhs cohn póh-yoh) - Saffron rice with chicken.
Asopao (ah-soh-páh-oh) - Soupy rice stew with chicken or shellfish.
Pernil (payr-néel) - Roast pork.
Arroz con gandules (ah-róhs cohn gahn-dóo-lays) -

Rice with pigeon peas.

Tostones (tohs-tóh-nays) - Sliced green bananas flattened and deep fried.

URUGUAY

Matambre relleno hervido (mah-táhm-bray ray-yáy-noh ayr-vée-doh) - Boiled beef stuffed with either vegetables or bread crumb dressing.

Puchero (poo-cháy-roh) - Slow-cooked beef stew with varied root vegetables, pumpkin, corn and cabbage.

Niños envueltos (née-nyohs ayn-vwáyl-tohs) - Steak rolls stuffed with bacon and bread crumb dressing, then sautéed in milk.

VENEZUELA

Tequeños (tay-káy-nyohs) - Mild cheese wrapped in dough and deep-fried.

Arepas (ah-ráy-pahs) - Deep-fried bun made of cornmeal, sometimes stuffed with cheese.

Hervido (ayr-vée-doh) - Soup made of beef or chicken and root vegetables.

Hallaca (ah-yáh-cah) - Mixture of cornmeal with meat, peppers, raisins, olives, onions and spices, wrapped in banana leaves and boiled.

ENGLISH - SPANISH

- A -

a /ei/ *art.* un; una
abandon /a-bán-don/ *v.* abandonar
abdomen /áb-do-men/ *n.* abdomen
ability /a-bíl-i-ti/ *n.* habilidad
able /éi-bl/ *adj.* capaz
abnormal /ab-nór-mal/ *adj.* anormal
aboard /a-bórd/ *adv.* a bordo
abolish /a-ból-ish/ *v.* abolir
abortion /a-bór-shon/ *n.* aborto
about /a bóut/ *adv.* alrededor; *prep.* acerca de
above /a-bóv/ *adv.* arriba; *prep.* sobre
abroad /a-bród/ *adv.* en el extranjero
absolute /áb-so-liut/ *adj.* absoluto
absolutely /ab-so-liút-li/ *adv.* absolutamente
absorb /ab-sórb/ *v.* absorber
abstract /áb-strakt/ *adj.* abstracto
abundant /a-bón-dant/ *adj.* abundante
accelerate /ak-sél-er-eit/ *v.* acelerar
accent /ák-sent/ *n.* acento
accept /ak-sépt/ *v.* aceptar
accident /ák-si-dent/ *n.* accidente
according to /a-kórd-ing tu/ *prep.* según
account /a-kóunt/ *n.* cuenta
accountant /a-káunt-ant/ *n.* contador
accuse /a-kiús/ *v.* acusar
accustom /a-kós-tom/ *v.* acostumbrar

ache /eik/ *n.* dolor; *v.* doler
acid /ás-id/ *n., adj.* ácido
acknowledge /ak-nól-ech/ *v.* reconocer
acknowledgment /ak-nól-ech-ment/ *n.* reconocimiento
across /a-krós/ *prep.* al través de
act /akt/ *n.* acto; *v.* actuar
action /ák-shon/ *n.* acción
active /ák-tiv/ *adj.* activo
activity /ak-tív-i-ti/ *n.* actividad
actor /ák-tor/ *n.* actor
actual /ák-tiul/ *adj.* real
actually /ák-tiu-li/ *adv.* realmente
addict /á-dikt/ *n.* adicto
addiction /a-dík-shon/ *n.* adicción
addition /a-dí-shon/ *n.* afición; hábito morboso
additional /a-di-shon-l/ *adj.* adicional
address /á-dres/ *n.* dirección
adequate /ád-i-kueit/ *adj.* adecuado
adjective /ád-ye-tif/ *n.* adjetivo
administer /ad-mín-is-ter/ *v.* administrar
admire /ad-máir/ *v.* admirar
admission /ad-mí-shon/ *n.* admisión
admit /ad-mít/ *v.* admitir
adult /á-dolt/ *n.* adulto
advance /ad-váns/ *n.* avance; *v.* avanzar
advantage /ad-ván-tich/ *n.* ventaja
adverb /ád-verb/ *n.* adverbio
advertisement /ad-ver-táis-ment/ *n.* anuncio comer-

cial
advice /ad-váis/ *n.* consejo
advise /ad-váiz/ *v.* aconsejar
affair /a-fér/ *n.* asunto
afford /a-fórd/ *v.* tener recursos para
after /áft-er/ *adv.* después; *prep.* después de
afternoon /aft-er-nún/ *n.* tarde
afterwards /áft-er-uerds/ *adv.* después
again /a-guéin/ *adv.* otra vez
against /a-guéinst/ *prep.* contra
age /eich/ *n.* edad
agency /éi-yen-si/ *n.* agencia
agent /éi-yent/ *n.* agente
ago /a-góu/ *adv.* hace ... (time period)
agree /a-grí/ *v.* estar de acuerdo
agreement /a-grí-ment/ *n.* acuerdo
ahead /a-jéd/ *adv.* adelante
aid /eid/ *n.* ayuda; *v.* ayudar
air /er/ *n.* aire
air conditioning /er kon-di-shon-ing/ *n.* aire acondicionado; *Mex.* clima
airplane /ér-plein/ *n.* avión
airport /ér-port/ *n.* aeropuerto
alarm /a-lárm/ *n.* alarma; *v.* poner sobre aviso
alarm clock /a-lárm klok/ *n.* despertador
alcohol /ál-ko jol/ *n.* alcohol
alert /a-lért/ *adj.* alerta; *v.* poner sobre aviso
alien /éi-lien/ *n., adj.* extranjero
alive /a-láiv/ *adj.* vivo

all /ol/ *adj., pron.* todo
all at once /ol at uans/ *adv.* de golpe
alley /ál-i/ *n.* callejón
allow /a-láu/ *v.* permitir
all right /ol rait/ está bien
almond /ál-mond/ *n.* almendra
almost /ól-moust/ *adv.* casi
alone /a-lóun/ *adj.* solo; *adv.* solamente
along /a-lóng/ *adv.* a lo largo
aloud /a-láud/ *adv.* en voz alta
already /ol-réd-i/ *adv.* ya
also /ól-sou/ *adv.* también
although /ol-dóu/ *conj.* aunque; sin embargo
altitude /ál-ti-tiud/ *n.* altura
always /ól-ueis/ *adv.* siempre
ambassador /am bás-a-dor/ *n.* embajador
amber /ám-br/ *n.* ámbar
ambulance /ám-biu-lans/ *n.* ambulancia
among /a-móng/ *prep.* entre
amount /a-móunt/ *n.* cantidad
ample /ám-pl/ *adj.* amplio
amplify /ám-pli-fai/ *v.* amplificar
amuse /a-miús/ *v.* divertir
amusing /a-miús-ing/ *adj.* divertido
an /an/ *art.* un; una
analysis /a-nál-i-sis/ *n.* análisis
analyze /án-a-lais/ *v.* analizar
anchovy /án-chou-vi/ *n.* anchoa
ancient /én-shent/ *adj.* antiguo

and /and/ *conj.* y; e
anger /án-guer/ *n.* enojo; coraje
angry /án-gri/ *adj.* enojado
animal /án-i-mal/ *n.* animal
ankle /án-kl/ *n.* tobillo
announce /a-náuns/ *v.* anunciar
announcement /a-náuns-ment/ *n.* aviso; anuncio
annoy /a-nói/ *v.* molestar; fastidiar
annual /á-niul/ *adj.* anual
another /a-nó-der/ *adj.* otro
answer /án-ser/ *n.* respuesta; contestación; *v.* contestar
antique /an-tik/ *n.* antigüedad; *adj.* antiguo
antiseptic /an-ti-sép-tik/ *adj.* antiséptico
anxious /ánk-shos/ *adj.* ansioso
any /én-i/ *pron., adj.* cualquier; alguno
anybody /én-i-bo-di/ *pron.* alguien
anyhow /én-i-jou/ *adv.* de cualquier modo
anything /én-i-thing/ *pron.* cualquier cosa
anyway /én-i-uei/ *adv.* de cualquier modo
anywhere /én-i-uer/ *adv.* donde quiera
apart /a-párt/ *adv.* aparte
apartment /a-párt-ment/ *n.* apartamento; *Mex.* departamento
apiece /a-pís/ *adv.* por persona
apologize /a-pól-a-yais/ *v.* disculpar
apology /a-pól-a-yi/ *n.* disculpa
apostrophe /a-pás-tro-fi/ *n.* apóstrofe
apparent /a-péi-rent/ *adj.* obvio; evidente

appear /a-pír/ *v.* aparecer
appearance /a-pir ans/ *n.* presentación; apariencia
applause /a-plós/ *n.* aplauso
apple /áp-l/ *n.* manzana
appliance /a-plái-ans/ *n.* aparato
apply /a-plái/ *v.* aplicar; solicitar
appointment /a-póint-ment/ *n.* cita
appreciate /a-prí-shi-eit/ *n.* apreciar
approach /a-próch/ *v.* acercarse
appropriate /a-próu-pri-et/ *adj.* apropiado
approve /a-prúv/ *v.* aprobar
approximate /a-próx-a-met/ *adj.* aproximado
apricot /éi-pri-kot/ *n.* albaricoque; *Arg.* groncho; *Chi., Uru.* damasco; *Mex.* chabacano
arch /arch/ *n.* arco
area /é-ri-a/ *n.* área
argue /ár-guiu/ *v.* discutir
argument /ár-guiu-ment/ *n.* discusión
arm /arm/ *n.* brazo; (mil.) arma; *v.* armar(se)
armchair /árm-cher/ *n.* butaca; sillón
around /a-ráund/ *adv.* alrededor
arrange /a-réinch/ *v.* arreglar
arrival /a-rái-vol/ *n.* llegada
arrive /a-ráiv/ *v.* llegar
art /art/ *n.* arte
article /ár-tik-l/ *n.* artículo
artificial /ar-ta-físh-ol/ *adj.* artificial
artist /ár-tist/ *n.* artista
as /as/ *conj.* como

ashamed /a-shéimd/ *adj.* avergonzado
ashtray /ásh-trei/ *n.* cenicero
ask /ask/ *v.* preguntar
ask for /ask for/ *v.* pedir
asparagus /as-pér-gos/ *n.* espárrago
assets /á-sets/ *n.* capital; valores
assist /a-síst/ *v.* ayudar; auxiliar
assistant /a-síst-ent/ *n.* asistente; ayudante
associate /a-sóu-shit/ *n.* socio
associate /a-sóu-shi-eit/ *v.* asociar
as soon as /as sun as/ tan pronto como
assortment /a-sórt-ment/ *n.* surtido; colección
as well /as uel/ *adv.* también
as well as /as uel as/ así como
at /at/ *prep.* a; en
at home /at joum/ *adv.* en casa
at least /at list/ al menos
at once /at uans/ *adv.* en seguida
attach /a-tách/ *v.* adjuntar; atar
attempt /a-témpt/ *v.* intentar
attend /a-ténd/ *v.* asistir
attention /a-tén-shon/ *n.* atención
at times /at taims/ a veces
attorney /a-tér-ni/ *n.* abogado; *Arg.* boga; *Mex.* licenciado
attract /a-trákt/ *v.* atraer
audience /ó-di-ens/ *n.* público
aunt /ant/ *n.* tía
authentic /o-thén-tik/ *adj.* auténtico

author /ó-thor/ *n.* autor; autora (female)
authority /o-thór-i-ti/ *n.* autoridad
automatic /o-to-mát-ik/ *adj.* automático
autumn /ó-tom/ *n.* otoño
available /a-véil-a-bl/ *adj.* disponible
avenue /áv-a-niu/ *n.* avenida
average /áv-rich/ *n.* promedio
avoid /a-vóid/ *v.* evitar
awake /a-uéik/ *adj.* despierto; *v.* despertar(se)
away /a-uéi/ *adv.* afuera; ausente
awful /ó-ful/ *adj.* terrible; horrible

- B -

baby /béi-bi/ *n.* bebé; nene; *Chi., Ec.* guagua; *Pe.* bebe; *Ven.* chamito
back /bak/ *n.* espalda; *v.* apoyar; *adv.* atrás
backward /bák-uerd/ *adj.* atrasado; *adv.* al revés
bacon /béi-kon/ *n.* tocino
bad /bad/ *adj.* mal; malo
bag /bag/ *n.* saco; bolsa
baggage /bág-ich/ *n.* equipaje
bait /beit/ *n.* carnada; anzuelo
bakery /béik-er-i/ *n.* panadería
ballet /bal-éi/ *n.* ballet; baile
balloon /ba-lún/ *n.* balón; globo
banana /ba-ná-na/ *n.* banana; plátano; *PR* guineo; *Ven.* cambur
bank /bank/ *n.* banco
bankruptcy /bánk-rop-si/ *n.* bancarrota; quiebra
bar /bar/ *n.* bar
barbecue /bár-bi-kiu/ *n. Mex.* barbacoa; *v.* asar un animal entero
barber /bár-ber/ *n.* barbero; *Arg., Mex., Uru.* peluquero
barely /bér-li/ *adv.* escasamente; apenas
bargain /bár-guin/ *n.* ganga; *Arg.* pichincha; *v.* regatear; *Chi.* pelear el precio
bargaining /bár-guin-ing/ *n.* regateo; *Bol.* trato
basis /béi-sis/ *n.* base

basket /bás-kit/ *n.* cesta; canasta
bath /bath/ *n.* baño
bathe /beith/ *v.* bañar; bañarse
bathroom /báth-rum/ *n.* sala de baño; baño
bathtub /báth-tob/ *n.* bañera; *Arg., Cuba* bañadera *Mex.* tina
battery /bá-ter-i/ *n.* batería; pila
be /bi/ *v.* ser; estar
be able /bi éi-bl/ *v.* poder
beach /bich/ *n.* playa
be afraid /bi a-fréid/ *v.* tener miedo
beans (dry) /bins/ *n. Arg., Bol., Chi., Ec., Uru.* porotos; *Bol., Ec.* fréjoles; *Cuba, Mex.* frijoles
beans (green) /bins/ *n. Bol., Uru.* habas; *Chi.* porotos verdes; *Cuba* habichuelas; *Ec.* vainitas; *Mex.* ejotes; *Pe.* fréjoles verdes; *PR* habichuelas tiernas; *RP* chauchas
beautiful /biú-ti-ful/ *adj.* hermoso; bello
beauty shop /biú-ti-shop/ *n.* salón de belleza; peluquería
be born /bi born/ *v.* nacer
because /bi-kós/ *conj.* porque
because of /bi-kós ov/ *prep.* a causa de
become /bi-kóm/ *v.* hacerse
bed /bed/ *n.* cama
bedroom /béd-rum/ *n.* cuarto de dormir; *Arg., Chi.* pieza; *Bol., Ec., Pe.* dormitorio; *Cuba, Uru., Ven.* habitación; *Mex.* recámara; *Uru.* cuarto
beef /bif/ *n.* carne de vaca; carne de res

beefsteak /bíf-steik/ *n.* bistec; *RP* bife
beer /bir/ *n.* cerveza
beet /bit/ *n.* remolacha; *Mex.* betabel; *Bol., Chi., Pe.* betarraga
before /bi-fór/ *prep., adv.* ante; *conj.* antes que; antes de que
beforehand /bi-fór-jend/ *adv.* de antemano
beggar /bég-ar/ *n.* mendigo; pordiosero; *Mex.* limosnero
begin /bi-guín/ *v.* empezar; comenzar
beginning /bi-guín-ing/ *n.* principio; comienzo
behind /bi-jáind/ *prep., adv.* detrás
be hungry /bi jón-gri/ *v.* tener hambre
be in charge /bi in charch/ *v.* estar a cargo
be in fashion /bi in fásh-on/ *v.* estar de moda
believe /bi-lív/ *v.* creer
bell /bel/ *n.* campana; timbre
bellhop /bél-jop/ *n.* botones; *Pe.* conserje
belong /bi-lóng/ *v.* pertenecer
belongings /bi-lóng-ings/ *n.* pertenencias
below /bi-lóu/ *adv.* debajo; *prep.* debajo de
belt /belt/ *n.* cinturón
bench /bench/ *n.* banco; *Mex.* banca
beneath /bi-nith/ *adv.* bajo; debajo; *prep.* debajo de
be on a diet /bi on a dái-et/ *v.* estar de dieta
be right /bi rait/ *v.* tener razón
beside /bi-sáid/ *adv.* junto; *prep.* al lado de
besides /bi-sáids/ *adv.* además; *prep.* además de
be sorry /bi sór-i/ *v.* sentirse

best /best/ *adj.* mejor
bet /bet/ *n.* apuesta; *v.* apostar
be thirsty /bi thérs-ti/ *v.* tener sed
better /bét-er/ *adv.* mejor
between /bi-tuín/ *prep.* entre
beverage /bév-er-ich/ *n.* bebida
be worth /bi uerth/ *v.* valer
be wrong /bi rong/ *v.* equivocarse
beyond /bi-yónd/ *adv.* más allá; *prep.* más allá de
Bible /baí-bl/ *n.* Biblia
bicycle /bái-si-kl/ *n.* bicicleta
big /big/ *adj.* grande
bill /bil/ *n.* cuenta; factura; (money) billete; *Col.* billullo
bill of fare /bil ov fer/ *n.* menú; carta; *Cuba* lista
bird /berd/ *n.* pájaro
birth /berth/ *n.* nacimiento
birthday /bérth-dei/ *n.* cumpleaños
bitter /bít-er/ *adj.* amargo
bitterness /bít-er-nes/ *n.* amargura
black /blak/ *adj.* negro
blanket /blán-ket/ *n.* frazada; colcha; *Bol.* manta; *Mex.* cobija
bleed /blid/ *v.* sangrar; echar sangre
blind /blaind/ *adj.* ciego
block /blok/ *n.* bloque; cuadra; manzana
blond /blond/ *n., adj.* rubio; *Chi.* rucio; *Ec.* suco, bermejo (fair complected); *Mex.* güero; *Pan.* fulo; *Ven.* catire; *Col.* mono

blood /blod/ *n.* sangre
blouse /blaus/ *n.* blusa
blue /blu/ *n., adj.* azul
boat /bout/ *n.* barco
bobby pin /bób-bi pin/ *n. Chi.* pinche; *Ec.* imperdible; *Mex., Uru.* pasador; *Pan.* gancho; *PR* horquilla
body /bód-i/ *n.* cuerpo
boil /boil/ *v.* hervir
bon appétit /boun a-pei-tí/ *interj.* que le aproveche
bone /boun/ *n.* hueso
book /buk/ *n.* libro
bookstore /búk-stor/ *n.* librería
boot /but/ *n.* bota
border /bór-der/ *n.* frontera
born /born/ *adj.* nacido
borrow /bár-ou/ *v.* pedir prestado
both /bouth/ *adj., n., pron.* ambos; los dos
bottle /bót-l/ *n.* botella
bottom /bá-tum/ *n.* fondo
bow /bou/ *n.* lazo
bow /bau/ *n.* proa
bowl /bol/ *n. Arg., Bol., Mex.* tazón; *Ven.* taza
box /baks/ *n.* caja
box office /boks óf-is/ *n.* taquilla
boy /boi/ *n.* niño; chico; muchacho; *Col.* chino
boyfriend /bói-frend/ *n.* novio; Chile, pololo; *Ec., Pe.* enamorado; *Ven.* empate
bracelet /bréis-lit/ *n.* pulsera; *Ven.* brazalete
braid /breid/ *n.* trenza

branch /branch/ *n.* rama; sucursal
brand /brand/ *n.* marca
brass /bras/ *n.* latón
brave /breiv/ *adj.* bravo; valiente
bread /bred/ *n.* pan
break /breik/ *v.* romper
breakfast /brék-fast/ *n.* desayuno
bridge /brich/ *n.* puente
brief /brif/ *adj.* breve
bright /brait/ *adj.* claro; brillante
brilliant /bríl-yant/ *adj.* brillante
bring /bring/ *v.* traer; llevar
broad /brod/ *adj.* ancho
broccoli /brák-o-li/ *n.* bróculi; brécol
broil /broil/ *v.* asar
broken /bróu-quen/ *adj.* roto; quebrado
bronze /brons/ *n.* bronce
brooch /broch/ *n.* broche
brother /bród-er/ *n.* hermano
brother-in-law /bród-er-in-lo/ *n.* cuñado
brown /broun/ *adj.* moreno; pardo; *Arg.* beige; *Mex.* café; *Pe., Uru., Ven.* marrón
brush /brosh/ *n.* cepillo; brocha
brussels sprouts /brós-els sprauts/ *n.* coles de Bruselas
bucket /bók-it/ *n.* balde; *Cuba, Pan.* cubo; *Mex.* cubeta
buckle /bók-l/ *n.* hebilla
buddy /bód-i/ *n. Arg., Bol., Uru.* compinche; *Cuba* so-

cio; *Ec., PR, Ven.* pana; *Mex.* cuate; *Pan.* pasiero; *Pe.* pata

budget /bóch-et/ *n.* presupuesto; *adj.* económico

bug /bog/ *n.* insecto; bicho (vulgar in *PR*)

bulb /bolb/ *n.* bombilla; *Mex.* foco

bureaucracy /biu-rók-ra-si/ *n.* burocracia

burn /bern/ *v.* quemar

bus (city) /bos/ *n. Arg., Bol.* colectivo; *Carib.* guagua; *Ec.* bus; *Col.* buseta; *Mex.* camión; *Pe., Uru.* ómnibus;

bus (intercity) /bos/ *n. Arg.* micro; *Bol.* flota; *Carib, Mex.* autobús; *Ec.* bus; *Pe., Uru.* ómnibus

business /bís-nes/ *n.* negocio

business card /bís-nes kard/ *n.* tarjeta de presentación

businessman /bís-nes-men/ *n.* hombre de negocios

businesswoman /bis-nes-u-man/ *n.* mujer de negocios

bus stop /bos stop/ *n.* parada; *Chi., Col.* paradero

but /bot/ *conj.* pero; sino

butter /bót-er/ *n.* mantequilla; *Arg.* manteca

butterfly /bót-er-flai/ *n.* mariposa

button /bót-n/ *n.* botón

buy /bai/ *v.* comprar

buyer /bái-er/ *n.* comprador

by /bai/ *prep.* por; a; de; con; en

- C -

cab /kab/ *n.* taxi; *Arg.* tacho; *Cuba* máquina; *Uru.* taxímetro
cabbage /káb-ich/ *n.* col; *Mex.* repollo
cabin /káb-in/ *n.* cabaña
cake /keik/ *n. Cuba* cake; *Chi., Ec., Uru.* torta; *Mex.* pastel; *PR* bizcocho
calculate /kál-kiu-leit/ *v.* calcular
calendar /kál-en-der/ *n.* calendario; almanaque
call /kol/ *n.* llamada; *v.* llamar
camera /kám-er-a/ *n.* cámara
camp /kamp/ *n.* campamento; *v.* acampar
can /kan/ *n.* lata; *Ven.* pote; *v.* poder
candle /kán-dl/ *n.* vela
candlestick /kán-del-stik/ *n.* candelero
candy /kán-di/ *n.* dulces; bombones
cane /kein/ *n.* bastón
canoe /ka-nú/ *n.* canoa
canyon /ká-nion/ *n.* cañón
capable /kéi-pa-bl/ *adj.* capaz
cape /keip/ *n.* cabo (land); capa
capital /káp-i-tl/ *n.* capital
car /kar/ *n.* automóvil; auto; carro; coche
carburetor /kár-bo-re-tor/ *n.* carburador
card /kard/ *n.* tarjeta; carta (playing)
care /ker/ *n.* cuidado
care for /ker for/ *n.* cuidar

careful /kér-ful/ *adj.* cuidadoso; cauteloso
cargo /kár-gou/ *n.* carga; cargamento
car horn /kar jorn/ *n.* bocina; *Ec.* pito; *Mex., Uru.* claxon; *Ven.* corneta
carnival /kár-ni-val/ *n.* carnaval
carpet /kár-pet/ *n.* alfombra; tapete
carrot /kár-ot/ *n.* zanahoria
carry /kár-i/ *v.* llevar
cart /kart/ *n.* carro; carreta
cartoon /kar-tún/ *n.* caricatura
case /keis/ *n.* caso
cash /kash/ *n.* efectivo; *Arg.* cash; *v.* cambiar
cashier /kash-ir/ *n.* cajero
cat /kat/ *n.* gato
catalogue /kát-a-log/ *n.* catálogo
catch /katch/ *v.* agarrar; tomar (bus, train, etc.)
catch up /katch op/ *v.* alcanzar
cathedral /ka-thí-dral/ *n.* catedral
catholic /káth-o-lik/ *n., adj.* católico
cauliflower /kó-li-fla-uer/ *n.* coliflor
cause /kos/ *n.* causa; *v.* causar
cave /keiv/ *n.* cueva; caverna
cease /sis/ *v.* cesar; dejar de
ceaseless /sís-les/ *adj.* incesante
cedar /sí-der/ *n.* cedro
celery /sél-e-ri/ *n.* apio
cellar /sél-ar/ *n.* sótano
cemetery /sém-i-te-ri/ *n.* cementerio
cent /sent/ *n.* centavo

central /sén-tral/ *adj.* central
central heating /sén-tral jí-ting/ *n.* calefacción; *Pe.* calefacción central
century /sén-chu-ri/ *n.* siglo
ceramics /ser-ám-iks/ *n.* cerámica
cereal /sí-ri-al/ *n.* grano; cereal
certain /sér-tin/ *adj.* cierto; seguro
certainly /sér-tin-li/ *adv.* seguramente
certificate /ser-tíf-i-ket/ *n.* certificado
certify /sér-ti-fai/ *v.* certificar
chair /cher/ *n.* silla
champagne /sham-péin/ *n.* champaña
chance /chans/ *n.* suerte; casualidad
change /cheinch/ *n.* cambio; suelto; *v.* cambiar
changeable /chéinch-a-bl/ *adj.* variable
channel /chán-l/ *n.* canal
chapel /cháp-l/ *n.* capilla
character /kár-ak-ter/ *n.* carácter
charge /charch/ *n.* carga; *v.* cobrar
chat /chat/ *n.* charla; plática; *v.* charlar; platicar
cheap /chip/ *adj.* barato
cheat /chit/ *v.* engañar; estafar
check /chek/ *n.* cheque (bank); cuenta (restaurant); *v.* comprobar
checkroom /chék-rum/ *n.* guardarropa
cheese /chis/ *n.* queso
cherry /chér-i/ *n.* cereza
chewing gum /chú-ing gom/ *n.* goma de mascar; chicle

chicken /chík-n/ *n.* pollo
child /chaild/ *n.* niño; niña (female)
chilli /chíl-i/ *n.* chile; *SA* ají
chilli sauce /chil-i sos/ *n.* salsa picante
china /chái-na/ *n.* loza
chocolate /chók-let/ *n.* chocolate
choice /chois/ *n.* selección; preferencia
choose /chus/ *v.* escoger
chop /chop/ *n.* chuleta
Christmas /krís-mas/ *n.* Navidad
Christmas tree /krís-mas tri/ *n.* árbol de Navidad
church /cherch/ *n.* iglesia
cigar /si-gár/ *n.* *Arg.* toscano; *Cuba, Ven.* tabaco; *Ec., PR* cigarro; *Mex., Pe.* puro
cigarette /sí-gar-et/ *n.* cigarrillo; *Cuba, Mex.* cigarro
cinema /sin-e-ma/ *n.* cine
cinnamon /sí-na-mon/ *n.* canela
circle /sír-kl/ *n.* círculo
circumstance /sér-kom-stans/ *n.* circunstancia
citizen /sít-i-sen/ *n.* ciudadano
citizenship /sít-i-sen-ship/ *n.* ciudadanía
city /sít-i/ *n.* ciudad
civil /sí-vil/ *adj.* civil
claim /kleim/ *n.* reclamación; *v.* reclamar
class /klas/ *n.* clase
classify /klás-i-fai/ *v.* clasificar
clay /klei/ *n.* barro
clean /klin/ *adj.* limpio; *v.* limpiar
cleaning /klín-ing/ *n.* limpieza

clear /klir/ *adj.* claro
clerk /klerk/ *n.* dependiente; *Arg.* vendedor; *Bol., Ec., Uru.* empleado
clever /klév-er/ *adj.* listo
client /klái-ent/ *n.* cliente
climate /klái-met/ *n.* clima
climb /klaim/ *v.* subir
clock /klok/ *n.* reloj
close /klos/ *adj.* cercano; *adv.* cerca
close /klous/ *n.* conclusión; cierre; *v.* cerrar; *adv.* de cerca
closet /klós-et/ *n.* armario; ropero; closet; *RP* placard
cloth /kloth/ *n.* tela; paño
clothes /kloz/ *n.* ropa
club /klob/ *n.* club
coat /kout/ *n.* abrigo
cock /kok/ *n.* gallo
cocoa /kó-ko/ *n.* cacao
coffee /kóf-i/ *n.* café
coffeehouse /kóf-i jaus/ *n.* café
coffeepot /kóf-i-pot/ *n.* cafetera
cognac /kó-ñac/ *n.* coñac
coin /koin/ *n.* moneda
cold /kould/ *n., adj.* frío (temperature); resfriado (head); catarro
collar /kál-r/ *n.* cuello
collarbone /kál-r-boun/ *n.* clavícula
color /kól-or/ *n.* color
column /kól-om/ *n.* columna

comb /koum/ *n.* peine
come /kom/ *v.* venir
come back /kom bak/ *v.* regresar; volver
come down /kom daun/ *v.* bajar
comedy /kóm-e-di/ *n.* comedia
come in /kom in/ *v.* entrar, pasar; *interj* pase
come out /kom aut/ *v.* salir
come up /kom op/ *v.* subir
comfort /kóm-fort/ *n.* comodidad
comfortable /kóm-fort-a-bl/ *adj.* cómodo
command /ko-mánd/ *n.* mando; *v.* mandar
comment /kó-ment/ *n.* observación; *v.* comentar
commerce /kóm-ers/ *n.* comercio
commercial /kom-mér-shal/ *adj.* comercial
commission /ko-mi-shon/ *n.* comisión
common /kóm-on/ *adj.* común; corriente
communication /ko-miu-ni-kéi-shon/ *n.* comunicación
companion /kom-pán-yon/ *n.* compañero
company /kóm-pa-ni/ *n.* compañía
compare /kom-pér/ *v.* comparar
comparison /kom-pár-i-son/ *n.* comparación
compartment /kom-párt-ment/ *n.* compartimiento
complain /kom-pléin/ *v.* quejarse
complaint /kom-pleínt/ *n.* queja
complete /kom-plít/ *adj.* completo; *v.* terminar; completar
comprehend /kom-pri-jénd/ *v.* comprender
comprehension /kom-pri-jén-shon/ *n.* comprensión

computer /kom-piú-ter/ *n.* computadora
concert /kón-sert/ *n.* concierto
conclude /kon-klúd/ *v.* concluir
conclusion /kon-klú-shon/ *n.* conclusión
condition /kon-dí-shon/ *n.* condición
conference /kón-fer-ens/ *n.* conferencia; congreso
confidence /kón-fi-dens/ *n.* confianza
conflict /kón-flikt/ *n.* conflicto
conflicting /kon-flíc-ting/ *adj.* contrario; contradictorio
confusion /kon-fiú-shon/ *n.* confusión
congratulate /kon-grát-yu-leit/ *v.* felicitar
congratulations /kon-grat-yu-leí-shons/ *n.* felicitaciones
congress /kón-gres/ *n.* congreso (pol.); conferencia
connect /ko-néct/ *v.* juntar; relacionar
connection /ko-nék-shon/ *n.* conexión
consciousness /kón-shos-nes/ *n.* conocimiento
consequence /kón-si-kuens/ *n.* consecuencia
consequently /kon-si-kuént-li/ *adv.* por consiguiente
consider /kon-síd-er/ *v.* considerar
considerable /kon-síd-er-a-bl/ *adj.* considerable
considerate /kon-síd-er-et/ *adj.* considerado; atento
consideration /kon-sid-er-é-shon/ *n.* consideración
consign /kon-sáin/ *v.* consignar; entregar
consignment /kon-sáin-ment/ *n.* consignación
consist /kon-síst/ *v.* consistir
consistent /kon-sís-tent/ *adj.* consistente
constant /kóns-tant/ *adj.* constante

constipation /kons-ti-pei-shon/ *n.* estreñimiento
constitute /kóns-ti-tiut/ *v.* constituir
construction /kons-trók-shon/ *n.* construcción
consul /kón-sel/ *n.* cónsul
consulate /kón-su-let/ *n.* consulado
consult /kon-sólt/ *v.* consultar
consume /kon-siúm/ *v.* consumir
consumer /kon-siúm-er/ *n.* consumidor
contact /kón-takt/ *n.* contacto; *v.* ponerse en contacto con
contain /kon-téin/ *v.* contener
container /kon-téin-er/ *n.* envase
content /kon-tént/ *adj.* contento; satisfecho
contents /kón-tents/ *n.* contenido
contest /kón-test/ *n.* concurso
continue /kon-tín-yu/ *v.* continuar
contraband /kón-tra-band/ *n.* contrabando
contract /kón-trakt/ *n.* contrato
contrary /kón-tra-ri/ *adj.* contrario
contrast /kón-trast/ *n.* contraste
contribute /kon-trí-biut/ *v.* contribuir
contribution /kon-tri-biú-shon/ *n.* contribución
control /kon-tróul/ *n.* control; *v.* controlar
convenience /kon-ví-niens/ *n.* conveniencia; comodidad
convenient /kon-ví-ni-ent/ *adj.* conveniente
convention /kon-vén-shon/ *n.* congreso
conversation /kon-ver-séi-shon/ *n.* conversación; plática

converse /kon-vérs/ *v.* conversar; platicar
cook /kuk/ *n.* cocinero; *v.* cocinar; guisar
cool /kul/ *adj.* fresco
copper /kóp-er/ *n.* cobre
copy /kóp-i/ *n.* copia; *v.* copiar
coral /kór-al/ *n.* coral
corn /korn/ *n.* maíz; *Arg., Chi., Ec., Pe.* choclo; *Ven.* jojoto
corner /kór-ner/ *n.* esquina; rincón
corporation /kor-po-réi-shon/ *n.* corporación
corrupt /ko-rópt/ *adj.* corrompido; corrupto
corruption /ko-róp-shon/ *n.* corrupción
cost /kost/ *n.* costo; precio; *v.* costar
costly /kóst-li/ *adj.* caro; costoso
costume /kós-tium/ *n.* traje; disfraz
cotton /kót-n/ *n.* algodón
cough /kof/ *n.* tos
count /kaunt/ *v.* contar
countless /káunt-les/ *adj.* innumerable
country /kón-tri/ *n.* país (nation); campo (rural area)
couple /kóp-l/ *n.* pareja
cousin /kós-n/ *n.* primo
cover /kóv-er/ *n.* cubierta; tapa; *v.* cubrir
crab /krab/ *n.* cangrejo
cracker /krá-ker/ *n.* galleta; *Arg.* galletita; *Cuba* galletica de sal
cramp /kramp/ *n.* calambre
crash /krash/ *n.* choque; *v.* estrellar; chocar
crazy /kréi-si/ *adj.* loco

credit /kréd-it/ *n.* crédito
creditor /kréd-it-er/ *n.* acreedor
crew /kru/ *n.* tripulación
crime /kraim/ *n.* crimen; delito
criminal /krím-i-nal/ *n., adj.* criminal
crisis /krái-sis/ *n.* crisis
cross /kros/ *n.* cruz; *v.* cruzar; atravesar
crossroad /krós-roud/ *n.* encrucijada
cry /krai/ *v.* llorar
crystal /krís-tl/ *n.* cristal
cucumber /kiú-kom-ber/ *n.* pepino
culture /kól-chiur/ *n.* cultura
cup /kop/ *n.* taza
cure /kiur/ *n.* cura; *v.* curar
curls /kerlz/ *n.* rizos; *Bol.* ondulación; *Ec.* churos; *Mex.* chinos; *Pe.* crespos; *Uru.* bucles
curly /kér-li/ *adj.* rizado
current /kér-ent/ *adj.* actual
curtain /kér-tin/ *n.* cortina
curve /kerv/ *n.* curva
cushion /kúsh-on/ *n.* cojín
custom /kós-tom/ *n.* costumbre
custom duty /kós-tom diú-ti/ *n.* derecho de aduana
customer /kós-tom-er/ *n.* cliente
custom house /kós-tom jaus/ *n.* aduana
customs /kós-toms/ *n.* aduana
cut /kot/ *n.* corte; *v.* cortar

- D -

daddy /dá-di/ *n.* papá
daily /deí-li/ *adj.* diario
damage /dám-ich/ *n.* daño; *v.* dañar
damp /damp/ *adj.* húmedo
dance /dans/ *n.* baile; *v.* bailar
dancer /dán-ser/ *n.* bailador; bailarín; bailarina
danger /déin-yer/ *n.* peligro
dangerous /déin-yer-os/ *adj.* peligroso
dare /der/ *n.* desafío; *v.* atreverse
dark /dark/ *adj.* oscuro
date /deit/ *n.* fecha; cita
daughter /dó-ter/ *n.* hija
daughter-in-law /dó-ter-in-lo/ *n.* nuera
day /dei/ *n.* día
daybreak /deí breik/ *n.* amanecer
dead /ded/ *adj.* muerto
deaf /def/ *adj.* sordo
deal /dil/ *n.* trato; negociación
dear /dir/ *adj.* querido
death /deth/ *n.* muerte
debt /det/ *n.* deuda
deceit /di-sít/ *n.* engaño
deceive /di-sív/ *v.* engañar
December /di-sém-br/ *n.* diciembre
decent /dí-sent/ *adj.* decente
decision /di-sí-shon/ *n.* decisión

declare /di-kléir/ *v.* declarar
decrease /di-krís/ *n.* reducción; *v.* disminuir
deep /dip/ *adj.* hondo; profundo
deer /dir/ *n.* venado
defect /di-fekt/ *n.* defecto
defective /di-fék-tiv/ *adj.* defectuoso
definite /déf-i-nit/ *adj.* preciso; definido
degree /di-grí/ *n.* grado; (in education) título
delay /di-léi/ *n.* retraso; demora; *v.* demorar; tardar
delicious /di-lísh-os/ *adj.* delicioso; sabroso; rico
deliver /di-lí-ver/ *v.* entregar
demand /di-mánd/ *n.* demanda; *v.* demandar
democratic /dem-o-krát-ik/ *adj.* democrático
demonstrate /dém-ons-treit/ *v.* demostrar
dense /dens/ *adj.* denso; espeso
dentist /dén-tist/ *n.* dentista
deny /di-nái/ *v.* negar
depart /di-párt/ *v.* irse; salir
department /di-párt-ment/ *n.* departamento
department store /di-párt-ment stor/ *n.* almacén; tienda de departamentos
depend /di-pénd/ *v.* depender; contar con
deposit /di-pós-it/ *n.* depósito; *v.* depositar
depth /depth/ *n.* profundidad
descend /di-sénd/ *v.* bajar
describe /dis-kráib/ *v.* describir
description /dis-kríp-shon/ *n.* descripción
desert /dés-ert/ *n.* desierto
deserve /di-sérv/ *v.* merecer

desire /di-sáir/ *n.* deseo; *v.* desear; querer
desk /desk/ *n.* escritorio
despite /dis-páit/ *prep.* a pesar de
dessert /di-sért/ *n.* postre
destroy /dis-trói/ *v.* destruir
destruction /dis-trók-shon/ *n.* destrucción
detail /dí-teil/ *n.* detalle
determine /di-tér-min/ *v.* determinar
develop /di-vél-op/ *v.* desarrollar; revelar (photo)
development /di-vél-op-ment/ *n.* desarrollo
devote /di-vóut/ *n.* dedicar
diabetes /dai-a-bí-tis/ *n.* diabetes
dialect /dái-a-lekt/ *n.* dialecto
dialogue /dái-a-log/ *n.* diálogo
diamond /dái-mond/ *n.* diamante
diary /dái-a-ri/ *n.* diario; jornal
dictionary /dík-shon-a-ri/ *n.* diccionario
die /dai/ *v.* morir
diet /dái-et/ *n.* dieta; *v.* estar a dieta
difference /díf-er-ens/ *n.* diferencia
different /díf-er-ent/ *adj.* diferente; distinto
diminish /di-mín-ish/ *v.* disminuir
dining car /dái-ning kar/ *n.* carro comedor; *Arg., Pe.* coche comedor; *Bol.* coche restaurante; *Uru.* vagón comedor
dining room /dái-ning rum/ *n.* comedor
dinner /dín-er/ *n.* cena; comida
direct /di-rékt/ *adj.* directo; *v.* dirigir
direction /di-rék-shon/ *n.* dirección

directly /di-rékt-li/ *adv.* directamente
director /di-rék-tor/ *n.* director
directory /di-rék-tor-i/ *n.* directorio; guía
dirt /dert/ *n.* suciedad; mugre; *Arg.* roña
dirty /dér-ti/ *adj.* sucio
disappear /dis-a-pir/ *v.* desaparecer
discomfort /dis-kóm-fort/ *n.* incomodidad
discontinue /dis-kon-tín-iu/ *v.* descontinuar
discotheque /dís-kou-tek/ *n.* discoteca; *Arg.* discotec; boliche
discount /dís-kaunt/ *n.* descuento
discover /dis-kóv-er/ *v.* descubrir
discuss /dis-kós/ *v.* cambiar opiniones
disease /di-sís/ *n.* enfermedad
dish /dish/ *n.* plato
dislike /dis-láik/ *v.* desagradar
display /dis-pléi/ *n.* exhibición; *v.* mostrar
dissolve /di-sólv/ *v.* disolver
distance /dís-tans/ *n.* distancia
distant /dís-tant/ *adj.* distante; lejano
distinguish /dis-tín-güish/ *v.* distinguir
distribute /dis-trí-biut/ *v.* distribuir
district /dís-trikt/ *n.* distrito
disturb /dis-térb/ *v.* molestar
disturbance /dis-térb-ans/ *n.* disturbio
divide /di-váid/ *v.* dividir
division /di-ví-shon/ *n.* división
do /du/ *v.* hacer
doctor /dók-tor/ *n.* médico; doctor

doctrine /dók-trin/ *n.* doctrina
document /dók-iu-ment/ *n.* documento
dog /dog/ *n.* perro
doll /dol/ *n.* muñeca
dollar /dó-lar/ *n.* dólar
dominate /dóm-i-neit/ *v.* dominar
donkey /dón-ki/ *n.* burro
door /dor/ *n.* puerta
door bell /dor bel/ *n.* timbre
double /dób-l/ *adj.* doble
doubt /dout/ *n.* duda; *v.* dudar
down /daun/ *adv.* abajo; *prep.* debajo de
down payment /daun péi-ment/ *n. Chi.* pie; *Cuba, PR, Uru.* adelanto; *Ec.* entrada; *Mex., Ven.* enganche; *Pe.* cuota inicial
downpour /dáun-por/ *n.* aguacero
downward /dáun-uerd/ *adv.* hacia abajo
dozen /dós-n/ *n.* docena
draw /dro/ *v.* dibujar
drawer /dró-er/ *n.* cajón
dream /drim/ *n.* sueño; *v.* soñar
dress /dres/ *n.* vestido; *v.* vestir
dressing /drés-ing/ *n.* salsa; aderezo
dressmaker /drés-meik-er/ *n.* costurera; modista
drink /drink/ *n.* bebida; trago; *Mex.* copa; *v.* beber; tomar
drive /draiv/ *v.* manejar; conducir
driver /drái-ver/ *n.* chofer; conductor
drop /drop/ *n.* gota; *v.* dejar caer

drop in /drop in/ *v.* visitar inesperadamente
drown /draun/ *v.* ahogarse
drug /drog/ *n.* droga; medicamento
druggist /dró-guist/ *n.* boticario; farmacеútico
drugstore /dróg-stor/ *n.* farmacia; *Col.* droguería; *Cuba* botica
drunk /dronk/ *n., adj.* borracho
drunkard /drónk-erd/ *n.* borracho
dry /drai/ *adj.* seco; *v.* secar
dryness /draí-nes/ *n.* sequedad
due /diu/ *adj.* debido; vencido
dumb /dom/ *adj.* tonto
during /dú-ring/ *prep.* durante
dust /dost/ *n.* polvo; *v.* despolvar; sacudir
duty /dú-ti/ *n.* deber
dye /dai/ *n.* tinte; *v.* teñir
dysentery /dís-n-te-ri/ *n.* disentería

- E -

each /ich/ *pron., adj.* cualquier; cada uno; cada
ear /ir/ *n.* oreja; oído
early /ér-li/ *adv.* temprano
earn /ern/ *v.* ganar
earnings /érn-ings/ *n.* ganancias
earrings /ír-ings/ *n.* aretes; pendientes; *Arg., Chi.,* aros; *Nic.* chapas; *PR* pantallas; *Uru.* caravanas; *Ven.* zarcillos
earth /erth/ *n.* tierra
earthenware /érth-in-uer/ *n.* loza de barro
earthquake /érth-kueik/ *n.* terremoto; temblor
easily /í-si-li/ *adv.* fácilmente
east /ist/ *n.* este
easy /í-si/ *adj.* fácil
easy chair /í-si cher/ *n.* butaca
eat /it/ *v.* comer
economical /i-ko-nóm-i-kal/ *adj.* económico
economy /i-kón-o-mi/ *n.* economía
effect /i-fékt/ *n.* efecto
efficient /i-fí-shent/ *adj.* eficiente
effort /éf-ort/ *n.* esfuerzo
egg /eg/ *n.* huevo; *Mex.* blanquillo
eight /eit/ *n., adj.* ocho

eighth /eith/ *adj.* octavo
eighty /éi-ti/ *n., adj.* ochenta
either /í-der/ *pron., adj.* uno u otro; *conj.* o; sea
elastic /i-lás-tik/ *n., adj.* elástico
elbow /él-bou/ *n.* codo
elderly /él-der-li/ *n.* ancianos; *adj.* anciano
element /él-i-ment/ *n.* elemento
elephant /él-i-fant/ *n.* elefante
elevator /é-le-vei-tor/ *n.* elevador; *SA* ascensor
eleven /i-lév-n/ *n., adj.* once
else /els/ *adj.* otro; cualquier(a); *adv.* más; además
embarrass /em-bér-as/ *v.* avergonzar
embassy /ém-ba-si/ *n.* embajada
embrace /em-bréis/ *n.* abrazo; *v.* abrazar(se)
emerald /ém-e-rald/ *n.* esmeralda
emphasis /ém-fa-sis/ *n.* énfasis
employ /em-plói/ *v.* emplear
employer /em-plói-er/ *n.* jefe; patrón
employment /em-plói-ment/ *n.* empleo
empties /ém-tis/ *n.* vacíos; envases; *Ven.* recipientes
empty /ém-ti/ *adj.* vacío
enamel /e-nám-l/ *n.* esmalte
enchant /en-chánt/ *v.* encantar
encounter /en-káun-ter/ *n.* encuentro; *v.* encontrar
encourage /en-kór-ich/ *v.* animar
encouragement /en-kór-ich-ment/ *n.* estímulo; incentivo
end /end/ *n.* fin; *v.* acabar; terminar
enemy /én-e-mi/ *n.* enemigo

energy /én-er-yi/ *n.* energía
engine /én-yin/ *n.* motor
enjoy /en-yói/ *v.* gozar de; disfrutar
enough /i-nóf/ *adj., adv.* bastante
enter /én-ter/ *v.* entrar
enterprise /én-ter-prais/ *n.* empresa
entertain /en-ter-téin/ *v.* festejar; agasajar
entertainment /en-ter-téin-ment/ *n.* diversión
enthusiasm /en-thú-si-as-m/ *n.* entusiasmo
entire /en-táir/ *adj.* entero
entrance /én-trans/ *n.* entrada
entry /én-tri/ *n.* entrada
envelope /én-vel-op/ *n.* sobre
environs /en-vái-rons/ *n.* alrededores
equal /í-kual/ *adj.* igual
equality /i-kuál-i-ti/ *n.* igualdad
equivalent /i-kuí-va-lent/ *n., adj.* equivalente
erase /i-réis/ *v.* borrar
error /ér-or/ *n.* error
especially /es-pésh-a-li/ *adv.* especialmente
essential /e-sén-shal/ *adj.* esencial
establish /es-táb-lish/ *v.* establecer
estimate /és-ti-met/ *n.* cálculo; presupuesto
estimate /és-ti-meit/ *v.* estimar; calcular
even /i-vn/ *adv.* aún
evening /ív-ning/ *n.* tarde; anochecer; noche
event /i-vént/ *n.* evento
eventually /i-vén-tiu-li/ *adv.* eventualmente
ever /év-er/ *adv.* siempre; en todo caso

every /év-ri/ *adj.* todo; cada uno
everybody /év-ri-bod-i/ *pron.* todo el mundo
everything /év-ri-thing/ *pron.* todo
everywhere /év-ri-juer/ *adv.* en todas partes
evidence /év-i-dens/ *n.* evidencia
evil /í-vil/ *n.* maldad; *adj.* malo
examination /ek-sam-i-néi-shon/ *n.* examen
examine /ek-sám-in/ *v.* examinar
example /ek-sám-pl/ *n.* ejemplo
excellent /ék-sel-ent/ *adj.* excelente
except /ek-sépt/ *prep.* excepto; a excepción de
exception /ek-sép-shon/ *n.* excepción
excess /ék-ses/ *n.* exceso
excessive /ek-sés-iv/ *adj.* excesivo
exchange /eks-chéinch/ *n.* cambio; *v.* cambiar
exclude /eks-klúd/ *v.* excluir
exclusive /eks-klú-siv/ *adj.* exclusivo
excursion /eks-kér-shon/ *n.* excursión; paseo
excuse /eks-kiúz/ *v.* perdonar; disculpar
excuse /eks-kiúz/ *n.* excusa
exempt /ek-sémpt/ *adj.* exento
exemption /eks-émp-shon/ *n.* exención
exercise /éks-er-sais/ *n.* ejercicio; *v.* hacer ejercicio
exhibition /eks-i-bí-shon/ *n.* exhibición
exit /ék-sit/ *n.* salida
expand /eks-pánd/ *v.* extender
expansion /eks-pán-shon/ *n.* expansión
expect /eks-pékt/ *v.* esperar
expense /eks-péns/ *n.* gasto; costo

expensive /eks-pén-siv/ *adj.* caro
experience /eks-pí-ri-ens/ *n.* experiencia; *v.* experimentar
experiment /eks-pér-i-ment/ *n.* experimento; *v.* experimentar
explain /eks-pléin/ *v.* explicar
explanation /eks-pla-neí-shon/ *n.* explicación
explore /eks-plór/ *v.* explorar
export /eks-pórt/ *v.* exportar
exports /éks-ports/ *n.* exportaciones
express /eks-prés/ *n.* expreso; *v.* expresar
expression /eks-pré-shon/ *n.* expresión
extensive /eks-tén-siv/ *adj.* extensivo
exterior /eks-tí-ri-or/ *n.* exterior; *adj.* exterior; externo
external /eks-tér-nal/ *adj.* exterior; externo
extra /éks-tra/ *n.* extra; *adj.* adicional
extraordinary /eks-tra-ór-di-na-ri/ *adj.* extraordinario
extreme /eks-trím/ *n., adj.* extremo
extremely /eks-trím-li/ *adv.* sumamente
eye /ai/ *n.* ojo
eyebrow /ái-brou/ *n.* ceja
eyeglasses /ái-glas-is/ *n.* anteojos; lentes; *Cuba* espejuelos
eyelash /ái-lash/ *n.* pestaña
eyesight /ái-sait/ *n.* vista

- F -

fabric /fá-brik/ *n.* tela
fabrication /fa-bri-kéi-shon/ *n.* construcción; ficción
face /feis/ *n.* cara; *v.* hacer frente
face cream /feis crim/ *n.* crema para la cutis
fact /fakt/ *n.* hecho
factor /fák-tor/ *n.* factor
factory /fák-to-ri/ *n.* fábrica
fail /feil/ *v.* fracasar
failure /féil-yur/ *n.* fracaso
fair (complected) /fer/ *n., adj.* rubio; *Chi.* rucio; *Ec.* bermejo; *Mex.* güero; *Ven.* catire
fall /fol/ *n.* otoño; *v.* caer(se)
false /fols/ *adj.* falso
family /fám-i-li/ *n.* familia
famous /féi-mos/ *adj.* famoso
fan /fan/ *n.* abanico; (elec.) ventilador
fantastic /fan-tás-tik/ *adj.* fantástico
far /far/ *adv.* lejos
fare /fer/ *n.* tarifa
farewell /fer-uél/ *n.* despedida; *interj.* adiós
farm /farm/ *n.* granja; *Cuba* finca; *RP* estancia
fashion /fásh-on/ *n.* moda
fast /fast/ *adj.* rápido
fasten /fás-n/ *v.* atar; amarrar
fat /fat/ *adj.* gordo
father /fá-der/ *n.* padre; *Col.* taita

father-in-law /fá-der-in-lo/ *n.* suegro
faucet /fó-sit/ *n.* llave; *Bol.* grifo; *Pe.* caño
fault /folt/ *n.* culpa
faultless /fólt-les/ *adj.* perfecto
fear /fir/ *n.* miedo; *v.* tener miedo; temer
fearful /fír-ful/ *adj.* miedoso
feather /fé-der/ *n.* pluma
February /féb-ru-a-ri/ *n.* febrero
fee /fi/ *n.* honorario
feel /fil/ *v.* sentir(se)
female /fí-meil/ *n.* hembra
feminine /fém-i-nin/ *adj.* femenino
ferry /fér-i/ *n.* transbordador; *Ec.* barcaza; gabarra; *Mex.* panga; *RP, Ven.* ferry
festival /fés-ti-val/ *n.* fiesta
festive /fés-tiv/ *adj.* festivo
fever /fí-ver/ *n.* fiebre; *Mex.* calentura
feverish /fí-ver-ish/ *adj.* febril
few /fiu/ *adj.* pocos; algunos; unos
fiber /fái-ber/ *n.* fibra
fifteen /fif-tín/ *n., adj.* quince
fifth /fifth/ *adj.* quinto
fifty /fif-ti/ *n., adj.* cincuenta
fig /fig/ *n.* higo
fight /fait/ *n.* lucha; pelea; *v.* luchar; pelear
figure /fí-guer/ *n.* figura; *v.* figurar
file /fail/ *n.* lima; archivo (for papers); *v.* limar; archivar (papers)
fill /fil/ *n.* llenar

film /film/ *n.* película; *v.* filmar
filter (cigarette) /fíl-ter/ *n.* filtro; *Mex., Pe.* boquilla
final /fái-nal/ *adj.* final
finance /fái-nans/ *n.* finanza; *v.* financiar
find /faind/ *v.* hallar; encontrar
fine /fain/ *adj.* fino; *interj.* muy bien
finger /fín-guer/ *n.* dedo
finish /fín-ish/ *v.* acabar; terminar
fire /fair/ *n.* fuego; *Cuba, Ven.* candela; *v.* despedir (from job)
fire alarm /fair a-lárm/ *n.* alarma de incendios
fire escape /fair es-kéip/ *n.* escalera de incendio
fireman /fáir-man/ *n.* bombero
fireplace /fáir-pleis/ *n.* chimenea
fireproof /fáir-pruf/ *adj.* incombustible
firm /firm/ *n.* (com.) firma; *adj.* firme
first /ferst/ *n., adj., adv.* primero
fish /fish/ *n.* pez; pescado (cooked)
fishbone /físh-boun/ *n.* espina (de pescado)
fisherman /físh-er-man/ *n.* pescador
fishhook /físh-juk/ *n.* anzuelo
fishing /físh-ing/ *n.* pesca
five /faiv/ *n., adj.* cinco
fix /fiks/ *v.* arreglar
flag /flag/ *n.* bandera
flat /flat/ *adj.* plano
flavor /fleí-vor/ *n.* sabor
flight /flait/ *n.* vuelo
floor /flor/ *n.* piso; suelo

florist /flór-ist/ *n.* florero
flour /flaur/ *n.* harina
flower /flaur/ *n.* flor
flu /flu/ *n.* gripe; *Mex.* gripa; *PR* influenza
fluency /flú-en-si/ *n.* fluidez
fluent /flú-ent/ *adj.* fluente
flush /flosh/ *v.* vaciar el agua
fly /flai/ *n.* mosca; *v.* volar
focus /fóu-kos/ *n.* foco; *v.* enfocar
fold /fould/ *v.* doblar
folk /fouk/ *n.* gente
follow /fól-ou/ *v.* seguir
food /fud/ *n.* comida
fool /ful/ *n.* tonto; *v.* engañar
foolish /fúl-ish/ *adj.* tonto
foot /fut/ *n.* pie
football (Amer.) /fút-bol/ *n.* fútbol; *Arg.* balompié
for /for/ *prep.* por; para
force /fors/ *n.* fuerza; *v.* forzar
foreign /fór-in/ *adj.* extranjero
foreigner /fór-in-er/ *n.* extranjero
forest /fór-est/ *n.* bosque
forget /for-guét/ *v.* olvidar(se)
forgetful /for-guét-ful/ *adj.* olvidadizo
forgive /for-guív/ *v.* perdonar
fork /fork/ *n.* tenedor; *Andes, Mex.* trinche
form /form/ *n.* forma; *v.* formar
formal /fór-mal/ *adj.* formal
former /fór-mer/ *adj.* anterior

forty /fór-ti/ *n., adj.* cuarenta
fountain /fáun-tin/ *n.* fuente
four /for/ *n., adj.* cuatro
fourteen /for-tín/ *n., adj.* catorce
fourth /forth/ *n., adj.* cuarto
fowl /faul/ *n.* ave
fox /foks/ *n.* zorro
fraud /frod/ *n.* fraude
free /fri/ *adj.* libre; *adv.* gratis (free of charge)
freedom /fri-dum/ *n.* libertad
freeze /friz/ *v.* congelar
freight /freit/ *n.* carga; flete
frequent /frí-kuent/ *adj.* frecuente
frequently /frí-kuent-li/ *adv.* frecuentemente
fresh /fresh/ *adj.* fresco
Friday /fraí-dei/ *n.* viernes
friend /frend/ *n.* amigo
friendship /frénd-ship/ *n.* amistad
fright /frait/ *n.* susto
from /from/ *prep.* de; desde
front /front/ *n.* frente
fruit /frut/ *n.* fruta
fry /frai/ *v.* freír
fuel /fiul/ *n.* combustible
full /ful/ *adj.* lleno
fun /fon/ *n.* diversión
fund /fond/ *n.* fondo; capital
fundamental /fond-a-mént-tl/ *adj.* fundamental
funny /fón-i/ *adj.* cómico; *Mex., Pe.* chistoso; raro

(strange)

furniture /fér-ni-chur/ *n.* muebles

future /fiú-chur/ *n.* futuro

- G -

gain /guein/ *v.* ganar
gallery /gál-er-i/ *n.* galería
gallon /gá-lon/ *n.* galón
gamble /gám-bl/ *v.* jugar
gambler /gám-bler/ *n.* jugador
gambling /gám-bling/ *n.* juego
game /gueim/ *n.* juego
garage /ga-rách/ *n.* garaje; *Arg.* garash; *Ec.* garage; *Mex.* cochera
garbage /gár-bich/ *n.* basura
garden /gár-den/ *n.* jardín
garlic /gár-lik/ *n.* ajo
garment /gár-ment/ *n.* prenda de vestir
gas /gas/ *n.* gas; gasolina; *Arg.* nafta; *Chi.* bencina
gate /gueit/ *n.* puerta; entrada
gather /gád-er/ *v.* recoger
gathering /gád-er-ing/ *n.* asamblea
gauze /gos/ *n.* gaza
gelatine /yél-a-tin/ *n.* gelatina
gem /yem/ *n.* joya
general /yén-er-al/ *n.* (mil.) general; *adj.* general
gentle /yén-tl/ *adj.* suave; dulce
gentleman /yén-tl-man/ *n.* caballero; señor
genuine /yén-iu-in/ *adj.* genuino
germ /yerm/ *n.* germen
gesture /yés-chur/ *n.* gesto

get /guet/ *v.* recibir; conseguir
get away /guet a-uéi/ *v.* escaparse; huirse
get down /guet daun/ *v.* bajar
get in /guet in/ *v.* entrar
get out /guet aut/ *v.* salir
get up /guet op/ *v.* subir; levantarse
giant /yái-ant/ *n., adj.* gigante
gift /guift/ *n.* regalo
gigantic /yai-gán-tik/ *adj.* gigantesco
gin /yin/ *n.* ginebra
girl /guerl/ *n.* muchacha; niña; *CA* chavala; *Mex.* chamaca
girl friend /guerl frend/ *n.* novia; *Chi.* polola; *Ec., Pe.* enamorada; *Ven.* empate
give /guiv/ *v.* dar; regalar
glad /glad/ *adj.* alegre; contento
glass /glas/ *n.* vidrio; vaso (tumbler)
glasses /glás-is/ *n.* anteojos; lentes; *Cuba* espejuelos
glassware /glás-uer/ *n.* cristalería
globe /gloub/ *n.* globo
glove /glov/ *n.* guante
glue /glu/ *n.* pegamento; *Arg.* cola; *Cuba* goma de pegar; *Uru.* goma; *Ven.* pega
go /gou/ *v.* ir
go away /gou a-uéi/ *v.* irse
go back /gou bak/ *v.* regresar
god /god/ *n.* dios
godfather /gód-fad-er/ *n.* padrino
godmother /gód-mod-er/ *n.* madrina

go down /gou daun/ *v.* bajar
gold /gould/ *n.* oro
golf /golf/ *n.* golf
good /gud/ *adj.* bueno; *interj.* bueno, bien
good-bye /gud-bái/ *n.* adiós
Good afternoon. /gud af-ter-nún/ Buenas tardes.
Good evening. /gud ív-ning/ Buenas noches.
Good morning. /gud mór-ning/ Buenos días.
goodness /gúd-nes/ *n.* bondad
goods /guds/ *n.* mercancías
goodwill /gud-uíl/ *n.* buena voluntad
go out /gou aut/ *v.* salir
go shopping /gou shóp-ing/ *v.* ir de compras
go up /gou op/ *v.* salir
govern /góv-ern/ *v.* gobernar
government /góv-ern-ment/ *n.* gobierno
governor /góv-er-ner/ *n.* gobernador
gown /gaun/ *n.* vestido
grab /grab/ *v.* agarrar
grade /greid/ *n.* grado
grain /grein/ *n.* grano; cereal
grammar /grám-er/ *n.* gramática
grand /grand/ *adj.* gran; grande
grandchild /gránd-chaild/ *n.* nieto
granddaughter /gránd-do-ter/ *n.* nieta
grandfather /gránd-fad-er/ *n.* abuelo
grandmother /gránd-mod-er/ *n.* abuela
grandson /gránd-son/ *n.* nieto
grape /greip/ *n.* uva

grapefruit /gréip-frut/ *n.* toronja; *Arg.* pomelo
grass /gras/ *n.* hierba; *Bol., Mex., Uru.* pasto; *RP* césped
grateful /gréit-ful/ *adj.* agradecido
gratuity /gra-tiú-i-ti/ *n.* gratificación; propina
gravy /gréi-vi/ *n.* salsa; jugo
gray /grei/ *n., adj.* gris
grease /gris/ *n.* grasa
great /greit/ *adj.* gran; grande
great deal /greit dil/ *adj., adv.* mucho
green /grin/ *n., adj.* verde
greet /grit/ *v.* saludar
greeting /grít-ing/ *n.* saludo
grief /grif/ *n.* tristeza
grill /gril/ *n.* parrilla; *v.* asar en parrilla
grocer /gróu-ser/ *n.* *Cuba* bodeguero; *Mex.* tendero; *SA* pulpero
groceries /gróu-ser-is/ *n.* víveres; *Mex.* abarrotes; *Uru.* comestibles; provisiones
grocery /gróu-ser-i/ *n.* *Cuba, PR, Ven.* bodega; *Mex.* abarrotes; *SA* pulpería; *Uru.* almacén de comestibles
ground /graund/ *n.* tierra; suelo
ground floor /graund flor/ *n.* piso bajo; *Mex.* planta baja; *Pe.* primer piso
group /grup/ *n.* grupo; *v.* agrupar
guarantee /ga-ran-tí/ *v.* garantizar
guaranty /gá-ran-ti/ *n.* garantía
guard /gard/ *n.* guardia; *v.* guardar

guess /gues/ *v.* adivinar
guest /guest/ *n.* huésped; invitado
guide /gaid/ *n.* guía; *v.* guiar
guidebook /gáid-buk/ *n.* guía
guilty /guíl-ti/ *adj.* culpable
guitar /gui-tár/ *n.* guitarra
gulf /golf/ *n.* golfo
gum /gom/ *n.* goma; chicle
gun /gon/ *n.* fusil
gymnasium /yim-néi-si-om/ *n.* gimnasio

- H -

habit /já-bit/ *n.* hábito; costumbre
haggle /jág-l/ *v.* regatear
hair /jer/ *n.* pelo; cabello
hairbrush /jér-brosh/ *n.* cepillo para la cabeza
hairdresser /jér-dres-er/ *n.* peluquero
hairpin /jér-pin/ *n.* horquilla; *Cuba* hebilla; *Ec.* invisible; *Ven.* gancho
half /jaf/ *n.* mitad; *adj.* medio
hall /jol/ *n.* pasillo; corredor; sala; salón
halt /jolt/ *v.* parar; *interj.* alto
ham /jam/ *n.* jamón
hamburger /jám-bur-guer/ *n.* hamburguesa; hamburger
hand /jand/ *n.* mano
handbag /jánd-bag/ *n.* cartera; *Ec.* bolso; *Mex.* bolsa
handbook /jánd-buk/ *n.* manual; guía
handful /jánd-ful/ *n.* puñado
handkerchief /jánd-ker-chif/ *n.* pañuelo
handle /ján-dl/ *n.* mango; manija; *Arg.* picaporte; *Ec.* perilla; *Ven.* manilla
handmade /jand-méid/ *adj.* hecho a mano
handrail /jánd-reil/ *n.* barandilla; pasamanos
handsome /jánd-som/ *adj.* guapo; bello; *Uru.* bien parecido
hang /jang/ *v.* colgar
hanger /jáng-er/ *n.* colgador; *Mex.* gancho; *Cuba* percherο

hangover /jáng-ou-ver/ *n. Bol., RP* resaca; *Chi.* caña; *Col.* guayabo; *Ec.* chuchaqui; *Mex.* cruda; *Pe.* perseguidora; *Ven.* ratón
happen /jáp-n/ *v.* pasar; suceder; ocurrir
happy /jáp-i/ *adj.* feliz
hard /jard/ *adj.* duro; difícil
hardly /járd-li/ *adv.* apenas
hardware store /járd-uer stor/ *n.* ferretería; quincallería
harm /jarm/ *n.* daño; *v.* dañar; lastimar
harmful /járm-ful/ *adj.* dañoso; nocivo
harmless /járm-les/ *adj.* inocuo
harp /jarp/ *n.* arpa
hat /jat/ *n.* sombrero
hate /jeit/ *n.* odio; *v.* odiar
have /jav/ *v.* tener; haber
have fun /jav fon/ *v.* divertirse
he /ji/ *pron.* él
head /jed/ *n.* cabeza; *v.* dirigir
headache /jéd-eik/ *n.* dolor de cabeza
head cold /jed kould/ *n.* resfriado
heads or tails /jedz or teils/ u cara o cruz; Mex: águila o sol
heal /jil/ *v.* sanar; curar
health /jelth/ *n.* salud
healthy /jél-thi/ *adj.* saludable; sano
hear /jir/ *v.* oír; escuchar
hearing /jír-ing/ *n.* oído
heart /jart/ *n.* corazón

heartless /járt-les/ *adj.* cruel
heat /jit/ *n.* calor
heaven /jév-n/ *n.* cielo
heavy /jév-i/ *adj.* pesado
heel /jil/ *n.* talón; tacón (shoe)
height /jait/ *n.* altura
hell /jel/ *n.* infierno
hello /jel-óu/ *interj.* hola
helmet /jél-met/ *n.* casco
help /jelp/ *n.* ayuda; socorro; *v.* ayudar
help /jelp/ *interj.* auxilio, socorro
helper /jélp-er/ *n.* ayudante; asistente
helpful /jélp-ful/ *adj.* útil
hem /jem/ *n.* dobladillo
hen /jen/ *n.* gallina
her /jer/ *pron.* ella; la; le; *adj.* su; de ella
herb /erb/ *n.* hierba
here /jier/ *adv.* aquí
hernia /jér-ni-a/ *n.* hernia
hers /jers/ *pron.* suyo; suya; de ella
herself /jer-sélf/ *pron.* ella misma
hesitate /jés-i-teit/ *v.* vacilar
hide /jaid/ *v.* esconder
high /jai/ *adj.* alto
highest /jái-est/ *adj.* el más alto
highway /jái-uei/ *n.* carretera
hike /jaik/ *v.* dar una caminata
hill /jil/ *n.* colina
him /jim/ *pron.* a él; le; lo; se

hire /jair/ *v.* alquilar; emplear; *CA, Col., Ven.* enganchar
his /jis/ *pron.* el suyo; *adj.* su; suyo
hit /jit/ *n.* golpe; *v.* golpear; pegar
hitchhike /hích-jaik/ *v. Arg., Chi., Uru.* hacer dedo; *Col.* echar dedo; *Mex.* pedir aventón
hold /jould/ *v.* aguantar
holder /jóul-der/ *n.* poseedor
hole /joul/ *n.* agujero; hueco
holiday /jál-i-dei/ *n.* día festivo
holy /jóu-li/ *adj.* santo
Holy Week /jóu-li uik/ *n.* Semana Santa
home /jom/ *n.* hogar; *adv.* a casa; en casa
homeland /jóm-land/ *n.* patria
honest /ón-est/ *adj.* honesto
honey /jón-i/ *n.* miel
honeymoon /jón-i-mun/ *n.* luna de miel
hook /juk/ *n.* gancho; *v.* enganchar
hope /joup/ *n.* esperanza; *v.* esperar
hopeless /jóup-les/ *adj.* desesperado
horrible /jór-i-bl/ *adj.* horrible
hors d'oeuvres /or dirvs/ *n.* entremeses; *Mex.* botanas
horse /jors/ *n.* caballo
horsepower /jórs-pau-er/ *n.* caballo de fuerza
hospital /jós-pi-tal/ *n.* hospital
hot /jot/ *adj.* caliente; picante (spicy)
hot dog /jot dog/ *n.* hot dog; perro caliente; *Arg.* pancho; *Uru.* frankfurter
hotel /jo-tél/ *n.* hotel

hour /auer/ *n.* hora
hourly /áuer-li/ *adv.* a cada hora
house /jaus/ *n.* casa
housekeeper /jáus-kip-er/ *n.* ama de llaves
how /jau/ *adv.* como
however /jau-év-er/ *adv.* en todo caso; *conj.* sin embargo
how many? /jau mén-i/ ¿cuántos?
how much? /jou moch/ ¿cuánto?
How much is it? /jau moch is it/ ¿Cuánto es?
how soon? /jau sun/ ¿cuándo?
huge /jiuch/ *adj.* enorme
human /jiú-man/ *n.* ser humano; *adj.* humano
humanity /jiu-mán-i-ti/ *n.* humanidad
humble /júm-bl/ *adj.* humilde
humorous /jiú-mor-os/ *adj.* chistoso; cómico
hundred /jón-dred/ *n., adj.* cien; ciento
hundredth /jón-dreth/ *adj.* centésimo
hunger /jón-ger/ *n.* hambre
hungry /jón-gri/ *adj.* hambriento
hunt /jont/ *v.* cazar
hunter /jónt-er/ *n.* cazador
hunting /jónt-ing/ *n.* caza
hurry /jér-i/ *v.* darse prisa
hurry up /jér-i op/ *imper.* dese prisa; apúrese; *Arg.* vaya; *PR* avanza; *Ven.* corre
hurt /jert/ *v.* herir; lastimar
husband /jós-band/ *n.* esposo; marido
hysterical /jis-tér-i-kal/ *adj.* histérico

- I -

I /ai/ *pron.* yo
ice /ais/ *n.* hielo
ice cream /ais krim/ *n.* helado; *PR* mantecado
idea /ai-dí-a/ *n.* idea
ideal /ai-díl/ *n., adj.* ideal
identity card /ai-dén-ti-ti kard/ *n.* cédula (de identidad)
idiom /íd-i-om/ *n.* modismo
idiot /íd-i-ot/ *n.* idiota
idol /ái-dol/ *n.* ídolo
if /if/ *conj.* si
ignore /ig-nór/ *v.* no hacer caso de
ill /il/ *adj.* malo; enfermo
illegal /i-lí-gal/ *adj.* ilegal
illness /íl-nes/ *n.* enfermedad
image /ím-ich/ *n.* imagen
imagine /i-mách-in/ *v.* imaginar
imitation /im-i-teí-shon/ *n.* imitación
immediately /i-mí-di-et-li/ *adv.* inmediatamente; en seguida; *Mex.* ahorita
immigrant /ím-a-grent/ *n.* inmigrante
immigrate /ím-a-greit/ *v.* inmigrar
immune /i-miún/ *adj.* inmune
impact /ím-pakt/ *n.* impacto
impatient /im-péi-shent/ *adj.* impaciente
impede /im-píd/ *v.* impedir

impel /im-pél/ *v.* impulsar
import /im-pórt/ *v.* importar
importance /im-pór-tans/ *n.* importancia
important /im-pór-tant/ *adj.* importante
import duty /ím-port diú-ti/ *n.* derecho de aduana
importer /ím-port-er/ *n.* importador
imports /ím-ports/ *n.* importaciones
impossible /im-pós-i-bl/ *adj.* imposible
impress /im-prés/ *v.* impresionar
impression /im-pré-shon/ *n.* impresión
impressive /im-prés-iv/ *adj.* impresionante
imprison /im-prís-n/ *v.* encarcelar
imprisonment /im-prís-n-ment/ *n.* encarcelación
improve /im-prúv/ *v.* mejorar
improvement /im-prúv-ment/ *n.* mejoramiento
inability /in-a-bíl-i-ti/ *n.* incapacidad
inadequate /in-ád-i-kuet/ *adj.* inadecuado
in advance /in ad-váns/ *adv.* por adelantado
incapable /in-kéi-pa-bl/ *adj.* incapaz
in case /in keis/ *conj.* en caso
inch /inch/ *n.* pulgada
incident /ín-si-dent/ *n.* incidente
include /in-klúd/ *v.* incluir
including /in-klúd-ing/ *prep.* incluso
income /ín-kom/ *n.* ingreso
income tax /ín-kom taks/ *n.* impuesto de utilidades
incomplete /in-kom-plít/ *adj.* incompleto
inconvenient /in-kon-ví-ni-ent/ *adj.* inconveniente
increase /in-krís/ *v.* aumentar

incredible /in-kréd-i-bl/ *adj.* increíble
indeed /in-díd/ *adv.* de veras; sí
indefinite /in-déf-i-nit/ *adj.* indefinido
independence /in-di-pén-dens/ *n.* independencia
independent /in-di-pén-dent/ *adj.* independiente
indicate /ín-di-keit/ *v.* indicar
indication /in-di-kéi-shon/ *n.* indicación
individual /in-di-ví-diu-al/ *n., adj.* individual
industrial /in-dós-tri-al/ *adj.* industrial
industry /ín-dos-tri/ *n.* industria
inefficient /in-i-físh-ent/ *adj.* ineficaz
inexpensive /in-eks-pén-siv/ *adj.* barato
infant /ín-fent/ *n.* nene; bebé; *Pe.* bebe; *Ven.* chamito
infect /in-fékt/ *v.* infectar
inferior /in-fí-ri-or/ *adj.* inferior
infinite /ín-fi-nit/ *adj.* infinito
influence /ín-flu-ens/ *n.* influencia
influenza /in-flu-én-sa/ *n.* influenza
injure /ín-yur/ *v.* dañar; lastimar
ink /ink/ *n.* tinta
inner /ín-er/ *adj.* interior
innocent /ín-o-sent/ *adj.* inocente
inquire /in-kuáir/ *v.* preguntar; informarse
inscription /in-skríp-shon/ *n.* inscripción
insect /ín-sekt/ *n.* insecto; bicho
inside /in-sáid/ *n., adj.* interior; *adv.* adentro
insist /in-síst/ *v.* insistir
inspect /in-spékt/ *v.* inspeccionar
instant /ín-stant/ *n.* instante; *adj.* inmediato

instead of /in-stéd ov/ *prep.* en vez de
institute /in-sti-tiut/ *n.* instituto; *v.* instituir
instruct /in-strókt/ *v.* instruir; enseñar
instruction /in-strók-shon/ *n.* instrucción
instrument /ín-stru-ment/ *n.* instrumento
insufficient /in-suf-ísh-ent/ *adj.* insuficiente
insult /ín-solt/ *n.* insulto
insult /in-sólt/ *v.* insultar
insurance /in-shúr-ans/ *n.* seguro
insure /in-shúr/ *v.* asegurar
intelligent /in-tél-i-yent/ *adj.* inteligente
interior /in-tí-ri-or/ *n., adj.* interior
internal /in-tér-nal/ *adj.* interno
interpreter /in-tér-pret-er/ *n.* intérprete
into /ín-tu/ *prep.* en; adentro
introduce /in-tro-diús/ *v.* presentar
invalid /in-vál-id/ *adj.* inválido
invitation /in-vi-téi-shon/ *n.* invitación
invite /in-váit/ *v.* invitar
involve /in-vólv/ *v.* involucrar
iron /ái-ern/ *n.* hierro (metal); plancha; *v.* planchar
island /ái-land/ *n.* isla
issue /í-shiu/ *n.* edición
it /it/ *pron.* él; ella; ello; lo; la; le
itch /ich/ *n.* picazón; *v.* picar
item /ái-tem/ *n.* artículo
its /its/ *adj.* su (de él, de ella, de ello)
itself /it-sélf/ *pron.* el mismo; la misma
ivory /ái-vor-i/ *n.* marfil

- J -

jack /yak/ *n.* gato
jacket /yák-it/ *n.* chaqueta; *Cuba* saco; *Mex.* chamarra; *Pe.* casaca; *RP* campera
jail /yeil/ *n.* cárcel; prisión
jam /yam/ *n.* mermelada
January /yán-iu-a-ri/ *n.* enero
jelly /yél-i/ *n.* jalea
jellyfish /yél-i-fish/ *n. Bol., Uru.* medusa; *Cuba, Mex.* agua mala; *Pe.* malagua; *PR, Uru.* aguaviva
jet /yet/ *n.* avión de reacción
jewel /yiú-l/ *n.* joya
jeweler /yiú-ler/ *n.* joyero
jewelry /yiú-el-ri/ *n.* joyería
jitney /yít-ni/ *n. Mex.* pesero
job /yob/ *n.* empleo
join /yoin/ *v.* unirse a; juntar
joke /youk/ *n.* broma; chiste; *v. Carib., Mex.* chotear
judge /yoch/ *n.* juez; *v.* juzgar
jug /yog/ *n.* jarro
juice /yus/ *n.* jugo; *CR* zumo
July /yu-lái/ *n.* julio
jump /yomp/ *v.* saltar; *Mex.* brincar
jungle /yón-gl/ *n.* jungla; selva
June /yun/ *n.* junio
jury /yú-ri/ *n.* jurado
just /yost/ *adj.* justo

justice /yóst-is/ *n.* justicia
justification /yost-i-fi-kéi-shon/ *n.* justificación
justify /yóst-i-fai/ *v.* justificar

- K -

keep /kip/ *v.* mantener; guardar
kennel /kén-l/ *n.* perrera
key /ki/ *n.* llave
keyboard /kí-bord/ *n.* teclado
kick /kik/ *v.* patear
kid /kid/ *n. Arg.* pibe; *Bol.,* muchacho; *Chi.,* cabro; *Cuba, Pe.* chico; *Ec.* guambra; *Mex.* chamaco; chavo; *Ven.* chamo; pavo
kidney /kíd-ni/ *n.* riñón
kill /kil/ *v.* matar
kilogram /kíl-ou-gram/ *n.* kilo(gramo)
kilometer /kil-á-ma-ter/ *n.* kilómetro
kilowatt /kíl-ou-uot/ *n.* kilovatio
kind /kaind/ *n.* clase; tripo; *adj.* bondadoso
kiss /kis/ *n.* beso; *v.* besar
kitchen /kích-n/ *n.* cocina
kitten /kít-n/ *n.* gatito; *Cuba* gatico
knee /ni/ *n.* rodilla
knife /naif/ *n.* cuchillo
knock /nok/ *v.* tocar; llamar
know /nou/ *v.* saber; conocer
know how /nou jau/ *v.* saber
knowledge /nál-ich/ *n.* conocimiento

- L -

label /léi-bel/ *n.* etiqueta
lace /leis/ *n.* encaje
lack /lak/ *n.* falta; *v.* faltar
ladder /lád-er/ *n.* escalera
lady /léi-di/ *n.* señora; dama
lake /leik/ *n.* lago
lamp /lamp/ *n.* lámpara
land /land/ *n.* tierra; *v.* aterrizar
landing /lánd-ing/ *n.* aterrizaje
landscape /lánd-skeip/ *n.* paisaje
lane (highway) /lein/ *n. Arg.* trocha; *Col.* vía; *Mex.* carril; *Ven.* canal
language /lán-güich/ *n.* lenguaje; idioma
large /larch/ *adj.* grande
last /last/ *adj.* último
late /leit/ *adv.* tarde
lately /léit-li/ *adv.* recientemente
latitude /lát-i-tiud/ *n.* latitud
latter /lát-er/ *adj.* posterior
laugh /laf/ *n.* risa; *v.* reírse
laughter /láf-ter/ *n.* risa
laundry /lón-dri/ *n.* lavandería
law /lo/ *n.* ley; derecho
lawn /lon/ *n.* césped; *Mex., PR* pasto; *Ven.* grama; *Andes* prado
lawsuit /ló-sut/ *n.* pleito

lawyer /lói-er/ *n.* abogado; *Mex.* licenciado
lay /lei/ *v.* poner
lazy /léi-si/ *adj.* flojo; vago; *Uru.* holgazán; *Ven.* perezoso
lead /lid/ *v.* guiar; dirigir
leader /líd-er/ *n.* guía; dirigente; líder
learn /lern/ *v.* aprender
least /list/ *adj.* menor; mínimo
leather /léd-er/ *n.* cuero; piel
leave /liv/ *v.* salir
leave out /liv aut/ *v.* omitir
left /left/ *adj.* izquierdo
leg /leg/ *n.* pierna
legal /li-gal/ *adj.* legal
legalize /li-gal-ais/ *v.* legalizar
lemon /lém-on/ *n.* limón
lemonade /lém-on-eid/ *n.* limonada
lend /lend/ *v.* prestar
length /length/ *n.* largo
lens /lens/ *n.* lente
lentils /lén-tils/ *n.* lentejas
less /les/ *adj., adv.* menos
letter /lét-er/ *n.* carta; letra (alphabet)
lettuce /lét-os/ *n.* lechuga
library /lái-bre-ri/ *n.* biblioteca
license (driver's) /lái-sens/ *n. Arg.* permiso de manejo; *Chi.* carnet de manejar; *Mex.* licencia (de conducir); *Pe.* brevete; *Uru.* libreta de conductor; *v.* licenciar

license plate /lái-sens pleit/ *n.* chapa; placa; *Chi.* patente
lid /lid/ *n.* tapa
lie /lai/ *n.* mentira
lie down /lai daun/ *v.* acostarse
life /laif/ *n.* vida
life insurance /laif in-shúr-ans/ *n.* seguro de vida
lift /lift/ *v.* levantar
lift (in car) /lift/ *n. Mex.* aventón; *PR* pon; *Ven.* cola
light /lait/ *n.* luz
light bulb /lait bolb/ *n.* bombilla; *Arg.* lamparita; *Mex.* foco
lighthouse /láit-jaus/ *n.* faro
lighting /láit-ing/ *n.* alumbrado
like /laik/ *v.* gustar; *adj.* parecido
lime /laim/ *n.* lima; limón
limit /lím-it/ *n.* límite; *v.* limitar
line /lain/ *n.* línea; cola; fila
linen /lín-en/ *n.* lino
lip /lip/ *n.* labio
lipstick /líp-stik/ *n.* lápiz de labios; *Arg., Chi., Pe.* rouge; *Col.* colorete; *Mex.* pintura de labios
liquor /lí-kor/ *n.* licor
liquid /lík-uid/ *n.* líquido
liqueur /li-kúr/ *n.* licor
list /list/ *n.* lista
listen /lís-n/ *v.* escuchar
little /lít-l/ *adj.* poco; pequeño; chico
live /liv/ *v.* vivir

live /laiv/ *adj.* vivo
lively /láiv-li/ *adj.* vivo
liver /lív-er/ *n.* hígado
living room /lív-ing rum/ *n.* sala; *Chi., RP* living; *Pe.* salón
lobster /lób-ster/ *n.* langosta
local /ló-kel/ *adj.* local
locate /lóu-keit/ *v.* encontrar
lock /lok/ *n.* cerradura; *v.* cerrar con llave
long /long/ *adj.* largo
look /luk/ *n.* mirada; *v.* mirar
look after /luk áf-ter/ *v.* cuidar
look at /luk at/ *v.* mirar
look for /luk for/ *v.* buscar
loose /lus/ *adj.* suelto; flojo
lose /luz/ *v.* perder
loss /los/ *n.* pérdida
lottery /lót-er-i/ *n.* lotería
loud /laud/ *adj.* alto; fuerte
loudspeaker /láud-spik-er/ *n.* altavoz
love /lov/ *n.* amor; *v.* amar; querer
low /lou/ *adj.* bajo
loyal /lói-al/ *adj.* leal
luck /lok/ *n.* suerte
luggage /lóg-ich/ *n.* equipaje
lunch (midday meal) /lonch/ *n. Arg.* morfi; *Bol., Cuba, Ven.* almuerzo; *Mex.* comida
luxury /lók-shor-i/ *n.* lujo

- M -

macaroni /mak-a-róu-ni/ *n.* macarrones
machine /ma-shín/ *n.* máquina
mad /mad/ *adj.* enojado
made /meid/ *adj.* hecho
madman /mád-man/ *n.* loco
madness /mád-ness/ *n.* locura
magazine /má-ga-sin/ *n.* revista
mahogany /ma-jóg-a-ni/ *n.* caoba
maid /meid/ *n.* criada; *Arg.* sierva; *Bol., Ec., Pan.* empleada; *Mex., Uru.* sirvienta; *Pe.* empleada doméstica
mail /meil/ *n.* correo; correspondencia; *v.* echar al correo
main /mein/ *adj.* principal
main square /mein skuer/ *n.* plaza mayor; *Mex.* zócalo
major /méi-yor/ *n.* (mil.) comandante; *adj.* mayor
majority /ma-yór-i-ti/ *n.* mayoría
make /meik/ *v.* hacer
make a mistake /meik a mis-téik/ *v.* equivocarse
male /meil/ *n., adj.* macho
man /man/ *n.* hombre
manage /mán-ich/ *v.* manejar
management /mán-ich-ment/ *n.* administración; gerencia
manager /mán-ich-er/ *n.* gerente

manicure /mán-i-kiur/ *n.* manicura
manner /mán-er/ *n.* manera
manners /mán-ers/ *n.* modales
manufacture /man-iu-fák-chur/ *n.* fabricación
many /mén-i/ *adj.* muchos
map /map/ *n.* mapa
marble /már-bl/ *n.* mármol
March /march/ *n.* marzo
margarine /már-ya-rin/ *n.* margarina
maritime /mér-i-taim/ *adj.* marítimo
mark /mark/ *n.* marca
market /már-ket/ *n.* mercado
marmalade /már-ma-leid/ *n.* mermelada
marriage /mér-ich/ *n.* matrimonio
married /mér-id/ *adj.* casado
marry /mér-i/ *v.* casarse con
masculine /más-kiu-lin/ *adj.* masculino
mass /mas/ *n.* masa; (rel.) misa
master /más-ter/ *n.* amo
masterpiece /más-ter-pis/ *n.* obra maestra
match /mach/ *n.* fósforo; Mex. cerillo
material /ma-tí-ri-al/ *n.* materia; adj. material
matter /mát-er/ *n.* materia; asunto; v. importar
May /mei/ *n.* mayo
may /mei/ *v.* poder
mayor /méi-yor/ *n.* alcalde; *Arg.* intendente; *Mex.* presidente municipal
me /mi/ *pron.* me; a mí
meal /mil/ *n.* comida

meaning /min-ing/ *n.* significado
measure /mésh-ur/ *n.* medida; *v.* medir
measurement /mésh-ur-ment/ *n.* medida
meat /mit/ *n.* carne
mechanic /me-kán-ik/ *n.* mecánico
medicine /méd-i-sin/ *n.* medicina
medium /mí-di-om/ *adj.* mediano
meet /mit/ *v.* conocer; encontrar
meeting /mít-ing/ *n.* reunión; junta
melon /mél-on/ *n.* melón
mend /mend/ *v.* remendar
menu /mén-iu/ *n.* menú; carta; *Cuba* lista
merchandise /mér-chan-dais/ *n.* mercancía
merchant /mér-chant/ *n., adj.* mercante
mess /mes/ *n.* desorden
message /més-ich/ *n.* recado
metal /mét-l/ *n.* metal
meter /mí-ter/ *n.* medidor; metro (measurement)
method /méth-od/ *n.* método
middle /míd-l/ *n., adj.* medio
middle-aged /mid-l-éicht/ *adj.* de edad mediana
middle class /míd-l klas/ *n.* la clase media
midnight /míd-nait/ *n.* medianoche
mile /mail/ *n.* milla
milk /milk/ *n.* leche
million /míl-yon/ *n.* millón
millionaire /míl-yon-er/ *n.* millonario
mind /maind/ *n.* mente
mine /main/ *n.* mina; *adj.* mío; *pron.* el mío

mineral /mín-er-al/ *n., adj.* mineral
minimum /mí-na-mom/ *n.* mínimo
minor /mái-nor/ *n., adj.* menor
minute /mín-it/ *n.* minuto
mirror /mír-or/ *n.* espejo
miss /mis/ *n.* señorita; *v.* extrañar
missing /mís-ing/ *adj.* perdido
missus /mís-us/ *n.* señora
mistake /mis-téik/ *n.* error
mister /mís-ter/ *n.* señor
mistrust /mis-tróst/ *v.* desconfiar de
misunderstand /mis-on-der-stánd/ *v.* entender mal
misunderstanding /mis-on-der-stánd-ing/ *n.* malentendido
mix /miks/ *v.* mezclar
mixture /míks-chur/ *n.* mezcla
modern /mód-ern/ *adj.* moderno
moment /móm-ent/ *n.* momento
monastery /món-as-ter-i/ *n.* monasterio
Monday /món-dei/ *n.* lunes
money /món-i/ *n.* dinero
money order /món-i ór-der/ *n.* giro; *Ven.* orden de pago
monkey /món-ki/ *n.* mono; *Mex.* chango
month /month/ *n.* mes
monument /món-iu-ment/ *n.* monumento
moon /mun/ *n.* luna
moral /mór-al/ *adj.* moral
more /mor/ *adj., adv.* más

morning /mór-ning/ *n.* mañana
mosquito /mos-kí-tou/ *n.* mosquito
most /moust/ *n.* la mayor parte (de)
mother /mód-er/ *n.* madre; *Mex.* mamá
motherhood /mód-er-jud/ *n.* maternidad
mother-in-law /mód-er-in-lo/ *n.* suegra
motion /móu-shon/ *n.* moción
motor /moú-ter/ *n., adj.* motor
motorboat /móu-ter-bout/ *n.* bote de motor
motorcycle /móu-ter-sai-kl/ *n.* motocicleta
motorist /moú-ter-ist/ *n.* automovilista
mountain /máun-tin/ *n.* montaña
mountainous /máun-tin-os/ *adj.* montañoso
mountain range /máun-tin rainch/ *n.* sierra
mouth /mauth/ *n.* boca
mouthful /máuth-ful/ *n.* bocado
move /muv/ *v.* mover
much /moch/ *adj.* mucho
municipal /miu-nís-i-pal/ *adj.* municipal
museum /miu-sí-om/ *n.* museo
mushroom /mósh-rum/ *n.* hongo; champiñón
music /miú-sik/ *n.* música
musician /miu-sí-shon/ *n.* músico
must /most/ *v.* deber; tener que
my /mai/ *adj.* mi; mío
myself /mai-sélf/ *pron.* yo mismo

- N -

nail /neil/ *n.* uña (finger); clavo; *v.* clavar
nail file /neil fail/ *n.* lima para uñas
name /neim/ *n.* nombre; *v.* nombrar
nap /nap/ *n.* siesta
napkin /náp-kin/ *n.* servilleta
narrow /nár-ou/ *adj.* estrecho
nation /néi-shon/ *n.* nación
national /násh-o-nal/ *adj.* nacional
native /néi-tiv/ *n., adj.* indígena; *adj.* nativo
natural /ná-chu-ral/ *adj.* natural
nature /néi-chur/ *n.* naturaleza
navy /néi-vi/ *n.* marina de guerra
near /nir/ *adv.* cerca; *prep.* cerca de
nearly /nír-li/ *adv.* casi
necessary /nés-es-a-ri/ *adj.* necesario
neck /nek/ *n.* cuello
need /nid/ *n.* necesidad; *v.* necesitar
needle /ní-dl/ *n.* aguja
needless /níd-les/ *adj.* innecesario
neighbor /néi-bor/ *n.* vecino
neighborhood /néi bor-jud/ *n.* vecindad; barrio
neither /ní-der/ *adj.* ninguno; *adv.* tampoco; *conj.* ni; tampoco
nephew /néf-iu/ *n.* sobrino
nervous /nér-vos/ *adj.* nervioso
net /net/ *n.* red

never /név-er/ *adv.* nunca; jamás
nevertheless /nev-er-da-lés/ *adv.* sin embargo
new /niu/ *adj.* nuevo
news /nius/ *n.* noticias
newspaper /niús-pei-per/ *n.* periódico; diario (daily)
next /nekst/ *adj.* próximo
nice /nais/ *adj.* simpático; amable
nickname /ník-neim/ *n.* apodo
niece /nis/ *n.* sobrina
night /nait/ *n.* noche
nightgown /náit-gaun/ *n.* camisa de dormir; *Cuba* bata de dormir
nightly /náit-li/ *adv.* cada noche
nightmare /náit-mer/ *n.* pesadilla
nine /nain/ *n., adj.* nueve
nineteen /nain-tín/ *n., adj.* diez y nueve
ninety /náin-ti/ *n., adj.* noventa
ninth /nainth/ *adj.* noveno
no /nou/ *adj.* ninguno; *adv.* no
nobody /nóu-bod-i/ *pron.* nadie
noise /nois/ *n.* ruido; bulla; *Arg.* bochinche
noisy /nói-si/ *adj.* ruidoso
none /non/ *pron.* ninguno
nonsense /nón-sens/ *n.* tontería
noon /nun/ *n.* mediodía
nor /nor/ *conj.* ni
normal /nór-ml/ *adj.* normal
north /north/ *n.* norte
nose /nous/ *n.* nariz

not /not/ *adv.* no
not at all /not at ol/ *adv.* de ninguna manera
note /nout/ *n.* nota; *v.* notar
notebook /nóut-buk/ *n.* cuaderno
nothing /ná-thing/ *pron.* nada
notice /nóu-tis/ *n.* aviso; *v.* notar
noun /naun/ *n.* nombre
nourishment /nór-ish-ment/ *n.* alimento
novel /náv-l/ *n.* novela
November /no-vém-br/ *n.* noviembre
now /nau/ *adv.* ahora
nowadays /náu-a-deis/ *adv.* hoy día
now and then /nau and den/ *adv.* de vez en cuando
nowhere /nóu-juer/ *adv.* en ninguna parte
number /nóm-ber/ *n.* número
numerous /niú-mer-os/ *adj.* numeroso
nurse /ners/ *n.* enfermera
nut /not/ *n.* nuez
nutrition /nu-trí-shon/ *n.* nutrición

- O -

oar /or/ *n.* remo
oatmeal /óut-mil/ *n.* avena
obey /o-béi/ *v.* obedecer
object /ob-yékt/ *v.* objetar
object /ób-yekt/ *n.* objeto
observatory /ob-sér-va-to-ri/ *n.* observatorio
observe /ob-sérv/ *v.* observar
obstacle /ób-sta-kl/ *n.* obstáculo
obstruct /ob-strókt/ *v.* obstruir; estorbar
obstruction /ob-strók-shon/ *n.* obstrucción
obtain /ob-téin/ *v.* obtener
occasion /o-kéi-shon/ *n.* ocasión
occasionally /o-kéi-shon-a-li/ *adv.* de vez en cuando
occupation /ok-iu-péi-shon/ *n.* ocupación
occupy /ók-iu-pai/ *v.* ocupar
occur /o-kér/ *v.* ocurrir
ocean /óu-shan/ *n.* océano
October /ok-tóu-br/ *n.* octubre
oculist /á-kiu-list/ *n.* oculista
odd /od/ *adj.* extraño
odor /óu-dor/ *n.* olor
of /ov/ *prep.* de
off /of/ *adv.* lejos; *prep.* de; desde
offend /o-fénd/ *v.* ofender
offense /o-féns/ *n.* ofensa
offensive /o-fén-siv/ *adj.* ofensivo

offer /óf-er/ *n.* ofrecimiento; *v.* ofrecer
office /óf-is/ *n.* oficina; *Arg., Ec., Pe.* (leg.) estudio jurídico; *Mex.* (leg.) bufete; (med.) consultorio
officer /óf-is-er/ *n.* oficial
official /o-físh-l/ *n., adj.* oficial
often /óf-n/ *adv.* frecuentemente
oil /oil/ *n.* aceite; *v.* engrasar
old /ould/ *adj.* viejo
olive /ól-iv/ *n.* aceituna
olive oil /ól-iv oil/ *n.* aceite de oliva
omit /o-mít/ *v.* omitir
on /on/ *prep.* en; sobre
once /uans/ *adv.* una vez
once more /uans mor/ *adv.* otra vez
one /uan/ *adj.* un; una; *pron.* uno
oneself /uan-sélf/ *pron.* se; sí mismo
on horseback /on jórs-bak/ *adv.* a caballo
onion /ón-yon/ *n.* cebolla
only /óun-li/ *adj.* sólo; único; *adv.* solamente
on top of /on top ov/ *prep.* encima de
onyx /ón-iks/ *n.* ónix
open /óu-pen/ *adj.* abierto; *v.* abrir
opening /oú-pen-ing/ *n.* inauguración
opera /óp-ra/ *n.* ópera
opinion /o-pín-yon/ *n.* opinión
opportunity /a-por-tiú-ni-ti/ *n.* oportunidad
oppose /a-póus/ *v.* oponer
opposite /áp-o-sit/ *adj.* opuesto
or /or/ *conj.* o

orange /ór-ench/ *n.* naranja
orange juice /ór-ench yus/ *n.* jugo de naranja; *PR* jugo de china
orchestra /ór-kes-tra/ *n.* orquesta
orchestra seat /ór kes-tra sit/ *n.* butaca
orchid /ór-kid/ n. orquídea
order /ór-der/ *n.* orden; *v.* pedir
ordinary /ór-di-na-ri/ *adj.* corriente
organization /or-ga-na-séi-shon/ *n.* organización
organize /ór-gan-ais/ *v.* organizar
ornament /ór-na-ment/ *n.* adorno
other /ód-er/ *adj., pron.* otro
otherwise /ód-er-uais/ *adv.* de otra manera
ought to /ot tu/ *v.* deber de
ounce /auns/ *n.* onza
our /aur/ *adj.* nuestro
ours /aurs/ *pron.* el nuestro
ourselves /aur-sélvs/ *pron.* nosotros mismos
out /aut/ *adv.* fuera
outlet /áut-let/ *n.* toma-corriente; *Mex.* contacto
out of /aut ov/ *prep.* fuera de
outside /aut-sáid/ *adv.* afuera
outstanding /aut-stánd-ing/ *adj.* destacado
over /óu-ver/ *prep.* sobre
overcharge /ou ver-chárch/ *v.* recargar; cobrar demasiado
overcoat /óu-ver-kout/ *n.* abrigo
overlook /ou-ver-lúk/ *v.* pasar por alto
overweight /ou-ver-uéit/ *n.* sobrepeso

owe /ou/ *v.* deber
owl /aul/ *n.* lechuza; buho; *Mex.* tecolote
own /oun/ *adj.* propio; *v.* poseer
owner /óu-ner/ *n.* dueño

- P -

pack /pak/ *v.* empacar
package /pák-ich/ *n.* paquete
page /peich/ *n.* página
pain /pein/ *n.* dolor
paint /peint/ *n.* pintura; *v.* pintar
paintbrush /péint-brosh/ *n.* brocha
painter /péint-er/ *n.* pintor
pair /per/ *n.* pareja; par
pajamas /pa-yá-mas/ *n.* pijamas
pale /peil/ *n.* pálido
palm /pam/ *n.* palma
pan /pan/ *n.* cazuela; *Mex.* olla
pancake /pán-keik/ *n., Ven.* panqué; *Mex.* hot cakes; *RP* panqueque
panties /pán-tis/ *n.* bragas; *Arg.* medibacha; *Chi., Pan., PR* panty; *Cuba* bloomers; *Ec., Pe.* calzón; *Mex.* pantaleta; *Uru.* bombacha
pants /pants/ *n.* pantalones; *Mex.* pantalón
pantyhose /pán-ti-jous/ *n. Mex.* pantimedia
paper /péi-per/ *n.* papel
parachute /pár-a-shut/ *n.* paracaídas
parade /pa-réid/ *n.* desfile
paradise /pár-a-dais/ *n.* paraíso
parasite /pár-a-sait/ *n.* parásito
pardon /pár-dn/ *n.* perdón; *v.* perdonar
parents /péi-rents/ *n.* padres

park /park/ *n.* parque; *v.* estacionar; *Cuba* parquear
parking /párk-ing/ *n.* estacionamiento; *Bol., Cuba* parqueo
parking lot /párk-ing lot/ *n.* estacionamiento; *Chi., RP* playa de estacionamiento; *Col., Ec.* parqueadero
parrot /pár-ot/ *n.* papagayo; loro
parsley /pár-sli/ *n.* perejil
part /part/ *n.* parte
participate /par-tís-a-peit/ *v.* participar
particular /par-tík-iu-lr/ *adj.* especial
party /pár-ti/ *n.* fiesta; (pol.) partido
pass /pas/ *n.* pase *v.* pasar; (in car) *Mex.* rebasar; *Pe.* sobrepasar; *Uru.* adelantar
passage /pás-ich/ *n.* pasaje
passenger /pás-in-yer/ *n.* pasajero
passport /pás-port/ *n.* pasaporte
past /past/ *n., adj.* pasado
pastry /péis-tri/ *n.* pastelería
path /path/ *n.* sendero
patient /péi-shent/ *n., adj.* paciente
pavement /péiv-ment/ *n.* pavimento
pay /pei/ *n.* pago; *v.* pagar
payment /péi-ment/ *n.* pago
pea /pi/ *n.* guisante; chícharo
peace /pis/ *n.* paz
peach /pich/ *n.* melocotón; *Arg., Mex., Pan.* durazno
peak /pik/ *n.* pico; cumbre
peanut /pí-not/ *n.* maní; *Mex.* cacahuate

pear /per/ *n.* pera
pearl /perl/ *n.* perla
peasant /pés-ant/ *n.* campesino; *Arg.* payuca; *Bol.* labrador; *Chi.* guaso; *Col.* paisa; *Cuba* guajiro; *PR* jíbaro;
pedestrian /pi-dés-tri-an/ *n.* caminante; peatón
peel /pil/ *n.* corteza; *v.* pelar
pen /pen/ *n.* pluma
penalty /pén-al-ti/ *n.* castigo
pencil /pén-sl/ *n.* lápiz
peninsula /pe-nín-su-la/ *n.* península
penny /pén-i/ *n.* centavo
pension /pén-shon/ *n.* retiro
people /pí-pl/ *n.* gente
pepper /pép-er/ *n.* pimienta
peppermint /pép-er-mint/ *n.* menta
peppers (green) /pép-ers/ *n.* ají; *Mex.* chile verde
per /per/ *prep.* por
percent /per-sént/ *n., adj.* por ciento
percentage /per-sén-tich/ *n.* porcentaje
perfect /pér-fikt/ *adj.* perfecto
perform /per-fórm/ *v.* ejecutar
performance /per-fórm-ans/ *n.* función
perfume /pér-fium/ *n.* perfume
perhaps /per-jáps/ *adv.* quizás; tal vez
period /pí-riod/ *n.* período
permanent /pér-ma-nent/ *n., adj.* permanente
permission /per-mísh-on/ *n.* permiso
permit /per-mít/ *v.* permitir

permit /pér-mit/ *n.* permiso
person /pér-son/ *n.* persona
personal /pér son-l/ *adj.* personal
personality /per-son-ál-i-ti/ *n.* personalidad
pet /pet/ *n.* animal doméstico; *Mex.* mascota
petroleum /pi-tróu-li-om/ *n.* petróleo
pheasant /fés-ant/ *n.* faisán
photograph /fóu-to-graf/ *n.* foto; *v.* sacar foto
photographer /fou-tóg-ra-fer/ *n.* fotógrafo
phrase /freis/ *n.* frase
physician /fi-sí-shan/ *n.* médico
piano /piá-nou/ *n.* piano
pick /pick/ *v.* escoger
pickle /pik-l/ *n.* encurtido
pickpocket /pík-pok-it/ *n.* carterista; ratero
pick up /pik op/ *v.* recoger
picnic /pík-nik/ *n.* día de campo; *Mex.* picnic
picture /pík-chur/ *n.* cuadro
pie /pai/ *n. Arg.* torta; *Bol.* tarta; *Chi.* kuchen; *Cuba* pastel; *Mex.* pay
piece /pis/ *n.* pedazo
pig /pig/ *n.* puerco; cerdo; cochino; *Arg., Bol.* chancho
pigeon /pích-on/ *n.* paloma
pill /pil/ *n.* píldora; *Arg., Mex.* pastilla
pillow /píl-ou/ *n.* almohada
pilot /pái-lot/ *n.* piloto
pin /pin/ *n.* alfiler; broche
pineapple /páin-ap-l/ *n.* piña; *Arg.* ananá
pink /pink/ *adj.* rosado

pint /paint/ *n.* pinta
pitcher /pí-chur/ *n.* cántaro; jarro
place /pleis/ *n.* lugar; *v.* poner
plain /plein/ *n.* llanura; *adj.* sencillo
plan /plan/ *n.* plan; *v.* planear
plane /plein/ *n.* avión
plant /plant/ *n.* planta; *v.* plantar
plantation /plan-téi-shon/ *n.* hacienda
plate /pleit/ *n.* plato
platform /plát-form/ *n.* plataforma
play /plei/ *n.* juego; drama; *v.* jugar
playground /pleí-graund/ *n.* campo de juego
playing cards /pleí-ing kards/ *n.* barajas; cartas; *Andes* naipes
pleasant /plés-ant/ *adj.* agradable
please /plis/ *v.* gustar; *interj.* por favor
plug /plog/ *n.* tapón; (elec.) enchufe
plum /plom/ *n.* ciruela
plumber /plóm-er/ *n.* plomero; *Andes* gasfitero; *Chi.* gasfiter; *Mex.* fontanero
plus /plos/ *adj., adv.* más
pneumonia /niu-móu-ni-a/ *n.* pulmonía
pocket /pók-it/ *n.* bolsillo
point /point/ *n.* punto; *v.* apuntar
police /po-lís/ *n.* policía; *Arg.* botón
policy /pól-i-si/ *n.* política
polite /po-láit/ *adj.* cortés
political /po-lít-i-kal/ *adj.* político
politician /pol-i-tí-shon/ *n.* político

politics /pól-i-tiks/ *n.* política
pool /pul/ *n.* piscina; alberca
poor /pur/ *adj.* pobre
pop /pop/ *n.* refresco; gaseosa
popcorn /póp-korn/ *n.* *Arg.* pochoclo; *Bol.* pipocas; *Chi.* cabritas; *Col.* cristetas; *Cuba* rositas de maíz; *Ec.* canguil; *Mex.* palomitas; *Pan., Pe.* popcorn; *Ven.* cotufas
popular /póp-iu-lr/ *adj.* popular
population /po-piu-leí-shon/ *n.* población
porcelain /pórs-lin/ *n.* porcelana
pork /pork/ *n.* carne de puerco
port /port/ *n.* puerto
portion /pór-shon/ *n.* porción
position /po-sí-shon/ *n.* posición
positive /pós-i-tiv/ *adj.* positivo
possess /po-sés/ *v.* poseer
possibility /pos-i-bíl-i-ti/ *n.* posibilidad
possible /pós-i-bl/ *adj.* posible
possibly /pós-i-bli/ *adv.* posiblemente
postage /póst-ich/ *n.* porte
postcard /póst-kard/ *n.* tarjeta postal
poster /póst-er/ *n.* cartel
postman /póst-man/ *n.* cartero
post office /post óf-is/ *n.* casa de correos; *Mex.* oficina de correos
potato /po-téi-to/ *n.* papa
pothole /pót-joul/ *n.* bache; *Pan., Ven.* hueco
poultry /póul-tri/ *n.* aves de corral

pound /paund/ *n.* libra
powder /páu-der/ *n.* polvo
powder puff /páu-der pof/ *n.* polvera; borla; *Ec., Mex., Pan.* mota; *RP* cisne
power /páu-er/ *n.* poder
powerful /páu-er-ful/ *adj.* poderoso
powerless /páu-er-les/ *adj.* impotente
practical /prák-ti-kl/ *adj.* práctico
practice /prák-tis/ *n.* práctica; *v.* practicar
prawn /pron/ *n.* langostino
precise /pri-sáis/ *adj.* exacto
precision /pri-sí-shon/ *n.* precisión
prefer /pri-fér/ *v.* preferir
preferable /préf-er-a-bl/ *adj.* preferible
preparation /pre-pa-réi-shon/ *n.* preparación
prepare /pri-pér/ *v.* preparar
prescribe /pri-skráib/ *v.* (med.) recetar
prescription /pris-kríp-shon/ *n.* (med.) receta
presence /prés-ens/ *n.* presencia
present /prés-ent/ *n.* presente; regalo; *adj.* actual
present /pre-sént/ *v.* presentar
presentation /pre-sen-teí-shon/ *n.* presentación
president /prés-i-dent/ *n.* presidente
press /pres/ *n.* prensa
pressure /présh-er/ *n.* presión
pretty /prí-ti/ *adj.* bonito; lindo
previous /prí-vi-os/ *adj.* anterior
price /prais/ *n.* precio
pride /praid/ *n.* orgullo

priest /prist/ *n.* cura; sacerdote
primary /prái-mei-ri/ *adj.* primario
primitive /prim-i-tiv/ *adj.* primitivo
principal /prín-si-pl/ *n., adj.* principal
principle /prín-si-pl/ *n.* principio
printer /prínt-er/ *n.* impresor
priority /prái-or-i-ti/ *n.* prioridad
prison /prí-sn/ *n.* prisión
prisoner /prí-son-er/ *n.* prisionero
privacy /prái-va-si/ *n.* privacidad
private /prái-vet/ *adj.* privado; particular
privilege /prí-vi-lich/ *n.* privilegio
probable /prób-a-bl/ *adj.* probable
problem /prób-lem/ *n.* problema
procedure /pro-sí-diur/ *n.* procedimiento
process /prá-ses/ *n.* proceso; *v.* procesar
produce /pró-dius/ *n.* productos agrícolas
produce /pro-diús/ *v.* producir
product /pród-okt/ *n.* producto
professor /pro-fés-or/ *n.* profesor
profit /próf-it/ *n.* ganancia; *v.* ganar
profitable /próf-it-ab-l/ *adj.* lucrativo
profound /pro-fáund/ *adj.* profundo
progress /pró-gres/ *n.* progreso
progress /pro-grés/ *v.* progresar
prohibit /pro-jíb-it/ *v.* prohibir
project /pró-yect/ *n.* proyecto
promise /pró-mis/ *n.* promesa; *v.* prometer
prompt /prompt/ *adj.* puntual

pronounce /pro-náuns/ *v.* pronunciar
pronunciation /pro-nun-si-éi-shon/ *n.* pronunciación
proof /pruf/ *n.* prueba
proper /próp-er/ *adj.* apropiado
property /próp-er-ti/ *n.* propiedad
propose /pro-poús/ *v.* proponer
prosecute /prós-i-kiut/ *v.* (leg.) procesar
prosecution /pros-i-kiú-shon/ *n.* prosecución
prostitute /prós-ti-tiut/ *n.* prostituta
protect /pro-téikt/ *v.* proteger
protection /pro-téik-shon/ *n.* protección
protest /pro-tést/ *v.* protestar
proud /praud/ *adj.* orgulloso
prove /pruv/ *v.* probar
proverb /próv-erb/ *n.* proverbio
provide /pro-váid/ *v.* proveer
province /próv-ins/ *n.* provincia
prune /prun/ *n.* ciruela pasa
public /pób-lik/ *n., adj.* público
publication /pob-li-kéi-shon/ *n.* publicación
publish /pób-lish/ *v.* publicar
pudding /púd-ing/ *n.* pudín; budín
pull /pul/ *v.* tirar; jalar
pump /pomp/ *n.* bomba
pumpkin /pómp-kin/ *n.* calabaza; *Andes, Chi., Pan., RP* zapallo; *Ven.* auyama
punch /ponch/ *n.* ponche
punctual /pónk-chu-al/ *adj.* puntual
punish /pón-ish/ *v.* castigar

punishment /pón-ish-ment/ *n.* castigo
puppet /póp-et/ *n.* títere; *Uru.* marioneta
purchase /pér-ches/ *n.* compra; *v.* comprar
pure /piur/ *adj.* puro
purify /piú-ri-fai/ *v.* purificar
purity /piú-ri-ti/ *n.* pureza
purple /pér-pl/ *n., adj.* morado
purpose /pér-pos/ *n.* propósito
purse /pers/ *n.* cartera; *Ec.* bolso; *Mex.* bolsa
pursue /per-siú/ *v.* perseguir
pus /pos/ *n.* pus
push /push/ *v.* empujar
put /put/ *v.* poner
put off /put of/ *v.* posponer
put on /put on/ *v.* ponerse
pyramid /pír-a-mid/ *n.* pirámide

- Q -

quaint /kueint/ *adj.* pintoresco
qualification /kual-i-fi-kéi-shon/ *n.* requisito
quality /kuál-i-ti/ *n.* calidad
quantity /kuán-ti-ti/ *n.* cantidad
quart /kuart/ *n.* cuarto de galón
quarter /kuár-ter/ *n.* cuarto
question /kués-chon/ *n.* pregunta;*v.* preguntar
quick /kuik/ *adj.* rápido
quiet /kuái-et/ *adj.* tranquilo
quit /kuit/ *v.* dejar de; renunciar
quite /kuait/ *adv.* bastante
quotation /kuou-téi-shon/ *n.* citación
quote /kuout/ *v.* citar

- R -

race /reis/ *n.* raza; carrera (horse, dog, etc.)
racket /rák-et/ *n.* raqueta
radio /réi-di-o/ *n.* radio
radish /rád-ish/ *n.* rábano
rail /reil/ *n.* riel
railway /réil-uei/ *n.* ferrocarril
rain /rein/ *n.* lluvia; *v.* llover
raincoat /réin-kout/ *n.* impermeable; *Pan.* capote
raise /reis/ *v.* levantar
raisin /réi-sin/ *n.* pasa; *Mex.* pasita
ranch /ranch/ *n.* rancho; hacienda; *Ven.* fundo
rancid /rán-sid/ *adj.* rancio
rank /rank/ *n.* rango
rape /reip/ *n.* violación; *v.* violar
rapid /ráp-id/ *adj.* rápido
rare /rer/ *adj.* medio crudo
rash /resh/ *n.* salpullido
rate /reit/ *n.* tarifa
rate of exchange /reit ov eks-chéinch/ *n.* tipo de cambio
rather /rád-er/ *adv.* más bien
raw /ro/ *adj.* crudo
razor /réi-sor/ *n.* máquina de afeitar
razor blade /réi-sor bleid/ *n.* hoja de afeitar; *Arg., Ec.* gillete; *Cuba* cuchillitos de afeitar; *Mex.* hoja de rasurar

reach /rich/ *v.* alcanzar
read /rid/ *v.* leer
reader /ríd-er/ *n.* lector
reading /ríd-ing/ *n.* lectura
ready /réd-i/ *adj.* listo
real /rí-al/ *adj.* verdadero
realize /ri-a-lais/ *v.* darse cuenta de
reason /rí-sn/ *n.* razón
reasonable /rí-sn-a-bl/ *adj.* razonable
rebate /rí-beit/ *n.* descuento
receipt /ri-sít/ *n.* recibo
receive /ri-sív/ *v.* recibir
recent /rí-sent/ *adj.* reciente
recently /rí-sent-li/ *adv.* recientemente
recipe /rés-a-pi/ *n.* receta
reclaim /ri-kléim/ *v.* reclamar
recognize /rék-og-nais/ *v.* reconocer
recommend /rek-o-ménd/ *v.* recomendar
recompense /rék-om-pens/ *n.* recompensa
record /rek-órd/ *v.* inscribir; grabar (sound)
record /rék-ord/ *n.* archivo; disco (phonograph)
recover /ri-kóv-er/ *v.* recobrar
red /red/ *n., adj.* rojo
reduce /ri-diús/ *v.* reducir
reduction /ri-dók-shon/ *n.* reducción
reef /rif/ *n.* arrecife
reel /ril/ *n.* carrete
refer /ri-fér/ *v.* referir
reference /réf-er-ens/ *n.* referencia

refresh /ri-frésh/ *v.* refrescar
refrigerator /ri-frí-ye-rei-tor/ *n.* refrigerador
refuse /ri-fiús/ *v.* rehusar
region /rí-yon/ *n.* región
register /ré-yis-ter/ *n.* registro; *v.* inscribir
registration /re-yis-tréi-shon/ *n.* inscripción; matrícula (school)
regret /ri-grét/ *v.* sentir
regular /ré-giu-lar/ *adj.* normal
reject /ri-yékt/ *v.* rechazar
relate /ri-léit/ *v.* relacionar; contar (tell)
relative /rél-a-tiv/ *n.* pariente; *adj.* relativo
relax /ri-láks/ *v.* relajar
release /ri-lís/ *v.* soltar
reliable /ri-lái-a-bl/ *adj.* confiable; *Mex.* formal
relief /ri-líf/ *n.* alivio
relieve /ri-lív/ *v.* aliviar
religion /ri-lí-yon/ *n.* religión
religious /ri-lí-yos/ *adj.* religioso
rely /ri-lái/ *v.* confiar
remain /ri-méin/ *v.* quedarse
remains /ri-méins/ *n.* restos
remember /rì-mém-ber/ *v.* recordar
remind /ri-máind/ *v.* recordar
remit /ri-mít/ *v.* remitir
remove /ri-múv/ *v.* quitar
renew /ri-niú/ *v.* renovar
renounce /ri-náuns/ *v.* renunciar
rent /rent/ *n.* renta; *v.* alquilar

repair /ri-pér/ *n.* reparación; *v.* reparar
repeat /ri-pít/ *v.* repetir
repetition /rep-i-tí-shon/ *n.* repetición
replace /ri-pléis/ *v.* reemplazar
reply /ri-plái/ *n.* respuesta; *v.* responder
report /ri-pórt/ *n.* informe; *v.* informar
reporter /ri-pór-ter/ *n.* periodista
represent /rep-ri-sént/ *v.* representar
reproduce /ri-pro-diús/ *v.* reproducir
reptile /rép-tail/ *n.* reptil
request /ri-kuést/ *n.* petición; *v.* pedir
require /ri-kuáir/ *v.* requerir
requirement /ri-kuáir-ment/ *n.* requisito
research /ri-serch/ *n.* investigación
reservation /re-ser-véi-shon/ *n.* reservación
reserve /ri-sérv/ *v.* reservar
resident /rés-i-dent/ *n., adj.* residente
resolve /ri-sólv/ *v.* resolver
resource /rí-sors/ *n.* recurso
respect /ris-pékt/ *n.* respeto; *v.* respetar
respond /ris-pónd/ *v.* responder
responsible /ris-pón-si-bl/ *adj.* responsable
rest /rest/ *n.* descanso; resto (remains); *v.* descansar
restaurant /rés-to-rant/ *n.* restaurante; restaurán
result /ri-sólt/ *n.* resultado
retail /rí-teil/ *n.* venta al menudeo; *v.* vender al menudeo
return /ri-térn/ *n.* regreso; *v.* volver; devolver (give back)

rheumatism /rú-ma-tis-m/ *n.* reumatismo
rib /rib/ *n.* costilla
ribbon /ríb-on/ *n.* cinta
rice /rais/ *n.* arroz
rich /rich/ *adj.* rico
ride /raid/ *v.* ir en coche (car); ir a caballo (horse)
ride (a lift) /raid/ *n.* *CA* ride; *Mex.* aventón; *Pe.* jalada; *PR* pon
rifle /rái-fl/ *n.* rifle
right /rait/ *n.* derecho; *adj.* correcto; derecho (direction)
right now /rait nou/ *adv.* ahora mismo; *Ec., Mex.* ahorita; *Pan.* momentito; *Uru.* pronto; enseguida
right there /rait der/ *adv.* allí mismo
ring /ring/ *n.* anillo; *v.* sonar
ripe /raip/ *adj.* maduro
rise /rais/ *v.* subir
risk /risk/ *n.* riesgo; *v.* arriesgar
river /rív-er/ *n.* río
road /roud/ *n.* camino
roast /roust/ *n.* asado; *v.* asar
rob /rob/ *v.* robar
robber /rób-er/ *n.* ladrón
robbery /rób-er-i/ *n.* robo
rock /rok/ *n.* roca
romance /róu-mans/ *n.* romance
room /rum/ *n.* cuarto; habitación; *Arg., Chi.* pieza
rose /rous/ *n.* rosa
rough /rof/ *adj.* áspero

round /raund/ *adj.* redondo
route /rut/ *n.* ruta
routine /ru-tin/ *n.* rutina
rubbish /rób-ish/ *n.* basura
ruby /rú-bi/ *n.* rubí
rude /rud/ *adj.* descortés; grosero; *Chi.,* roto; *Ven.* tosco
rug /rog/ *n. Arg.* alfombrita; *Chi.* choapino; *Mex.* tapete
rule /rul/ *n.* regla; *v.* mandar
rum /rom/ *n.* ron
run /ron/ *v.* correr
rush /rosh/ *n.* prisa; *v.* ir de prisa

- S -

sad /sad/ *adj.* triste
saddle /sád-l/ *n.* silla de montar
safe /seif/ *n.* caja de seguridad; *adj.* seguro
safety /séif-ti/ *n.* seguridad
sail /seil/ *n.* vela; *v.* navegar
sailor /séil-or/ *n.* marinero
saint /seint/ *n.* santo
salad /sál-ad/ *n.* ensalada
salary /sál-a-ri/ *n.* salario
sale /seil/ *n.* venta; *Arg.* pichincha; *Mex.* barata; oferta
salesman /séils-man/ *n.* vendedor
salmon /sá-mon/ *n.* salmón
salt /solt/ *n.* sal
salvage /sál-vich/ *n.* salvamento
same /seim/ *adj.* mismo
sample /sám-pl/ *n.* muestra
sanction /sánk-shon/ *n.* sanción; *v.* sancionar
sanctuary /sánk-chu-a-ri/ *n.* santuario
sand /sand/ *n.* arena
sandal /sán-dl/ *n.* sandalia; *Arg.* osota
sandwich /sánd-uich/ *n.* sandwich; emparedado; *Arg.* sanguche; *Cuba* bocadito; *Ec.* sánduche
sanitary /sán-i-ta-ri/ *adj.* sanitario
sapphire /sáf-air/ *n.* zafiro
sardine /sar-din/ *n.* sardina
satin /sát-in/ *n.* raso

satisfaction /sat-is-fák-shon/ *n.* satisfacción
satisfactory /sat-is-fák-to-ri/ *adj.* satisfactorio
satisfy /sát-is-fai/ *v.* satisfacer
Saturday /sát-er-dei/ *n.* sábado
sauce /sos/ *n.* salsa
saucer /sós-er/ *n.* platillo
sausage /só-sich/ *n.* salchicha (frankfurter); chorizo (hot sausage); longaniza
save /seiv/ *v.* salvar; ahorrar
savings /séi-vings/ *n.* ahorros
say /sei/ *v.* decir
saying /séi-ing/ *n.* dicho; refrán
scar /skar/ *n.* cicatriz
scarce /skers/ *adj.* escaso
scarcity /skér-ci-ti/ *n.* escasez
scare /sker/ *v.* asustar
scene /sin/ *n.* escena
scenery /sí-ner-i/ *n.* paisaje
scent /sent/ *n.* olor
schedule /skéd-iul/ *n.* horario
scholarship /skól-er-ship/ *n.* beca
school /skul/ *n.* escuela
science /sái-ns/ *n.* ciencia
scientific /sai-n-tí-fik/ *adj.* científico
scissors /sís-ers/ *n.* tijeras
scrape /skreip/ *v.* raspar
scratch /skrach/ *n.* rasguño; *v.* rascar
screen /skrin/ *n.* biombo; pantalla (movie, TV)
screw /skru/ *n.* tornillo

screwdriver /skrú-drai-ver/ *n.* destornillador
scrub /skrob/ *v.* fregar
sculptor /skólp-tor/ *n.* escultor
sculpture /skólp-chur/ *n.* escultura
sea /si/ *n.* mar
seal /sil/ *n.* sello; (zool.) foca; *v.* sellar
seam /sim/ *n.* costura
search /serch/ *n.* búsqueda; *v.* buscar
season /sí-sn/ *n.* estación; temporada
seasoning /sí-son-ing/ *n.* sazón
seat /sit/ *n.* asiento; *v.* sentar
second /sék-ond/ *n., adj.* segundo
secondhand store /sek-ond-jánd stor/ *n.* tienda de segunda mano; *Mex.* bazar; *Pan.* patio sale
secret /sí-krit/ *n., adj.* secreto
secretary /sék-ri-ta-ri/ *n.* secretario; secretaria
section /sék-shon/ *n.* sección
secure /si-kíur/ *adj.* seguro
security /si-kiú-ri-ti/ *n.* seguridad
sedative /séd-a-tiv/ *n., adj.* calmante
see /si/ *v.* ver
seed /sid/ *n.* semilla
seek /sik/ *v.* buscar
seem /sim/ *v.* parecer
seldom /sél-dm/ *adv.* raramente
select /si-lékt/ *v.* escoger
selection /si-lék-shon/ *n.* selección
self /self/ *adj.* mismo
sell /sel/ *v.* vender

senate /sén-et/ *n.* senado
send /send/ *v.* enviar
send back /send bak/ *v.* devolver
sender /sénd-er/ *n.* remitente
senior /sí-ni-or/ *n.* anciano; *adj.* mayor
sensation /sen-séi-shon/ *n.* sensación
sense /sens/ *n.* sentido
sensitive /sén-si-tiv/ *adj.* sensible
sensual /sén-shu-al/ *adj.* sensual
sentence /sén-tens/ *n.* (gram.) frase; sentencia; *v.* condenar
sentiment /sén-ti-ment/ *n.* sentimiento
separate /sép-ret/ *adj.* separado
separate /sep-a-réit/ *v.* separar
separation /sep-a-réi-shon/ *n.* separación
September /sep-tém-br/ *n.* septiembre
serenade /sér-i-néid/ *n.* serenata
series /sí-ris/ *n.* serie
serpent /sér-pent/ *n.* serpiente
servant /sér-vant/ *n.* criado; sirviente
serve /serv/ *v.* servir
service /sér-vis/ *n.* servicio
session /sé-shon/ *n.* sesión
set /set/ *n.* juego; *v.* poner
seven /sév-n/ *n., adj.* siete
seventh /sev-n-th/ *adj.* séptimo
seventy /sév-n-ti/ *n., adj.* setenta
several /sév-er-al/ *adj.* varios
severe /si-vír/ *adj.* severo; grave

sew /so/ *v.* coser
sewing /só-ing/ *n.* costura
sex /seks/ *n.* sexo
shack /shak/ *n.* choza; *Arg.* tapera; *Bol., Ven.* cabaña; *Cuba* bohío; *Mex.* jacal
shade /sheid/ *n.* sombra
shadow /shád-ou/ *n.* sombra
shake /sheik/ *v.* sacudir
shame /sheim/ *n.* vergüenza
shampoo /sham-pú/ *n.* champú
shape /sheip/ *n.* forma; *v.* dar forma
share /sher/ *n.* (com.) acción; *v.* compartir
shareholder /shér-joul-der/ *n.* (com.) accionista
shark /shark/ *n.* tiburón
sharp /sharp/ *adj.* agudo
shave /sheiv/ *v.* afeitar(se); *CA, Mex.* rasurar
she /shi/ *pron.* ella
sheep /ship/ *n.* oveja
sheet /shit/ *n.* hoja (paper); sábana (bed)
shelf /shelf/ *n.* estante
shell /shel/ *n.* casco; concha (sea)
shellfish /shél-fish/ *n.* marisco
shelter /shél-ter/ *n.* albergue
sheriff /shér-if/ *n.* sheriff; alguacil
sherry /shér-i/ *n.* vino de jerez
shine /shain/ *n.* brillo; *v.* lucir; brillar
shipment /shíp-ment/ *n.* envío
shirt /shert/ *n.* camisa
shock /shok/ *n.* choque

shoe /shu/ *n.* zapato
shoelace /shú-leis/ *n.* cordón de zapato
shoe polish /shu pól-ish/ *n.* betún; *Mex.* pintura para zapatos
shoeshine boy /shú-shain boi/ *n.* limpiabotas; *Chi., Ec., Pe., Uru.* lustrabotas; *Mex.* boleros
shoot /shut/ *v.* tirar
shop /shop/ *n.* tienda; *v.* ir de compras
shopping /shóp-ing/ *n.* compras
shopping bag /shóp-ing bag/ *n. Chi., Ec., Pe., Uru.* bolsa (para compras); *Cuba* jaba; *Mex.* morral; *PR* bolso de compras
shore /shor/ *n.* costa; ribera
short /short/ *adj.* corto; bajo (stature)
short person /short pér-son/ *n. Arg., Bol., Uru.* petizo; *Chi., Ven.* enano; *Cuba* bajito; *Ec.* omoto; *Mex.* chaparro
shortage /shórt-ich/ *n.* escasez
shortly /shórt-li/ *adv.* pronto
shot /shot/ *n.* tiro
shoulder /shóul-der/ *n.* hombro
shout /shaut/ *v.* gritar
show /shou/ *n.* espectáculo; *v.* mostrar
shower /sháu-er/ *n.* ducha; *Mex.* regadera (bath); aguacero (rain)
shrimp /shrimp/ *n.* camarones
shrine /shrain/ *n.* relicario
shrink /shrink/ *v.* encogerse
shut /shot/ *v.* cerrar(se)

shy /shai/ *adj.* tímido
sick /sik/ *adj.* malo; enfermo
sickness /sík-nes/ *n.* enfermedad
side /said/ *n.* lado
sidewalk /sáid-uok/ *n.* acera; Andes, RP, Uru. vereda; *Chi.* cuneta; *CA, Col.* andén
sigh /sai/ *n.* suspiro; *v.* suspirar
sight /sait/ *n.* vista
sign /sain/ *n.* letrero; *v.* firmar
signal /síg-nal/ *n.* señal
signature /síg-na-chur/ *n.* firma
silent /sái-lent/ *adj.* silencioso
silk /silk/ *n.* seda
silly /síl-i/ *adj.* tonto
silver /síl-ver/ *n.* plata
similar /sím-i-ler/ *adj.* similar
simple /sím-pl/ *adj.* sencillo
simplify /sím-pla-fai/ *v.* simplificar
sin /sin/ *n.* pecado; *v.* pecar
since /sins/ *adv.* desde; *conj.* puesto que
sincere /sin-sír/ *adj.* sincero
sing /sing/ *v.* cantar
singer /síng-er/ *n.* cantante
single /sín-gl/ *adj.* único; *n., adj.* soltero
singular /sín-guiu-lar/ *adj.* singular
sink (bathroom) /sink/ *n. Bol., Chi., Ven.* lavamanos; *Mex.* lavabo; *Pe.* lavatorio; *RP* pileta
sink (kitchen) /sink/ *n. Bol., Ven.* lavaplatos; *Chi., Pe., RP* lavadero; *Mex.* fregadero; *Uru.* pileta; *v.*

hundir
sirloin /sér-loin/ *n.* lomo
sister /sís-ter/ *n.* hermana
sister-in-law /sís-ter-in-lo/ *n.* cuñada
sit /sit/ *v.* sentar
sit down /sit daun/ *v.* sentarse
situated /sit-iu-ei-tid/ *adj.* situado
situation /sit-iu-éi-shon/ *n.* situación
six /six/ *n., adj.* seis
sixth /síx-th/ *adj.* sexto
sixty /síx-ti/ *n., adj.* sesenta
size /sais/ *n.* tamaño
skill /skil/ *n.* habilidad
skillful /skíl-ful/ *adj.* hábil
skin /skin/ *n.* piel; cutis
skirt /skert/ *n.* falda; *Cuba* saya; *RP* pollera
skunk /skonk/ *n.* mofeta; *Arg., Bol., Guat., Hond., Mex.* zorrillo
sky /skai/ *n.* cielo
slang /slang/ *n.* jerga; *Arg.* lunfardo; *Ec., Pan.* trapeador; *Mex.* caló; *Uru.* argot
sleep /slip/ *n.* sueño; *v.* dormir
sleeping car /slíp-ing kar/ *n. Arg.* camarote; *Chi.* cochecama; *Ec.* vagón; *Mex.* camarín; *Pe.* coche dormitorio; *Uru.* cabina de dormir; *Ven.* camerino
sleeve /sliv/ *n.* manga
slice /slais/ *n.* rebanada; *v.* rebanar
slip /slep/ *n.* combinación; *Chi., PR* enagua; *Cuba* sayuela; *Mex.* fondo; *Pan.* peticote

slow /slou/ *adj.* lento
slowly /slóu-li/ *adv.* despacio
slum /slom/ *n.* barrio pobre; *Arg.* villa; *Mex.* colonia; *Pe.* barriada
small /smol/ *adj.* pequeño; chico
smallpox /smól-poks/ *n.* viruela
smart /smart/ *adj.* inteligente
smell /smel/ *n.* olor; *v.* oler
smile /smail/ *n.* sonrisa; *v.* sonreir(se)
smoke /smouk/ *n.* humo; *v.* fumar
smooth /smuth/ *adj.* liso
snack /snak/ *n.* merienda; *Arg.* faivocló; *CA* bocas; *Chi.* las onces; *Cuba, Pe.* bocadito; *Mex.* botana; *Ven.* pasapalos
snake /sneik/ *n.* culebra; *Mex.* víbora
snow /snou/ *n.* nieve; *v.* nevar
so /sou/ *adv.* así
soak /souk/ *v.* mojar
soap /soup/ *n.* jabón
social /só-shal/ *adj.* social
society /so-sái-i-ti/ *n.* sociedad
sock /sok/ *n.* calcetín; media
soda /só-da/ *n.* soda; gaseosa
soft /soft/ *adj.* suave
soft drink /soft drink/ *n.* refresco; *Pan.* soda; *Pe.* gaseosa
soldier /sól-yer/ *n.* soldado
sole /soul/ *n.* suela (shoe); lenguado (fish); *adj.* solo; único

solid /sól-id/ *adj.* sólido
solution /so-lú-shon/ *n.* solución
solve /solv/ *v.* resolver
some /som/ *adj.* algunos; unos
somebody /sóm-bod-i/ *n., pron.* alguien
somehow /sóm-jau/ *adv.* de alguna manera
someone /sóm-uan/ *pron.* alguien
something /sóm-thing/ *n., pron.* algo
sometimes /sóm-taims/ *adv.* a veces
somewhere /sóm-juer/ *adv.* en alguna parte
son /son/ *n.* hijo
song /song/ *n.* canción
son-in-law /són-in-lo/ *n.* yerno
soon /sun/ *adv.* pronto
sore /sor/ *n.* herida; *adj.* doloroso
soul /soul/ *n.* alma
sound /saund/ *n.* sonido; *v.* sonar
soup /sup/ *n.* sopa
sour /saur/ *adj.* agrio
south /sauth/ *n.* sur
South American /sauth a-mér-i-kan/ *n., adj.* sudamericano
souvenir /su-ve-nír/ *n.* recuerdo
space /speis/ *n.* espacio
spare parts /sper parts/ *n.* piezas de repuesto; *Arg., Ven.* reparaciones; *Mex.* refacciones
speak /spik/ *v.* hablar
spear /spir/ *n.* arpón (de pesca)
special /spé-shal/ *adj.* especial

speech /spich/ *n.* discurso
speed /spid/ *n.* rapidez; velocidad
speed bumps /spid bomps/ *n.* *CR* muertos; *Ec.* policía acostado; *Mex.* topes; *Pan.* policía muerto; *Pe.* rompemuelles; *Uru.* lomo de burro
spend /spend/ *v.* gastar
spice /spais/ *n.* especia
spicy /spái-si/ *adj.* picante
spill /spil/ *v.* derramar(se)
spinach /spín-ich/ *n.* espinacas
spool /spul/ *n.* carrete
spoon /spun/ *n.* cuchara
spoonful /spún-ful/ *n.* cucharada
sport /sport/ *n.* deporte
spot /spot/ *n.* lugar (place); mancha
spotless /spót-les/ *adj.* sin mancha
spouse /spaus/ *n.* esposo
spread /spred/ *v.* extender
spring /spring/ *n.* primavera; manantial (water)
square /skuer/ *n., adj.* cuadrado
stable /stéi-bl/ *n.* establo; *adj.* estable
staff /staf/ *n.* personal
stage /steich/ *n.* escena
stain /stein/ *n.* mancha; *v.* manchar
stairs /sters/ *n.* escalera
stamp /stamp/ *n.* estampilla; *Arg., Cuba* sello; *Mex.* timbre
stand /stand/ *n.* puesto; *v.* estar de pie
standard /stán-dard/ *n.* norma

star /star/ *n.* estrella
starch /starch/ *n.* almidón
start /start/ *n.* comienzo; *v.* comenzar; empezar
state /steit/ *n.* estado
statement /stéit-ment/ *n.* declaración; (com.) estado de cuenta
station /stéi-shon/ *n.* estación
stationery /stéi-shon-e-ri/ *n.* papelería
station wagon /stéi-shon uág-n/ *n.* *Mex.* camioneta; *CA* camionetilla
statue /stá-chu/ *n.* estatua
stay /stei/ *v.* quedarse
steak /steik/ *n.* biftec; *RP* bife
steal /stil/ *v.* robar
steam /stim/ *n.* vapor
steel /stil/ *n.* acero
step /step/ *n.* paso; *v.* pisar
stepfather /stép-fa-der/ *n.* padrastro
stepmother /stép-mo-der/ *n.* madrastra
stew /stiu/ *n.* *Cuba* carne con papas; *Mex.* guisado; *Pe.* estofado; *RP* guiso
stewardess /stiú-er-des/ *n.* azafata; aeromoza
still /stil/ *adv.* todavía
stockbroker /stók-brouk-er/ *n.* corredor de bolsa
stock exchange /stok eks-chéinch/ *n.* bolsa
stockings /stók-ings/ *n.* medias
stomach /stóm-ak/ *n.* estómago
stomachache /stóm-ak-eik/ *n.* dolor de estómago
stone /stoun/ *n.* piedra

stool /stul/ *n.* taburete
stop /stop/ *n.* parada; *v.* detener
store /stor/ *n.* tienda
storm /storm/ *n.* tormenta
story /stó-ri/ *n.* cuento
stove /stouv/ *n.* estufa; cocina
straight /streit/ *adj., adv.* derecho
strange /strench/ *adj.* raro
stranger /strén-cher/ *n.* desconocido
straw (drinking) /stro/ *n. Bol.* bombilla; *Chi., Uru.* pajita; *Cuba* sorbente; *Ec.* sorbete; *Mex.* popote; *Pe.* cañita; *Pan.* carrizo; *PR* sorbeto; *Ven.* pitillo
strawberry /stró-ber-i/ *n.* fresa
street /strit/ *n.* calle
strike /straik/ *n.* huelga (work); *v.* golpear (hit)
string /string/ *n.* cuerda; *Ven.* cordón; cinta
strong /strong/ *adj.* fuerte
struggle /strόg-l/ *n.* lucha; *v.* luchar
student /stiú-dent/ *n.* estudiante
studio /stú-di-ou/ *n.* estudio
study /stód-i/ *n.* estudio; *v.* estudiar
stupid /stiú-pid/ *adj.* estúpido
style /stail/ *n.* estilo
subject /sób-yekt/ *n.* tema
submission /sob-mí-shon/ *n.* sumisión
submit /sob-mít/ *v.* someter(se)
subscribe /sob-skráib/ *v.* subscribir(se)
subscription /sob-skríp-shon/ *n.* subscripción
substitute /sób-sti-tiut/ *n.* sustituto; *v.* sustituir

subtract /sob-trákt/ *v.* restar
suburb /sób-erb/ *n.* suburbio
subway /sób-uei/ *n.* subterráneo; *Mex.* metro
succeed /sok-síd/ *v.* tener éxito
success /sok-sés/ *n.* éxito
such /soch/ *adj., pron.* tal
sudden /sód-n/ *adj.* repentino
suddenly /sód-n-li/ *adv.* de repente
suffer /sóf-er/ *v.* sufrir
sufficient /so-físh-ent/ *adj.* suficiente; bastante
sugar /shú-ger/ *n.* azúcar
suggest /sog-yést/ *v.* sugerir
suggestion /sog-yést-shon/ *n.* sugestión
suit /sut/ *n.* traje; (leg.) pleito
suitable /sút-ab-l/ *adj.* apropiado
summer /sóm-er/ *n.* verano
summit /sóm-it/ *n.* cumbre
sun /son/ *n.* sol
Sunday /són-dei/ *n.* domingo
sunrise /són-rais/ *n.* salida del sol
sunset /són-set/ *n.* puesta del sol
sunstroke /són-strouk/ *n.* insolación
superficial /su-per-físh-l/ *adj.* superficial
superintendent /su-per-in-tén-dent/ *n.* superintendente
superior /su-pí-ri-or/ *n., adj.* superior
superstitious /su-per-stí-shous/ *adj.* supersticioso
supervise /sú-per-vais/ *v.* supervisar
supplement /sóp-li-ment/ *n.* suplemento

supply /so-plái/ *n.* suministro; *v.* abastecer
support /so-pórt/ *n.* apoyo; *v.* apoyar
suppose /so-póus/ *v.* suponer
sure /shur/ *adj.* seguro
surface /sér-fis/ *n.* superficie
surgeon /sér-yon/ *n.* cirujano
surgery /sér-yer-i/ *n.* cirugía
surname /sér neim/ *n.* apellido
surprise /ser-práis/ *n.* sorpresa; *v.* sorprender
survey /sér-vei/ *n.* encuesta
suspect /sos-pékt/ *v.* sospechar
swallow /suá-lou/ *n.* trago; *v.* tragar
sweat /suet/ *n.* sudor; *v.* sudar
sweater /sué-ter/ *n.* suéter
sweep /suip/ *v.* barrer
sweet /suit/ *adj.* dulce
sweetheart /suít-jart/ *n.* novio
sweet potato /suit pou-téi-tou/ *n.* *Arg., PR* batata; *Cuba* boniato; *Mex.* camote
swelling /suél-ing/ *n.* hinchazón
swim /suim/ *v.* nadar
swimmer /suím-mer/ *n.* nadador
swimming pool /suím-ing pul/ *n.* piscina; *Arg.* pileta; *Mex.* alberca
switch /suich/ *n.* interruptor
symbol /sím-bol/ *n.* símbolo
symptom /sím-tom/ *n.* sintoma
syrup /sír-op/ *n.* *Cuba, Pan.* sirope; *Mex.* miel
system /sis-tem/ *n.* sistema

- T -

table /téi-bl/ *n.* mesa
tablecloth /téi-bl-kloth/ *n.* mantel
tablespoon /téi-bl-spun/ *n.* cucharada
tablet /táb-let/ *n.* tableta; pastilla (medicine)
tail /teil/ *n.* cola
tailor /téil-r/ *n.* sastre
take /teik/ *v.* tomar; llevar
take away /teik a-uéi/ *v.* quitar
take care /teik ker/ *v.* tener cuidado
take care of /teik ker ov/ *v.* cuidar
take off /teik of/ *v.* quitarse
talk /tok/ *n.* plática; charla; *v.* hablar; platicar
tall /tol/ *adj.* alto
tangerine /tan-yer-ín/ *n.* mandarina; *Uru.* tangerina
tape /teip/ *n.* cinta; *Ec.* scotch; *Pan.* tape; *Ven.* teipe
tariff /tár-if/ *n.* tarifa; arancel
taste /teist/ *n.* gusto; *v.* saborear
tasty /téis-ti/ *adj.* sabroso; rico
tax /taks/ *n.* impuesto
taxi /ták-si/ *n.* taxi; *Arg.* tacho; *Cuba* máquina
tea /ti/ *n.* té
teach /tich/ *v.* enseñar
team /tim/ *n.* equipo
technical /ték-ni-kl/ *adj.* técnico
telegram /tél-e-gram/ *n.* telegrama
telephone /tél-e-foun/ *n.* teléfono; *v.* llamar por telé-

fono

telephone directory /tél-e-foun di-rék-to-ri/ *n.* guía telefónica; *Mex.* directorio telefónico

temperature /tém-per-a-chur/ *n.* temperatura; (med.) fiebre; calentura

temporary /tém-po-ra-ri/ *adj.* temporal

ten /ten/ *n., adj.* diez

tennis /tén-is/ *n.* tenis

tent /tent/ *n.* tienda de campaña

tenth /tenth/ *adj.* décimo

term /term/ *n.* término; plazo

terms /terms/ *n.* condiciones

terrible /tér-i-bl/ *adj.* terrible

terrific /ter-í-fik/ *adj.* tremendo

territory /tér-i-to-ri/ *n.* territorio

test /test/ *n.* prueba; *v.* probar

than /dan/ *conj.* que

thank /thenk/ *v.* agradecer

thankful /thénk-ful/ *adj.* agradecido

thank you /thenk iu/ *interj.* gracias

that /dat/ *adj., conj.* que

that's it /dats it/ *interj* eso es

the /di/ *art.* el, la, los, las

theater /thí-a-ter/ *n.* teatro

theater box /thía-ter boks/ *n.* palco

their /der/ *adj.* su

theirs /ders/ *pron.* el suyo

them /dem/ *pron.* ellos; las

themselves /dem-sélvs/ *pron.* ellos mismos

then /den/ *adv.* entonces
there /der/ *adv.* allí
therefore /dér-for/ *adv.* por eso
there is (are) /der is (ar)/ *v.* hay
these /dis/ *adj.* estos; *pron.* éstos
they /dei/ *pron.* ellos
thief /thif/ *n.* ladrón
thin /thin/ *adj.* delgado; flaco
thing /thing/ *n.* cosa; *Col., Dom.* vaina
think /think/ *v.* pensar
third /therd/ *n.* tercera parte; *adj.* tercer(o)
thirst /therst/ *n.* sed
thirteen /thér-tin/ *n., adj.* trece
thirty /thér-ti/ *n., adj.* treinta
this /dis/ *adj.* este; *pron.* éste
those /dous/ *adj.* esos; aquellos (in distance); *pron.* ésos; áquellos
though /dou/ *conj.* aunque
thought /thot/ *n.* pensamiento
thousand /tháu-sand/ *n., adj.* mil
thread /thred/ *n.* hilo
threat /thret/ *n.* amenaza
three /thri/ *n., adj.* tres
throat /throut/ *n.* garganta
through /thru/ *prep.* a través de
throw /throu/ *v.* echar; tirar
Thursday /thérs-dei/ *n.* jueves
thus /dos/ *adv.* así
ticket /tík-it/ *n.* boleto; *Bol.* entrada; *Col.* boleta; *Cu-*

ba ticket; *Ven.* tique
tide /taid/ *n.* marea
tie /tai/ *n.* corbata; *v.* amarrar; *Arg.* atar
tight /tait/ *adj.* apretado; estrecho
tile /tail/ *n.* azulejo
till /til/ *prep.* hasta; *conj.* hasta que
time /taim/ *n.* tiempo; hora (of day)
tin /tin/ *n.* estaño
tiny /tái-ni/ *adj.* muy pequeño
tip /tip/ *n.* propina
tire /tair/ *n.* llanta; *Chi., Uru.* neumático; *Cuba* goma; *Ven.* caucho
tired /taird/ *adj.* cansado
to /tu/ *prep., adv.* a
toast /toust/ *n.* pan tostado; brindis (drink to health)
tobacco /to-bák-ou/ *n.* tabaco
today /tu-déi/ *adv.* hoy
toe /tou/ *n.* dedo del pie
together /to-gué-der/ *adv.* juntos
toilet /tói-let/ *n.* inodoro
toll /toul/ *n.* tarifa; derechos de paso; *Ec., Uru., Ven.* peaje
tomato /to-méi-tou/ *n.* tomate; *Mex.* jitomate
tomb /tum/ *n.* tumba
tomorrow /tu-mór-ou/ *adv.* mañana
ton /ton/ *n.* tonelada
tongue /tong/ *n.* lengua
tonight /tu-náit/ *n., adv.* esta noche
too /tu/ *adv.* también

tool /tul/ *n.* herramienta
too much /tu moch/ *adv.* demasiado
tooth /tuth/ *n.* diente; muela
toothache /túth-eik/ *n.* dolor de muela
toothbrush /túth-brosh/ *n.* cepillo para dientes
toothpaste /túth-peist/ *n.* pasta dentrífica
toothpick /túth-pick/ *n. Bol., Chi.* mondadientes; *Mex.* palillo; *Pe.* palo de dientes
top /top/ *n.* cumbre
total /tóu-tl/ *n.* total; *v.* sumar
touch /toch/ *v.* tocar
tough /tof/ *adj.* duro
tour /tur/ *n.* excursión
towards /tords/ *prep.* hacia
towel /táu-el/ *n.* toalla
tower /táu-er/ *n.* torre
town /taun/ *n.* pueblo
toy /toi/ *n.* juguete
trade /treid/ *n.* comercio; *v.* comerciar; cambiar
trade union /trid iún-yon/ *n.* sindicato
traffic /tráf-ik/ *n.* tráfico
trailer /tréil-er/ *n. Mex.* camión de carga
train /trein/ *n.* tren; *v.* entrenar
transfer /tráns-fer/ *n.* transferencia; *v.* transferir
translate /tráns-leit/ *v.* traducir
translation /trans-léi-shon/ *n.* traducción
transmit /trans-mít/ *v.* transmitir
transport /trans-pórt/ *v.* transportar
travel /tráv-l/ *v.* viajar

tray /trei/ *n.* bandeja; *Ec.* charol; *Mex.* charola; *Pe.* azafate
treatment /trít-ment/ *n.* tratamiento
treaty /trí-ti/ *n.* tratado
tree /tri/ *n.* árbol
tremendous /tri-mén-dos/ *adj.* tremendo
tribe /traib/ *n.* tribu
trick /trik/ *n.* trampa; truco; *v.* engañar
trip /trip/ *n.* viaje
tropic /tró-pik/ *n.* trópico
tropical /tróp-i-kal/ *adj.* tropical
trouble /tráb-l/ *n.* apuro; molestia; *v.* molestar
trousers /tráu-sers/ *n.* pantalones
trout /traut/ *n.* trucha
truck /trok/ *n.* camión
true /tru/ *adj.* verdadero
trunk /tronk/ *n.* baúl (chest)
trust /trost/ *n.* confianza; *v.* confiar
truth /truth/ *n.* verdad
try /trai/ *v.* probar; intentar
try on /trai on/ *v.* probarse
Tuesday /tús-dei/ *n.* martes
tunnel /tón-l/ *n.* túnel
turkey /tér-ki/ *n.* pavo; *CA* jolote; *Col.* pisco; *Mex.* guajolote
turn /tern/ *n.* turno; *v.* volver(se)
turn into /tern ín-tu/ *v.* convertir(se)
turn off /tern of/ *v.* apagar; cenar
turn on /tern on/ *v.* poner; encender

turtle /tér-tl/ *n.* tortuga; jicotea
twelve /tuelv/ *n., adj.* doce
twenty /tuén-ti/ *n., adj.* veinte
twice /tuais/ *adv.* dos veces
twin /tuin/ *n.* gemelo; mellizo; *Cuba* jimagua; *Mex.* cuate; *Ven.* morocho
two /tu/ *n., adj.* dos
typewriter /táip-rai-ter/ *n.* máquina de escribir
typical /típ-i-kal/ *adj.* típico

- U -

ugly /óg-li/ *adj.* feo
ultimate /ól-ti-met/ *adj.* fundamental
umbrella /om-brél-a/ *n.* paraguas
unable /on-éi-bl/ *adj.* incapaz
unbreakable /on-bréik-a-bl/ *adj.* irrompible
uncertain /on-sér-tin/ *adj.* incierto
uncle /ón-kl/ *n.* tío
uncomfortable /on-kóm-for-ta-bl/ *adj.* incómodo
uncommon /on-kóm-on/ *adj.* poco común
unconscious /on-kón-shos/ *adj.* inconsciente
under /ón-der/ *prep.* debajo de
underneath /on-der níth/ *adv.* debajo
understand /on-der-stánd/ *v.* entender; comprender
understanding /on-der-stánd-ing/ *n.* entendimiento
underwear /ón-der-uer/ *n.* ropa interior
uneducated /on-éd-iu-kei-tid/ *adj.* inculto
unemployed /on-em-plóid/ *adj.* desempleado
unemployment /on-em-plói-ment/ *n.* desempleo
uneven /on-í-vn/ *adj.* desigual
unexpected /on-eks-pék-tid/ *adj.* inesperado
unfair /on-fér/ *adj.* injusto
unfaithful /on-féith-ful/ *adj.* infiel
unfasten /on-fás-n/ *v.* desatar
unforeseen /on-fore-sín/ *adj.* imprevisto
unfortunate /on-fór-chu-net/ *adj.* desafortunado
unhappy /on-jáp-i/ *adj.* infeliz

uniform /íu-ni-form/ *n., adj.* uniforme
unimportant /on-im-pór-tant/ *adj.* poco importante
union /iú-nion/ *n.* unión; sindicato (trade)
unit /iú-nit/ *n.* unidad
university /iu-ni-vér-si-ti/ *n.* universidad
unjust /on-yóst/ *adj.* injusto
unknown /on-noún/ *adj.* desconocido
unlawful /on-ló-ful/ *adj.* ilegal
unless /on-lés/ *conj.* a menos (de) que
unlimited /on-lím-i-ted/ *adj.* ilimitado
unlucky /on-lók-i/ *adj.* desafortunado
unmarried /on-már-id/ *adj.* soltero
unnecessary /on-nés-ses-a-ri/ *adj.* innecesario
unoccupied /on-ók-iu-paid/ *adj.* desocupado
unpleasant /on-plés-ant/ *adj.* desagradable
unreasonable /on-rí-son-a-bl/ *adj.* irrazonable
unsafe /on-séif/ *adj.* inseguro
unsatisfactory /on-sat-is-fák-to-ri/ *adj.* poco satisfactorio
until /on-tíl/ *prep.* hasta; *conj.* hasta que
untrue /on-trú/ *adj.* falso
unusual /on-iú-shu-al/ *adj.* poco común
unwrap /on-ráp/ *v.* desenvolver
up /op/ *adv.* arriba
upon /o-pón/ *prep.* sobre
upper /óp-er/ *adj.* superior
upstairs /ops-térs/ *adv.* arriba
upwards /óp-uerds/ *adv.* hacia arriba
urban /ér-bon/ *adj.* urbano

urgent /ér-yent/ *adj.* urgente
us /os/ *pron.* nos; nosotros
use /ius/ *n.* uso
use /iuz/ *v.* usar
useful /iús-ful/ *adj.* útil
usual /iú-shual/ *adj.* usual

- V -

vacancy /véi-kan-si/ *n.* vacancia
vacant /véi-kant/ *adj.* vacante
vaccinate /vák-si-neit/ *v.* vacunar
valid /vál-id/ *adj.* válido
valise /va-lís/ *n.* maleta; *Mex.* petaca
valley /vál-i/ *n.* valle
valuable /vál-iu-bl/ *adj.* valioso
valuables /vál-iu-bls/ *n.* objetos de valor
value /vál-iu/ *n.* valor; *v.* valuar
vanilla /va-níl-a/ *n.* vainilla
varied /vé-rid/ *adj.* variado
variety /va-rái-i-ti/ *n.* variedad
various /vé-ri-os/ *adj.* varios
veal /vil/ *n.* ternera
vegetable /véch-ta-bl/ *n., adj.* vegetal
vegetarian /vech-i-téi-ri-an/ *n., adj.* vegetariano
vehicle /ví-a-kl/ *n.* vehículo
velocity /ve-ló-ci-ti/ *n.* velocidad
vendor /vén-dr/ *n.* vendedor
verb /verb/ *n.* verbo
verbal /vér-bl/ *adj.* verbal
versatile /vér-sa-til/ *adj.* versátil
very /vér-i/ *adv.* muy
via /vái-a/ *n.* vía; *prep.* por
viaduct /vái-a-dokt/ *n.* viaducto
vicinity /vi-sín-i-ti/ *n.* vecindad

victim /vík-tim/ *n.* víctima
view /viu/ *n.* vista; *v.* mirarm; ver
vinegar /vín-i-gher/ *n.* vinagre
violence /vái-o-lens/ *n.* violencia
violent /vái-o-lent/ *adj.* violento
visa /ví-sa/ *n.* visa
visit /vís-it/ *n.* visita; *v.* visitar
visitor /vís-i-tor/ *n.* visitante
voice /vois/ *n.* voz
void /void/ *adj.* nulo
volt /volt/ *n.* voltio
volume /vól-ium/ *n.* volumen
vomit /vóm-it/ *n.* vómito; *v.* vomitar
vote /vout/ *n.* voto; *v.* votar

- W -

wages /uéi-chis/ *n.* sueldo
waist /ueist/ *n.* cintura
wait /ueit/ *n.* demora *v.* esperar
waiter /uéit-er/ *n.* mozo; *Cuba* camarero; *Ec.* salonero; *Mex.* mesero; *Uru.* garçon; *Ven.* mesonero
wait for /ueit for/ *v.* esperar
waitress /uéit-res/ *n.* *Cuba* camarera; *Mex.* mesera; *Ven.* mesonera
waive /ueiv/ *v.* renunciar
wake /ueik/ *v.* despertar
waken /uéi-ken/ *v.* despertar(se)
walk /uok/ *n.* paseo; *v.* caminar
wall /uol/ *n.* pared
wallet /uól-it/ *n.* billetera; *Mex., Uru.* cartera
walnut /uól-not/ *n.* nuez; nogal
waltz /uolts/ *n.* vals
want /uant/ *v.* desear; querer
war /uor/ *n.* guerra
warehouse /uér-jaus/ *n.* almacén; bodega
warm /uorm/ *adj.* caliente
warn /uorn/ *v.* advertir
warrant /uár-ant/ *n.* garantía
warrant for arrest /uár-ant for a-rést/ *n.* orden de arresto
warranty /uár-an-ti/ *n.* garantía
wart /uort/ *n.* verruga

wash /uash/ *v.* lavar(se)
wasp /uasp/ *n.* avispa
waste /ueist/ *n.* desperdicios; *v.* malgastar
wastebasket /uéist-bas-kit/ *n. Chi.* tarro de basura; *Ec., Pe.* basurero; *Mex.* bote de basura; *PR* zafacón; *RP* tacho de basura; *Ven.* pipote de basura
watch /uach/ *n.* reloj; *v.* mirar; vigilar
water /uá-tr/ *n.* agua
waterfall /uá-tr-fol/ *n.* cascada
watermelon /uá-tr-mel-on/ *n.* melón (de agua); *Col., Ven.* patilla; *Mex.* sandía
waterproof /uá-tr-pruf/ *adj.* impermeable
wave /ueiv/ *n.* ola
wax /uaks/ *n.* cera
way /uei/ *n.* vía; manera
we /ui/ *pron.* nosotros
weak /uik/ *adj.* débil
wealth /uelth/ *n.* riqueza
wealthy /uél-thi/ *adj.* rico
weapon /uép-n/ *n.* arma
wear /uer/ *v.* llevar
weariness /uí-ri-nes/ *n.* cansancio
weary /uí-ri/ *adj.* cansado
weather /uéd-er/ *n.* tiempo
weather report /uéd-er ri-pórt/ *n.* boletín meteorológico
wedding /uéd-ing/ *n.* boda
Wednesday /uéins-dei/ *n.* miércoles
weed /uid/ *n.* mala hierba

week /uik/ *n.* semana
weekday /uíc-dei/ *n.* día laborable
weekend /uík-end/ *n.* fin de semana
weekly /uík-li/ *adj.* semanal; *adv.* cada semana
weep /uip/ *v.* llorar
weigh /uei/ *v.* pesar
weight /ueit/ *n.* peso
weird /uird/ *adj.* raro
welcome /uél-kom/ *adj.* bienvenido
welfare /uél-fer/ *n.* bienestar
well /uel/ *n.* pozo (water); *adj., adv.* bien
well done /uel don/ *adj.* bien cocido
west /uest/ *n.* oeste
wet /uet/ *adj.* mojado
whale /jueil/ *n.* ballena
what /juat/ *interr.* ¿qué?; *pron.* lo que
whatever /juat-év-er/ *adj.* cualquier; *pron.* cualquiera
wheat /juit/ *n.* trigo
wheel /juil/ *n.* rueda
when /juen/ *adv.* cuando; *interr.* ¿cuándo?
whenever /juen-év-er/ *conj.* siempre que
where /juer/ *adv.* donde; *conj.* donde; *interr.* ¿dónde?
wherever /juer-év-er/ *adv.* donde quiera
whether /juéd-er/ *conj.* si
which /juich/ *pron.* que; cual; *interr.* ¿qué?
whichever /juich-év-er/ *pron.* cualquiera
while /juail/ *n.* rato; *conj.* mientras que
whip /juip/ *n.* látigo
whiskers /juís-kers/ *n.* bigotes

whisky /juís-ki/ *n.* whisky
whisper /juís-per/ *n.* susurro; *v.* susurrar
whistle /juís-l/ *n.* silbato; *v.* silbar
white /juait/ *n., adj.* blanco
who /ju/ *pron.* quien; el que; *interr.* ¿quién?
whoever /ju-év-er/ *pron.* quienquiera que
whole /joul/ *adj.* entero
wholesale /jóul-seil/ *adj., adv.* al por mayor
whom /jum/ *pron.* que; el que; el cual; quien; *interr.* ¿quién?
whore /jor/ *n.* prostituta
whose /jus/ *pron.* cuyo; de quien; *interr.* ¿de quién?
why /juai/ *adv.* por qué; *interr.* ¿por qué?
wide /uaid/ *adj.* ancho
widow /uíd-ou/ *n.* viuda
widower /uíd-ou-er/ *n.* viudo
width /uíd-th/ *n.* ancho
wife /uaif/ *n.* esposa
wild /uaild/ *adj.* salvaje
will /uil/ *n.* voluntad; (leg.) testamento
willing /uíl-ing/ *adj.* dispuesto
win /uin/ *v.* ganar
wind /uind/ *n.* viento; aire
window /uín-dou/ *n.* ventana
wine /uain/ *n.* vino
wineglass /uáin-glas/ *n.* copa
wing /uing/ *n.* ala
winter /uín-ter/ *n.* invierno
wire /uair/ *n.* alambre

wisdom /uís-dm/ *n.* sabiduría
wise /uais/ *adj.* sabio
wish /uish/ *n.* deseo; *v.* desear; querer
witch /uich/ *n.* bruja
witchcraft /uích-kraft/ *n.* brujería
with /uith/ *prep.* con
without /uith-áut/ *prep.* sin
without fail /uith-áut feil/ *adv.* sin falta
witness /uít-nes/ *n.* testigo; *v.* atestiguar
wolf /uolf/ *n.* lobo
woman /uó-man/ *n.* mujer
wonder /uón-der/ *n.* admiración; *v.* preguntarse
wonderful /uón-der-ful/ *adj.* maravilloso
wood /uud/ *n.* madera
wooden /uúd-n/ *adj.* de madera
woods /uuds/ *n.* bosque; monte
wool /uul/ *n.* lana
word /uerd/ *n.* palabra
work /uerk/ *n.* trabajo; *v.* trabajar
world /uerld/ *n.* mundo
worry /uér-i/ *n.* preocupación; *v.* preocupar(se)
worse /uers/ *adj., adv.* peor
worst /uerst/ *adj., adv.* peor
wound /uund/ *n.* herida; *v.* herir
wreath /rith/ *n.* corona
wrench /rench/ *n.* llave
wrinkle /rín-kl/ *n.* arruga; *v.* arrugar(se)
wrist /rist/ *n.* muñeca
write /rait/ *v.* escribir

writer /rái-ter/ *n.* escritor
writing /rái-ting/ *n.* escritura
written /rít-n/ *adj.* escrito
wrong /rong/ *adj.* equivocado

- X -

X-ray /éks-rei/ *n.* rayos X
xylophone /sái-lo-foun/ *n.* xilófono

- Y -

yacht /yat/ *n.* yate
year /yir/ *n.* año
yearly /yír-li/ *adj.* anual
yellow /yél-ou/ *n., adj.* amarillo
yes /yes/ *adv.* sí
yesterday /yés-ter-dei/ *adv.* ayer
yet /yet/ *adv.* aún; todavía; *conj.* sin embargo
you /yu/ *pron.* tú; usted; ustedes
young /yong/ *adj.* joven
youngster /yóngs-ter/ *n.* joven
your /yur/ *adj.* su; tu
yours /yurs/ *pron.* el suyo; el tuyo
youth /yuth/ *n.* juventud

- Z -

zero /sí-rou/ *n.* cero
zipper /síp-er/ *n. CA, Cuba* zipper; *Mex., Uru.* cierre
zone /soun/ *n.* zona
zoo /su/ *n.* zoológico

SPANISH-ENGLISH

- A -

a /ah/ *prep.* at; to; in; on; by; for
abajo /ah-báh-hoh/ *adv.* below; under; underneath
abajo ... /ah-báh-hoh/ *interj.* down with ...
abandonar /ah-bahn-doh-náhr/ *v.* abandon; leave
abanico /ah-bah-née-coh/ *n.* hand fan
abarrotes /ah-bah-róh-tays/ *n. Mex.* groceries
abastecer /ah-bahs-tay-sáyr/ *v.* supply; provide
abdomen /ahb-dóh-mayn/ *n.* abdomen
abierto /ah-bee-áyr-toh/ *adj.* open
abogado /ah-boh-gáh-doh/ *n.* lawyer
abolir /ah-boh-léer/ *v.* abolish
abordo /ah-bóhr-doh/ on board
aborto /ah-bóhr-toh/ *n.* abortion; miscarriage
abrazar /ah-brah-sáhr/ *v.* embrace
abrazo /ah-bráh-soh/ *n.* embrace; hug
abrigo /ah-brée-goh/ *n.* coat
abril /ah-bréel/ *n.* April
abrir /ah-bréer/ *v.* open
absolutamente /ahb-soh-loo-tah-máyn-tay/ *adv.* absolutely
absoluto /ahb-soh-lóo-toh/ *adj.* absolute
absorber /ahb-sohr-báyr/ *v.* absorb
abstracto /ahb-stráhk-toh/ *adj.* abstract
abuela /ah-bwáy-lah/ *n.* grandmother
abuelita /ah-bway-lée-tah/ *n. Mex.* grandmother

abuelito /ah-bway-lée-toh/ *n. Mex.* grandfather
abuelo /ah-bwáy-loh/ *n.* grandfather
abundante /ah-boon-dáhn-tay/ *adj.* abundant
a caballo /ah kah-báh-yoh/ *adv.* on horseback
a cada hora /ah káh-dah óh-rah/ *adv.* every hour; hourly
a cara o cruz /ah káh-rah oh kroos/ heads or tails
acabar /ah-kah-báhr/ *v.* finish; end; *CA, Mex., RP* age; fail in health
acabar de /ah-kah-báhr day/ *v.* have just
a casa /ah káh-sah/ *adv.* home
a causa de /ah káh-oo-sah day/ *prep.* because of
accidente /ahk-see-dáyn-tay/ *n.* accident
acción /ahk-see-óhn/ *n.* action; (com.) stock certificate
accionista /ahk-see-oh-nées-tah/ *n.* (com.) stockholder
aceite /ah-sáy-tay/ *n.* oil
aceite de oliva /ah-sáy-tay day oh-lée-vah/ *n.* olive oil
aceituna /ah-say-tóo-nah/ *n.* olive
acelerar /ah-say-lay-ráhr/ *v.* accelerate
acento /ah-sáyn-toh/ *n.* accent
aceptar /ah-sayp-táhr/ *v.* accept
acera /ah-sáy-rah/ *n.* sidewalk (except *Mex., RP*)
acerca de /ah-sáyr-cah day/ *prep.* about; relating to
acercar /ah-sayr-cáhr/ *v.* approach; get nearer
acero /ah-sáy-roh/ *n.* steel
ácido /áh-see-doh/ *n., adj.* acid
aconsejar /ah-kohn-say-háhr/ *v.* advise

acostarse /ah-coh-stáhr-say/ *v.* lie down
acostumbrar /ah-coh-stoom-bráhr/ *v.* accustom
acreedor /ah-cray-ay-dór/ *n.* creditor
actividad /ahk-tee-vee-dáhd/ *n.* activity
activo /ahk-tée-voh/ *adj.* active
acto /áhk-toh/ *n.* act; ceremony
actor /ahk-tóhr/ *n.* actor
actual /ahk-too-áhl/ *adj.* present-day
actualidad /ahk-too-ah-lee-dáhd/ *n.* present time
actuar /ahk-too-áhr/ *v.* act; perform
acuerdo /ah-kuáyr-doh/ *n.* agreement
acusar /ah-koo-sáhr/ *v.* accuse; prosecute
adecuado /ah-day-kwáh-doh/ *adj.* adequate
adelantar /ah-day-lahn-táhr/ *v.* advance; pass in car
adelantarse /ah-day-lahn-táhr-say/ *v. Arg.* pass in car
adelante /ah-day-láhn-tay/ *adv.* ahead; *interj.* come in
adelanto /ah-day-láhn-toh/ *n. PR, Uru.* down payment
además /ah-day-máhs/ *adv.* besides
además de /ah-day-máhs day/ *prep.* besides
adentro /ah-dáyn-troh/ *adv.* within
aderezo /ah-day-ráy-soh/ *n.* dressing; seasoning
adición /ah-dee-see-óhn/ *n.* addition
adicional /ah-dee-see-oh-náhl/ *adj.* additional
adicto /ah-déek-toh/ *n.* addict; *LA* fan; supporter
adiós /ah-dee-óhs/ *interj.* good-bye
adivinar /ah-dee-vee-náhr/ *v.* guess
adjetivo /ahd-hay-tée-voh/ *n.* adjective
administración /ahd-mee-nee-strah-see-óhn/ *n.* admi-

nistration
administrar /ahd-mee-nee-stráhr/ *v.* manage
admiración /ahd-me-rah-see-óhn/ *n.* admiration
admirar /ahd-mee-ráhr/ *v.* admire
admisión /ahd-mee-see-óhn/ *n.* admission
admitir /ahd-mee-téehr/ *v.* admit; allow
adorno /ah-dóhr-noh/ *n.* adornment; ornament
aduana /ah-dwáh-nah/ *n.* customhouse
adulto /ah-dóol-toh/ *n.* adult
adverbio /ahd-váyr-bee-oh/ *n.* adverb
advertir /ahd-vayr-téehr/ *v.* warn; inform
aeromoza /ah-ay-roh-móh-sah/ *n.* airline stewardess
aeropuerto /ah-ay-roh-pwáyr-toh/ *n.* airport
a excepción de /ah ex-sayp-see-óhn day/ *prep.* with the exception of
afeitarse /ah-fay-táhr-say/ *v.* shave
afuera /ah-fwáy-rah/ *adv.* outside
agarrar /ah-gah-ráhr/ *v.* seize; take hold of
agasajar /ah-gah-sah-háhr/ *v.* honor (at social event)
agencia /ah-háyn-see-ah/ *n.* agency; *Chi.* pawnshop
agente /ah-háyn-tay/ *n.* agent; police officer
agosto /ah-góhs-toh/ *n.* August
agradable /ah-grah-dáh-blay/ *adj.* pleasant
agradecer /ah-grah-day-sáyr/ *v.* thank for
agradecido /ah-grah-day-sée-doh/ *adj.* grateful
agrio /áh-gree-oh/ *adj.* sour
agrupar /ah-groo-páhr/ *v.* group together
agua /áh-gwah/ *n.* water
aguacero /ah-gwah-sáy-roh/ *n.* rain shower

aguamala /ah-gwah-máh-lah/ *n. Carib., Mex.* jelly fish
aguantar /ah-gwahn-táhr/ *v.* tolerate; stand
aguaviva /ah-gwah-vée-vah/ *n. PR, RP* jelly fish
agudo /ah-góo-doh/ *adj.* sharp
águila o sol /áh-ghee-lah oh sohl/ *Mex.* heads or tails
aguja /ah-góo-hah/ *n.* needle
agujero /ah-goo-háy-roh/ *n.* hole (bored)
ahí mismo /ah-ée mées-moh/ *adv.* right there
ahogarse /ah-oh-gáhr-say/ *v.* drown
ahora mismo /ah-óh-rah mées-moh/ *adv.* right now
ahorita /ah-oh-rée-tah/ *adv. LA* right away
ahorros /ah-óh-rohs/ *n.* savings
aire /áh-ee-ray/ *n.* air; wind
aire acondicionado /áh-ee-ray ah-cohn-dee-see-oh--náh-doh/ *n.* air conditioning
ají /ah-hée/ *n. Cuba, Ven.* bell pepper
ajo /áh-hoh/ *n.* garlic
ajuste /ah-hóos-tay/ *n.* adjustment; *Mex.* car engine overhaul
ala /áh-lah/ *n.* wing; row
alambre /ah-láhm-bray/ *n.* wire
alarma /ah-láhr-mah/ *n.* alarm
alarma de incendios /ah-láhr-mah day een-sáyn-dee-ohs/ *n.* fire alarm
alarmar /ah-lahr-máhr/ *v.* alarm; alert
albaricoque /ahl-bah-ree-cóh-kay/ *n.* apricot (except *Arg., Mex., Uru.*)
alberca /ahl-báyr-cah/ *n. Mex.* swimming pool
albergue /ahl-báyr-gay/ *n.* shelter; lodging

alborotos /ahl-boh-róh-tohs/ *n. CA* caramel popcorn
alcalde /ahl-cáhl-day/ *n.* mayor
alcanzar /ahl-cahn-sáhr/ *v.* reach; catch up
alcoba /ahl-cóh-bah/ *n.* small bedroom; roomette on train
alcohol /ahl-cóhl/ *n.* alcohol
alegre /ah-láy-gray/ *adj.* merry
alerta /ah-léhr-tah/ *n.* alert; (mil.) watchword
alfiler /ahl-fee-láyr/ *n.* pin
alfombra /ahl-fóhm brah/ *n.* carpet
alfombrita /ahl-fohm brée-tah/ *n. RP* throw rug
algo /áhl-goh/ *pron.* something; *adv.* somewhat
algodón /ahl-goh-dóhn/ *n.* cotton
alguacil /ahl-gwah-séel/ *n.* bailiff; sheriff
alguien /áhl-ghee-ayn/ *pron.* someone; anyone
alguno /ahl-góo-noh/ *adj.* some; any
algunos /ahl-góo-nohs/ *pron.* some
alimento /ah-lee-máyn-toh/ *n.* food
aliviar /ah-lee-vee-áhr/ *v.* relieve; soothe
alivio /ah-lée-vee-oh/ *n.* relief
al lado de /ahl láh-doh day/ *prep.* beside
alma /áhl-mah/ *n.* soul
almacén /ahl-mah-sáyn/ *n.* warehouse; store; *Arg.* food store; *Mex.* department store; *Gua.* fabric store
almanaque /ahl-mah-náh-kay/ *n.* almanac; calendar
almendra /ahl-máyn-drah/ *n.* almond
al menos /ahl máy-nohs/ at least
almíbar /ahl-mée-bahr/ *n.* sugar syrup

almidón /ahl-mee-dóhn/ *n.* starch; *Col., Ven.* paste (glue)
almohada /ahl-moh-áh-dah/ *n.* pillow
almuerzo /ahl-moo-áyr-soh/ *n.* lunch; midday meal (except Mex.)
al por mayor /ahl pohr mah-yóhr/ *adv.* wholesale
alquilar /ahl-key-láhr/ *v.* rent
alrededor /ahl-ray-day-dóhr/ *adv.* around; about
alrededor de /ahl-ray-day-dóhr day/ *prep.* about; around
alrededores /ahl-ray-day-dóh-rays/ *n.* environs
al revés /ahl ray-váys/ *adv.* backwards
altavoz /ahl-tah-vóhs/ *n.* loud-speaker
alto /áhl-toh/ *adj.* tall; high; *interj.* stop, halt
al través de /ahl trah-váys day/ *prep.* through
altura /ahl-tóo-rah/ *n.* altitude; height
alumbrado /ah-loom-bráh-doh/ *n.* lighting system; *adj.* lighted
allí /ah-ée/ *adv.* over there
ama de llaves /áh-mah day yáh-vays/ *n.* housekeeper
amanecer /ah-mah-nay-sáyr/ *n.* dawn; *v.* dawn
amar /ah-máhr/ *v.* love
amargo /ah-máhr-goh/ *adj.* bitter
amargura /ah-mahr-góo-rah/ *n.* bitterness
amarillo /ah-mah-rée-yoh/ *n., adj.* yellow
amarrar /ah-mah-ráhr/ *v.* tie up (especially in *Arg., Chi., Uru., Mex.*)
ámbar /áhm-bahr/ *n.* amber
ambiente /ahm-bee-áyn-tay/ *n.* atmosphere; ambi-

ance; *Andes* room
ambos /áhm bohs/ *adj.* both
ambulancia /ahm-boo-láhn-see-ah/ *n.* ambulance
amenazar /ah-may-nah-sáhr/ *v.* threaten
a menos que /ah máy-nohs kay/ *conj.* unless
amiga /ah-mée-gah/ *n.* friend (female)
amigo /ah-mée-goh/ *n.* friend (male)
amistad /ah-mees-táhd/ *n.* friendship
amo /áh-moh/ *n.* master; owner
amor /ah-móhr/ *n.* love
amplificar /ahm-plee-fee-cáhr/ *v.* amplify; enlarge
amplio /áhm-plee-oh/ *adj.* spacious; roomy
análisis /ah-náh-lee-sees/ *n.* analysis
analizar /ah-nah-lee-sáhr/ *v.* analyze
ananá /ah-nah-náh/ *n. Arg.* pineapple
ancho /áhn-choh/ *adj.* broad; wide; *Col., Ven.* conceited
anchoa /ahn-chóh-ah/ *n.* anchovy
andale /áhn-dah-lay/ *interj. Mex.* hurry up
andén /ahn-dáyn/ *n.* platform of train station; *Gua., Hon.* sidewalk
anillo /ah-née-yoh/ *n.* ring
animal /ah-nee-máhl/ *n.* animal
animal doméstico /ah-nee-máhl doh-máys-teecoh/ *n.* pet (except Mex.)
animar /ah-nee-máhr/ *v.* encourage
anochecer /ah-noh-chay-sáyr/ *v.* to get dark
anormal /ah-nohr-máhl/ *adj.* abnormal
ansioso /ahn-see-óh-soh/ *adj.* anxious; eager

ante /áhn-tay/ *prep.* before; in the presence of
anteayer /ahn-tay-ah-yéhr/ *adv.* day before yesterday
anteojos /ahn-tay-óh-hohs/ *n. RP* eyeglasses
anterior /ahn-tay-ree-óhr/ *adj.* former
antes (de) que /áhn-tays (day) kay/ *conj.* before
antigüedad /ahn-tee-gway-dáhd/ *n.* antique; seniority
antiguo /ahn-tée-gwoh/ *adj.* ancient
antiséptico /ahn-tee-sáyp-tee-coh/ *n., adj.* antiseptic
antualito /ahn-too-ah-lée-toh/ *adv. Col.* right now
anual /ah-noo-áhl/ *adj.* annual
anunciar /ah-noon-see-áhr/ *v.* announce; advertise
anuncio /ah-nóon-see-oh/ *n.* announcement
anuncio comercial /ah-nóon-see-oh coh-mayr--see-áhl/ *n.* advertisement
anzuelo /ahn-swáy-loh/ *n.* fishhook; bait
año /áhn-yoh/ *n.* year
apagar /ah-pah-gáhr/ *v.* put out; turn off
aparato /ah-pah-ráh-toh/ *n.* apparatus
aparecer /ah-pah-ray-sáyr/ *v.* appear; show up
apariencia /ah-pah-ree-áyn-see-ah/ *n.* appearance
apartamento /ah-pahr-tah-máyn-toh/ *n.* apartment (except Mex.)
aparte /ah-páhr-tay/ *adv.* apart
aparte de /ah-páhr-tay day/ *prep.* apart from
apellido /ah-pay-yée-doh/ *n.* last name; surname
apenas /ah-páy-nahs/ *adv.* scarcely
a pesar de /ah pay-sáhr day/ *prep.* in spite of
apio /áh-pee-oh/ *n.* celery
aplauso /ah-pláh-oo-soh/ *n.* applause

aplicar /ah-plee-cáhr/ *v.* apply
apodo /ah-póh-doh/ *n.* nickname
apostar /ah-pohs-táhr/ *v.* bet
apóstrofe /ah-póhs-troh-fay/ *n.* apostrophe
apoyar /ah-poh-yáhr/ *v.* support
apoyo /ah-póh-yoh/ *n.* support
apreciar /ah-pray-see-áhr/ *v.* appreciate; be grateful for; like
aprender /ah-prayn-dáyr/ *v.* learn
apretado /ah-pray-tah-doh/ *adj.* tight
apretar /ah-pray-táhr/ *v.* compress; tighten
aprobar /ah-proh-báhr/ *v.* approve; pass (course or exam)
apropiado /ah-proh-pee-áh-doh/ *adj.* appropriate
aproximado /ah-proks-ee-máh-doh/ *adj.* approximate
apuesta /ah-pwáys-tah/ *n.* bet
apuntar /ah-poon-táhr/ *v.* take a note; aim
apurarse /ah-poo-ráhr-say/ *v.* hurry
apúrate /ah-póo-rah-tay/ *imper. Bol., Ec., Pe., Ven.* hurry up
apuro /ah-póo-roh/ *n.* need; affliction; *LA* hurry; rush
aquel /ah-káyl/ *adj.* that...over there
aquél /ah-káyl/ *pron.* that one over there
aquí /ah-kéy/ *adv.* here
arancel /ah-rahn-sáyl/ *n.* custom duties; tariff
árbol /áhr-bohl/ *n.* tree
árbol de Navidad /áhr-bohl day nah-vee-dáhd/ *n.* Christmas tree

arco /áhr-coh/ *n.* arc; arch; bow
archivar /ahr-chee-váhr/ *v.* file
archivo /ahr-chée-voh/ *n.* archives; file; *Col.* office
área /áh-ray-ah/ *n.* area
arena /ah-ráy-nah/ *n.* sand; arena
aretes /ah-ráy-tays/ *n. Cuba, Mex.* earrings
argot /ahr-gót/ *n. Uru.* slang
arma /áhr-mah/ *n.* arm; weapon
armar /ahr-máhr/ *v.* arm; put together; assemble
armario /ahr-máh-ree-oh/ *n.* free-standing piece of furniture for clothes; armoire
aros /áh-rohs/ *n. Arg., Chi.* earrings
arpa /áhr-pah/ *n.* harp
arpón /ahr-póhn/ *n.* harpoon
arrecife /ah-ray-sée-fay/ *n.* reef
arreglar /ah-ray-gláhr/ *v.* arrange; fix
arriba /ah-rée-bah/ *adv.* above; upstairs
arriesgar /ah-ree-ays-gáhr/ *v.* risk
arrojar /ah-roh-háhr/ *v.* throw; throw up; throw out
arroz /ah-róhs/ *n.* rice
arruga /ah-róo-gah/ *n.* wrinkle
arrugar /ah-roo-gáhr/ *v.* wrinkle; *Carib.* annoy
arrugarse /ah-roo-gáhr-say/ *v.* get wrinkled
arte /áhr-tay/ *n.* art
articulo /ahr-tée-coo-loh/ *n.* article
artificial /ahr-tee-fee-see-áhl/ *adj.* artificial
artista /ahr-tées-tah/ *n.* artist; entertainer
asado /ah-sáh-doh/ *adj.* roasted; *n. RP* steak; barbecue

asamblea /ah-sahm-bláy-ah/ *n.* assembly
asar /ah-sáhr/ *v.* roast
ascensor /ah-sayn-sóhr/ *n. Arg., Ecu., Pe., Uru., Ven.* elevator
asegurar /ah-say-goo-ráhr/ *v.* secure; insure
así /ah-sée/ *adv.* so; thus
asiento /ah-see-áyn-toh/ *n.* seat; chair
así no más /ah-sée noh mahs/ *Andes, Mex., RP* so so; just so
asistente /ah-sees-táyn-tay/ *n.* assistant; *Col., PR, Ven.* servant
asistir /ah-sees-téer/ *v.* be present; serve
asociar /ah-soh-see-áhr/ *v.* associate
áspero /áhs-pay-roh/ *adj.* rough
asunto /ah-sóon-toh/ *n.* matter; affair
asustar /ah-soos-táhr/ *v.* scare
atar /ah-táhr/ *v.* tie; *Arg.* tie up
atención /ah-tayn-see-óhn/ *n.* attention
atento /ah-táyn-toh/ *adj.* attentive; courteous
aterrizaje /ah-tay-ree-sáh-hay/ *n.* landing
aterrizar /ah-tay-ree-sáhr/ *v.* land
atornillar /ah-tohr-nee-yáhr/ *v.* to screw on
atraer /ah-trah-áyr/ *v.* attract
atrasado /ah-trah-sáh-doh/ *adj.* late; behind
atravesar /ah-trah-vay-sáhr/ *v.* cross; go across
a través de /ah trah váys day/ *prep.* through; across
atreverse /ah-tray-váyr-say/ *v.* dare
aumentar /ah-oo-mayn-táhr/ *v.* increase; enlarge
aun /ah-óon/ *adv.* even

aún /ah-óon/ *adv.* still; yet
aunque /ah-óon-kay/ *conj.* although
ausente /ah-oo-sáyn-tay/ *adj.* absent
auténtico /ah-oo-táyn-tee-coh/ *adj.* authentic; real
auto /áh-oo-toh/ *n.* car
autobús /ah-oo-toh-bóoz/ *n. Ven.* city bus; *Arg., Chi., Cuba, Mex., Ven.* intercity bus
automático /ah-oo-toh-máh-tee-coh/ *adj.* automatic
automóvil /ah-oo-toh-móh-veel/ *n.* auto; car
autor /ah-oo-tóhr/ *n.* author
autora /ah-oo-tóh-rah/ *n.* authoress
autoridad /ah-oo-toh-ree-dáhd/ *n.* authority
auxiliar /ah-ook-see-lee-áhr/ *n.* assistant; *adj.* auxiliary; *v.* help; aid
auxilio /ah-ook-sée-lee-oh/ *interj.* help
auyama /ah-oo-yáh-mah/ *n. Ven.* pumpkin
avance /ah-váhn-say/ *n.* advance payment
avanza /ah-váhn-sah/ *imper. PR* hurry up
avanzar /ah-vahn-sáhr/ *v.* advance
ave /áh-vay/ *n.* bird; fowl
a veces /ah váy-says/ *adv.* sometimes; at times
avellana /ah-vay-yáh-nah/ *n.* hazelnut
avena /ah-váy-nah/ *n.* oats; oatmeal
avenida /ah-vay-née-dah/ *n.* avenue
aventón /ah-vayn-tóhn/ *n. Mex.* lift (in car); *Gua., Mex., Pe.* push; shove
avergonzado /ah-vayr-gohn-sáh-doh/ *adj.* ashamed; embarrassed
avergonzar /ah-vayr-gohn-sáhr/ *v.* shame; embarrass

avión /ah-vee-óhn/ *n.* airplane
avión de reacción /ah-vee-óhn day ray-ahk-see-óhn/ *n.* jet plane
aviso /ah-vée-soh/ *n.* information; warning; *LA* advertisement
avispa /ah-vées-pah/ *n.* wasp
ayer /ah-yáyr/ *adv.* yesterday
ayuda /ah-yóo-dah/ *n.* help; aid
ayudante /ah-yoo-dáhn-tay/ *n.* helper; assistant
ayudar /ah-yoo-dáhr/ *v.* help
azafata /ah-sah-fáh-tah/ *n.* airline stewardess
azafate /ah-sah-fáh-tay/ *n. Pe.* tray
azúcar /ah-sóo-cahr/ *n.* sugar
azul /ah-sóol/ *n., adj.* blue
azulejo /ah-soo-láy-hoh/ *n.* glazed tile

- B -

bache /báh-chay/ *n. Mex., Ven.* pothole
bailador /bah-ee-lah-dóhr/ *n.* dancer
bailar /bah-ee-láhr/ *v.* dance
bailarín /bah-ee-lah-réen/ *n.* dancer (professional)
bailarina /bah-ee-lah-rée-nah/ *n.* ballerina; dancer (female)
baile /báh-ee-lay/ *n.* dance
bajar /bah-hár/ *v.* go down; lessen
bajar el agua /bah-hár el áh-gwah/ *v. Mex.* flush (toilet)
bajito /bah-hée-toh/ *adj.* low; *Cuba, Uru.* short (person) *adv.* softly
bajo /báh-hoh/ *adj.* short; low; *adv.* under; below; *n. Pe.* short person
balcón /bahl-cóhn/ *n.* balcony
balde /báhl-day/ *n. Arg., Bol., Ec., Pe.* bucket
balompié /bah-lohm-pee-áy/ *n. Arg.* football
balón /bah-lóhn/ *n.* large ball; football
ballena /bah-yáy-nah/ *n.* whale
banana /bah-náh-nah/ *n.* banana
bancarrota /bahn-cah-róh-tah/ *n.* bankruptcy
banca /báhn-cah/ *n. Mex.* bench
banco /báhn-coh/ *n.* bench; bank
bandeja /banh-dáy-hah/ *n. Bol., Chi., Cuba, Ecu., Uru., Ven.* tray
bandera /bahn-dáy-rah/ *n.* flag

banqueta /bahn-káy-tah/ *n. Arg., CA, Mex.* sidewalk
bañadera /bah-nyah-dáy rah/ *n. Arg., Cuba* bathtub
bañar /bah-nyáhr/ *v.* bathe
bañarse /bah-nyáhr-say/ *v.* take a bath
bañera /bah-nyáy-rah/ *n. PR, Uru., Ven.* bathtub
baño /báh-nyoh/ *n.* bath; bathroom
bar /bahr/ *n.* bar
barajas /bah-ráh-hahs/ *n. Cuba, Mex., Pe., Uru., Ven.* playing cards
barandilla /bah-rahn-dée-yah/ *n.* handrail
barata /bah-ráh-tah/ *n. Mex.* sale
barato /bah-ráh-toh/ *adj.* cheap
barbacoa /bahr bah-cóh-ah/ *n.* barbecue
barbero /bahr-báy-roh/ *n.* barber
barcaza /bahr-cáh-sah/ *n. Ec.* ferry
barco /báhr-coh/ *n.* boat; ship
barrer /bah-ráyr/ *v.* sweep
barriada /bah-ree-áh-dah/ *n. Pe.* slum
barrio /báh-ree-oh/ *n.* quarter or neighborhood of city; *Ec.* slum
barrio pobre /báh-ree-oh póh-bray/ *n. Mex., Uru.* slum
barro /báh-roh/ *n.* clay
base /báh-say/ *n.* base; basis; *Mex.* permanent (hair)
bastante /bah-stáhn-tay/ *adv.* enough
bastón /bahs-tóhn/ *n.* cane
basura /bah-sóo-rah/ *n.* garbage
basurero /bah-soo-ráy-roh/ *n. Ec., Pe.* wastebasket
batata /bah-táh-tah/ *n. Arg., PR* sweet potato

batería /bah-tay-rée-ah/ *n.* battery
baúl /bah-óol/ *n.* trunk; chest
bazar /bah-sáhr/ *n.* bazaar; *RP* kitchen supply store; *Mex.* secondhand store; garage sale
bebe /báy-bay/ *n. Pe.* baby; infant
bebé /bay-báy/ *n.* baby; infant
beber /bay-báyr/ *v.* drink
bebida /bay-bée-dah/ *n.* drink; beverage
beca /béy-cah/ *n.* scholarship
beige /báy-sh/ *n., adj. Arg.* brown
bello /báy-yoh/ *adj.* beautiful; handsome
bencina /bayn-sée-nah/ *n. Chi.* gasoline
bermejo /bayr-máy-hoh/ *n., adj. Ec.* blond
besar /bay-sáhr/ *v.* kiss
beso /báy-soh/ *n.* kiss
betabel /bay-tah-báyl/ *n. Mex.* beet
betarraga /bay-tah-ráh-gah/ *n. Bol., Chi., Pe.* beet
betún /bay-tóon/ *n.* shoe polish; *Mex.* cake frosting
Biblia /béeb-lee-ah/ *n.* Bible
biblioteca /beeb-lee-oh-táy-cah/ *n.* library
bicicleta /bee-see-cláy-tah/ *n.* bicycle
bicho /bée-choh/ *n.* insect; small animal; *Cuba* shrewd operator; *PR* (vulgar)
bien /bee-áyn/ *adv.* well; very; *interj.* good, fine
bien cocido /bee-áyn coh-sée-doh/ *adj.* well done (meat)
bienestar /bee-ayn-ess-táhr/ *n.* well-being
bienvenido /bee-ayn-vay-née-doh/ *interj.* welcome
bife /bée-fay/ *n. RP* steak

biftec /beef táyk/ *n.* beefsteak
bigote /bee-góh-tay/ *n.* mustache
billete /bee-yáy-tay/ *n.* banknote; bill (money)
billetera /bee-yay-táy-rah/ *n. Bol., Chi., Cuba, Ec., Pe.* wallet
billullo /bee-yóo-yoh/ *n. Col.* bill (money)
bistec /bees-táyk/ *n. Cuba, Mex., Pe.* beefsteak
bizcocho /bees-cóh-choh/ *n. Cuba* ladyfinger; *PR* cake, *Mex.* (vulgar)
blanco /bláhn-coh/ *n., adj.* white; *n.* target
blanquillo /blahn-kéy-yoh/ *n. Gua., Mex.* egg (euphemism for huevo, which has double meaning)
bloque /blóh-kay/ *n.* block
blusa /blóo-sah/ *n.* blouse
boca /bóh-cah/ *n.* mouth
bocadillo /boh-cah-dée-yoh/ *n. Ven.* fruitcake
bocaditos /boh-cah-dée-tohs/ *n. Cuba* little sandwiches; *Pe.* snacks
bocas /bóh-cahs/ *n. CA* snacks
bocina /boh-sée-nah/ *n. Cuba, Ecu., PR, RP* car horn
bochinche /boh-chéen-chay/ *n. Arg.* noise; commotion
boda /bóh-dah/ *n.* wedding
bodega /boh-dáy-gah/ *n.* store; warehouse; *Cuba, Pe., PR, Ven.* grocery store
bodeguero /boh-day-gáy-roh/ *n. Cuba, Pe., PR, Ven.* grocer
boga /bóh-gah/ *n. Arg.* attorney
bohío /boh-ée-oh/ *n.* thatched hut

boina /bóy-nah/ *n.* beret; *Ec.* powder puff
bol /bohl/ *n. Arg.* bowl
bolero /boh-láy-roh/ *n. Mex.* shoeshine boy
boleta /boh-láy-tah/ *n. Col.* ticket
boletín meteorológico /boh-lay-téen may-tay-oh-roh--lóh-hee-coh/ *n.* weather report
boleto /boh-láy-toh/ *n.* ticket
boliche /boh-lée-chay/ *n. Arg.* corner bar; discotheque; *Cuba* cut of meat; *Mex.* bowling; bowling alley
bolsa /bóhl-sah/ *n.* bag; stock market; *Mex.* purse; *Ec., Pe., Uru.* shopping bag
bolsillo /bohl-sée-yoh/ *n.* pocket
bolso /bóhl-soh/ *n. Ec.* purse; *Chi., PR* shopping bag
bomba /bóhm-bah/ *n.* pump; bomb
bombacha /bohm-báh-chah/ *n. Uru.* panty
bombero /bohm-báy-roh/ *n.* fireman
bombilla /bohm-bée-yah/ *n.* light bulb (except Mex.); *Bol., RP* drinking straw
bombones /bohm-bóh-nays/ *n.* bonbons
bondad /bohn-dáhd/ *n.* kindness
bondadoso /bohn-dah-dóh-soh/ *adj.* kind
boniato /boh-nee-áh-toh/ *n. Cuba* sweet potato
bonito /boh-née-toh/ *n.* tuna fish; *adj.* pretty
boquilla /boh-kéy-yah/ *n. Mex., Pe.* cigarette filter
borla /bóhr-lah/ *n. Ec., Mex.* powder puff
borracho /boh-ráh-choh/ *n., adj.* drunk
borrar /boh-ráhr/ *v.* scratch out; erase
bosque /bóhs-kay/ *n.* woods

bota /bóh-tah/ *n.* boot
botana /boh-táh-nah/ *n. Mex.* snack
bote /bóh-tay/ *n.* can; *Mex.* empty returnable bottle
bote de basura /bóh-tay day bah-sóo-rah/ *n. Mex.* wastebasket
botella /boh-táy-yah/ *n.* bottle; *Cuba* sinecure
botica /boh-tée-cah/ *n. Carib.* drug store
boticario /boh-tee-cáh-ree-oh/ *n.* druggist
botón /boh-tóhn/ *n.* button; *Arg.* policeman
botones /boh-tóh-nays/ *n.* bellboy
bragas /bráh-gahs/ *n.* panties
bravo /bráh-voh/ *adj.* brave; *Andes, CA, Carib.* angry
brazalete /brah-sah-láy-tay/ *n.* bracelet
brazo /bráh-soh/ *n.* arm
brécol /bráy-cohl/ *n.* broccoli
breve /bráy-vay/ *adj.* brief
brevete /bray-váy-tay/ *n. Pe.* driver's license
brillante /bree-yáhn-tay/ *adj.* brilliant
brillo /brée-yoh/ *n.* shine; sparkle
brincar /breen-cáhr/ *v.* jump
brindis /bréen-dees/ *n.* toast to one's health
bróculi /bróh-coo-lee/ *n.* broccoli
brocha /bróh-chah/ *n.* wide brush
broche /bróh-chay/ *n.* clasp; *Chi.* paper clip
broma /bróh-mah/ *n.* joke
bromista /broh-mées-tah/ *n.* joker; *adj. Arg.* funny
bronce /bróhn-say/ *n.* bronze
bruja /bróo-hah/ *n.* witch
brujería /broo-hay-rée-ah/ *n.* witchcraft

bucles /bóo-clays/ *n. Uru.* curls
budín /boo-déen/ *n. Arg., Mex., Uru.* pudding
buena voluntad /bwáy-nah voh-loon-táhd/ *n.* good will
bueno /bwáy-noh/ *adj.* good; *Ven.* fair complected
Buenos días. /bwáy-nohs dée-ahs/ Good morning.
Buenas noches. /bwáy-nahs nóh-chays/ Good evening. Good night.
Buenas tardes. /bwáy-nahs táhr-days/ Good afternoon.
bufete /boo-fáy-tay/ *n.* law office
buho /bóo-oh/ *n.* owl
bulla /bóo-yah/ *n.* noise
buque /bóo-kay/ *n.* ship
burocracia /boo-roh-cráh-see-ah/ *n.* bureaucracy
burro /bóo-roh/ *n.* donkey; *Mex.* ironing board
bus /boos/ *n. Ec.* city and intercity bus; *Pan.* city bus
buscar /boos-cáhr/ *v.* look for
buseta /boo-sáy-tah/ *n. Col.* bus
búsqueda /bóos-kay-dah/ *n.* search
butaca /boo-táh-cah/ *n.* easy chair; box seat (theater)

- C -

caballero /cah-bah-yáy-roh/ *n.* gentleman
caballo /cah-báh-yoh/ *n.* horse
cabaña /cah-báh-nyah/ *n.* cabin; hut *Arg.* cattle breeding ranch
cabello /cah-báy-yoh/ *n.* hair
cabeza /cah-báy-sah/ *n.* head
cabina de dormir /cah-bée-nah day dohr-méer/ *n.* *Uru.* sleeping car
cabo /cáh-boh/ *n.* cape; (mil.) corporal
cabritas /cah-brée-tahs/ *n. Chi.* popcorn
cabrito /cah-brée-toh/ *n.* kid; baby goat
cabro /cáh-broh/ *n. Chi.* kid
cacahuates /cah-cah-oo-áh-tays/ *n. Mex.* peanuts
cacao /cah-cáh-oh/ *n.* cocoa; chocolate
cada /cáh-dah/ *adj.* each; every
caer /cah-áyr/ *v.* fall
café /cah-fáy/ *n.* coffee; café; *n., adj. Mex.* brown
cafetera /cah-fay-táy-rah/ *n.* coffee pot; *Arg., Mex.* jalopy
cafetería /cah-fay-tay-rée-ah/ *n.* coffee house
caja /cáh-hah/ *n.* box; safe; cashier's window
caja de seguridad /cáh-hah day say-goo-ree-dáhd/ *n.* safe-deposit box
cajero /cah-háy-roh/ *n.* cashier; teller
cajón /cah-hón/ *n.* drawer
calabaza /cah-lah-báh-sah/ *n. Cuba, Mex., Pe., Uru.*

pumpkin
calambre /cah-láhm bray/ *n.* cramp
calcetín /cahl-say-téen/ *n.* sock
calcular /cahl-coo-láhr/ *v.* calculate
calefacción /cah-lay-fahk-see-óhn/ *n.* central heating
calendario /cah-layn-dáh-ree-oh/ *n.* calendar
calentura /cah-layn-tóo-rah/ *n. Mex.* fever
calidad /cah-lee-dáhd/ *n.* quality
caliente /cah-lee-áyn-tay/ *adj.* hot
calmante /cahl-máhn-tay/ *n.* sedative; tranquilizer; *adj.* soothing
caló /cah-lóh/ *n. Mex.* underworld slang
calor /cah-lóhr/ *n.* heat
calzón /cahl-sóhn/ *n. Ec., Pe., Uru.* panties
calle /cáh-yay/ *n.* street
callejón /cah-yay-hón/ *n.* alley
cama /cáh-mah/ *n.* bed
cámara /cáh-mah-rah/ *n.* camera; chamber; inner tube (tire)
camarera /cah-mah-ráy-rah/ *n.* waitress; chambermaid
camarero /cah-mah-ráy-roh/ *n.* waiter
camarín /cah-mah-réen/ *n. Mex.* sleeping car
camarón /cah-mah-róhn/ *n.* shrimp; *CA, Col.,* tip; *Ven.* nap
camarote /cah-mah-róh-tay/ *n. Arg.* sleeping car
cambiar /cahm-bee-áhr/ *v.* change; exchange
cambiar opiniones /cahm-bee-áhr oh-pee-nee-óh-nays/ *v.* discuss

cambio /cáhm-bee-oh/ *n.* change; exchange
cambur /cahm-bóor/ *n. Ven.* banana
camerino /cah-may-rée-noh/ *n. Ven.* sleeping car
caminante /cah-mee-náhn-tay/ *n.* walker
caminar /cah-mee-náhr/ *v.* walk
camino /cah-mée-noh/ *n.* road
camión /cah-mee-óhn/ *n.* truck; *Mex.* city bus
camioneta /cah-mee-oh-náy-tah/ *n.* light truck; pickup
camisa /cah-mée-sah/ *n.* shirt
camisa de dormir /cah-mée-sah day dohr-méer/ *n.* nightshirt
camote /cah-móh-tay/ *n. Mex.* sweet potato; *Chi.* lie; *Chi., Pe.* sweetheart; *LA* onion
campamento /cahm-pah-máyn-toh/ *n.* camp
campana /cahm-páh-nah/ *n.* bell; *Andes, RP* spy; lookout
campera /cahm-páy-rah/ *n. RP* jacket
campesino /cahm-pay-sée-noh/ *n.* farmer; peasant
campo /cáhm-poh/ *n.* country (rural area)
campo de juego /cáhm-poh day hwáy-goh/ *n.* playground
canal /cah-náhl/ *n.* canal; channel
canasta /cah-náhs-tah/ *n.* basket
canción /cahn-see-óhn/ *n.* song
candela /cahn-dáy-lah/ *n.* candle; fire
canela /cah-náy-lah/ *n.* cinnamon
cangrejo /cahn-gráy-hoh/ *n.* crab
canguil /cahn-ghéel/ *n. Ec.* popcorn

canoa /cah-nóh-ah/ *n.* canoe
cansado /cahn-sáh-doh/ *adj.* tired
cansancio /cahn-sáhn-see-oh/ *n.* weariness
cantante /cahn-táhn-tay/ *n.* singer
cantar /cahn-táhr/ *v.* sing
cántaro /cáhn-tah-roh/ *n.* jug; pitcher
cantidad /cahn-tee-dáhd/ *n.* amount
caña /cáh-nyah/ *n.* sugar cane; *Chi.* hangover
cañita /cah-nyée-tah/ *n. Pe.* drinking straw
caño /cáh-nyoh/ *n.* pipe; tube; *Col.* stream; *Pe.* faucet
cañón /cah-nyóhn/ *n.* canyon; (mil.) cannon
caoba /cah-óh-bah/ *n.* mahogany
capa /cáh-pah/ *n.* cape; layer
capaz /cah-páhs/ *adj.* capable
capilla /cah-pée-yah/ *n.* chapel
capital /cah-pee-táhl/ *n.* capital (investment); *adj.* main; principal
capote /cah-póh-tay/ *n. Pan.* raincoat
cara /cáh-rah/ *n.* face
carácter /cah-ráhk-tayr/ *n.* character
caravanas /cah-rah-váh-nahs/ *n. Uru.* earrings
carburador /cahr-boo-rah-dóhr/ *n.* carburetor
cárcel /cáhr-sayl/ *n.* jail
carga /cáhr-gah/ *n.* freight; cargo
cargamento /cahr-gah-máyn-toh/ *n.* load; shipment
cargar /cahr-gáhr/ *v.* load; charge
caricatura /cah-ree-cah-tóo-rah/ *n.* cartoon
carnada /cahr-náh-dah/ *n.* bait
carnaval /cahr-nah-váhl/ *n.* carnival

carne /cáhr-nay/ *n.* meat
carne de puerco /cáhr-nay day pwáyr-coh/ *n.* pork
carne de res /cáhr-nay day rays/ *n.* beef
carne de vaca /cáhr-nay day váh-cah/ *n.* beef
carnet de identidad /cahr-náyt day ee-dayn-tee-dáhd/ *n.* ID card
carnet de manejar /cahr-náyt day mah-nay-háhr/ *n.* *Chi.* driver's license
caro /cáh-roh/ *adj.* expensive
carrera /cah-ráy-rah/ *n.* race; career
carreta /cah-ráy-tah/ *n.* cart
carrete /cah-ráy-tay/ *n.* reel; spool
carretera /cah-ray-táy-rah/ *n.* highway
carril /cah-réel/ *n.* rail; *Mex.* lane; *Chi.* train
carrizo /cah-rée-soh/ *n.* *Pan.* straw (drinking)
carro /cáh-roh/ *n.* car
carro comedor /cáh-roh coh-may-dóhr/ *n.* *Mex.* dining car
carta /cáhr-tah/ *n.* letter; menu
cartas /cáhr-tahs/ *n.* playing cards
cartel /cahr-táyl/ *n.* poster
cartera /cahr-táy-rah/ *n.* wallet; *Bol., Chi., Cuba, Ec., Pe., RP, Ven.* woman's purse
carterista /cahr-tay-rées-tah/ *n.* pickpocket
cartero /cahr-táy-roh/ *n.* postman
cartilla /cahr-tée-yah/ *n.* *Mex.* ID card (mil. service)
casa /cáh-sah/ *n.* house; home
casaca /cah-sáh-cah/ *n.* *Pe.* jacket
casa de correos /cáh-sah day coh-ráy-ohs/ *n.* post of-

fice (except Mex.)
casado /cah-sáh-doh/ *adj.* married
casarse con /cah-sáhr-say cohn/ *v.* get married to
cascada /cahs-cáh-dah/ *n.* waterfall
casco /cáhs-coh/ *n.* helmet
casi /cáh-see/ *adv.* almost
caso /cáh-soh/ *n.* case; event
castigar /cah-stee-gáhr/ *v.* punish
castigo /cah-stée-goh/ *n.* punishment
casualidad /cah-soo-ah-lee-dáhd/ *n.* accident; chance
catálogo /cah-táh-loh-goh/ *n.* catalogue
catarro /cah-táh-roh/ *n.* head cold; *CA, Mex.* flu
catedral /cah-tay-dráhl/ *n.* cathedral
catire /cah-tée-ray/ *n., adj. Ven.* blond
católico /cah-tóh-lee-coh/ *n., adj.* catholic
catorce /cah-tóhr-say/ *n., adj.* fourteen
caucho /cáh-oo-choh/ *n.* rubber; *Col.* rubber raincoat; *Ven.* tire
causa /cáh-oo-sah/ *n.* cause; lawsuit; *Chi.* snacks; *Pe.* potato salad
causar /cah-oo-sáhr/ *v.* cause
cauteloso /cah-oo-tay-lóh-soh/ *adj.* cautious
caverna /cah-váyr-nah/ *n.* cave
caza /cáh-sah/ *n.* hunt; hunting
cazador /cah-sah-dóhr/ *n.* hunter
cazar /cah-sáhr/ *v.* hunt
cazuela /cah-swáy-lah/ *n.* cook pot; casserole; *SA* chicken stew
cebolla /say bóh-yah/ *n.* onion

cedro /sáy-droh/ *n.* cedar
cédula de identidad /sáy-doo-lah day ee-dayn-tee--dáhd/ *n. Bol., Ec., Mex., Pe., RP* ID card
ceja /sáy-hah/ *n.* eyebrow
cementerio /say-mayn-táy-ree-oh/ *n.* cemetery
cena /sáy-nah/ *n.* supper; dinner
cenicero /say-nee-sáy-roh/ *n.* ashtray
centavo /sayn-táh-voh/ *n.* cent
central /sayn-tráhl/ *n.* sugar mill; *adj.* central
cepillo /say-pée-yoh/ *n.* brush (for grooming)
cepillo de dientes /say-pée-yoh day dee-áyn-tays/ *n.* toothbrush
cepillo para la cabeza /say-pée-yoh páh-rah lah cah--báy-sah/ *n.* hairbrush
cera /sáy-rah/ *n.* wax
cerámica /say-ráh-mee-cah/ *n.* ceramics
cerámico /say-ráh-mee-coh/ *adj.* ceramic
cerca /sáyr-cah/ *n.* fence; *adv.* near
cerca de /sáyr-cah day/ *prep.* near
cerdo /sáyr-doh/ *n.* pig
cereal /say-ray-áhl/ *n., adj.* cereal
cereza /say-ráy-sah/ *n.* cherry
cerillo /say-rée-yoh/ *n. Mex.* match
cero /sáy-roh/ *n.* zero
cerradura /say-rah-dóo-rah/ *n.* lock
cerrar /say-ráhr/ *v.* close
cerrar con llave /say-ráhr cohn yáh vay/ *v.* lock
certificado /sayr-tee-fee-cáh-doh/ *n.* certificate; *adj.* registered

certificar /sayr-tee-fee-cáhr/ *v.* certify; register
cerveza /sayr-váy-sah/ *n.* beer
cesar /say-sáhr/ *v.* stop; cease
césped /sáys-payd/ *n.* lawn
cesta /sáys-tah/ *n.* basket
chabacano /chah-bah-cáh-noh/ *n. Mex.* apricot
chamaco /chah-máh-coh/ *n. Mex., PR* kid
chamarra /chah-máh-rah/ *n. Mex.* jacket
chamba /chám-bah/ *n. Ec.* lawn; *Mex.* work
chamito /chah-mée-toh/ *n. Ven.* baby
chamo /cháh-moh/ *n. Ven.* kid
champaña /chahm-páh-nyah/ *n.* champagne
champiñón /chahm-pee-nyóhn/ *n. Mex.* mushroom
champú /chahm-póo/ *n.* shampoo
chancho /cháhn-choh/ *n. Arg., Bol.* pig
chango /cháhn-goh/ *n. Mex.* monkey; *adj. Chi.* stupid
chapa /cháh-pah/ *n.* plate; *Chi., Mex.* lock; *Ec.* door handle
chaparro /chah-páh-roh/ *adj. CA, Mex.* short (person)
chaqueta /chah-káy-tah/ *n.* jacket
charla /cháhr-lah/ *n.* chat; talk
charlar /chahr-láhr/ *v.* chat; talk
charol /chah-róhl/ *n. Ec.* tray
charola /chah-róh-lah/ *n. Mex.* tray
chauchas /cháh-oo-chahs/ *n. RP* green beans
chavo /cháh-voh/ *n. Mex.* kid
cheque /cháy-kay/ *n.* check
chicle /chée-clay/ *n.* chewing gum

chico /chée-coh/ *n.* kid; *adj.* small
chicharo /chée-chah-roh/ *n.* pea; *Col.* poor grade cigar
chile /chée-lay/ *n.* chilli pepper
chile verde /chée-lay váyr-day/ *n. Mex.* bell pepper
chimenea /chee-may-náy-ah/ *n.* chimney; fireplace
chino /chée-noh/ *n. Col.* boy; *Mex.* curl; *n., adj.* Chinese
chiquillo /chee-kéy-yoh/ *n. Pan.* kid
chiste /chée-stay/ *n.* joke
chistoso /chee-stóh-soh/ *adj. Mex., Pe.* funny
chiva /chée-vah/ *n. Pan.* intercity bus
choapino /choh-ah-pée-noh/ *n. Chi.* throw rug
chocar /choh-cáhr/ *v.* collide; irritate
choclo /chóh-cloh/ *n. Arg., Chi., Ec., Pe.* corn (on cob)
chocolate /choh-coh-láh-tay/ *n.* chocolate
chofer /choh-fáyr/ *n.* driver
choque /chóh-kay/ *n.* shock; clash
chorizo /choh-rée-soh/ *n. Mex.* salami-type sausage
choza /chóh-sah/ *n.* hut
chuchaqui /choo-cháh-key/ *n. Ec.* hangover
chuleta /choo-láy-tah/ *n.* chop; cutlet
cicatriz /see-cah-trées/ *n.* scar
ciego /see-áy-goh/ *adj.* blind
cielo /see-áy-loh/ *n.* sky; heaven
cien /see-áyn/ *n., adj.* one hundred
ciencia /see-áyn-see-ah/ *n.* science
científico /see-ayn-tée-fee-coh/ *n.* scientist; *adj.* scien-

tific
ciento /see-áyn-toh/ *n., adj.* one hundred
cierre /see-áy-ray/ *n.* closing; *Mex., Uru.* zipper
cierre relámpago /see-áy-ray ray-láhm-pah-goh/ *n. Uru.* zipper
cierto /see-áyr-toh/ *adj.* certain
cigarrillo /see-gah-rée-yoh/ *n. Ec., Pan., Pe., PR, RP* cigarette
cigarro /see-gáh-roh/ *n.* cigarette; *Ec., PR* cigar
cinco /séen-coh/ *n., adj.* five
cincuenta /seen-kwáyn-tah/ *n., adj.* fifty
cine /sée-nay/ *n.* movies; movie theater
cinta /séen tah/ *n.* ribbon; tape; *Ven.* string
cintura /seen-tóo-rah/ *n.* waist
cinturón /seen-too-róhn/ *n.* belt
círculo /séer-coo-loh/ *n.* circle
circunstancia /seer-coon-stáhn-see-ah/ *n.* circumstance
ciruela /see-roo-áy-lah/ *n.* plum
ciruela pasa /see-roo-áy-lah páh-sah/ *n.* prune
cirugía /see-roo-hée-ah/ *n.* surgery
cirujano /see-roo-háh-noh/ *n.* surgeon
cisne /sées-nay/ *n.* swan; *RP* powder puff
cita /sée-tah/ *n.* appointment; date
citación /see-tah-see-óhn/ *n.* citation; quotation
citar /see-táhr/ *v.* summon; quote
ciudad /see-oo-dáhd/ *n.* city
ciudadanía /see-oo-dah-dah-née-ah/ *n.* citizenship
ciudadano /see-oo-da-dáh-noh/ *n.* citizen

civil /see-véel/ *adj.* civil; *n.* civilian
claro /kláh-roh/ *adj.* clear; *adv.* clearly; *interj.* sure, of course
clase /kláh-say/ *n.* class; kind
clasificar /klah-see-fee-cáhr/ *v.* classify
clavar /klah-váhr/ *v.* nail; *Mex.* dive
clavícula /klah-vée-coo-lah/ *n.* collarbone
clavo /kláh-voh/ *n.* nail; clove
claxon /kláhk-sohn/ *n. Mex., Uru.* car horn
cliente /klee-áyn-tay/ *n.* customer; client
clima /klée-mah/ *n.* climate; *Mex.* air conditioning
club /kloob/ *n.* club
cobija /coh-bée-hah/ *n. Mex.* blanket
cobre /cóh-bray/ *n.* copper
cocina /coh-sée-nah/ *n.* kitchen; cuisine; stove
cocinar /coh-see-náhr/ *v.* cook
cocinero /coh-see-náy-roh/ *n.* cook
coco /cóh-coh/ *n.* coconut; *Carib., Mex., RP* head
coche /cóh-chay/ *n.* car
coche cama /cóh-chay cáh-mah/ *n.* sleeping car
coche comedor /cóh-chay coh-may-dóhr/ *n.* dining car
coche dormitorio /cóh-chay dohr-mee-tóh-ree-oh/ *n. Pe.* sleeping car
cochera /coh-cháy-rah/ *n.* garage
coche restaurante /cóh-chay rays-tah-oo-ráhn-tay/ *n. Bol.* dining car
cochino /coh-chée-noh/ *n.* pig; *adj.* dirty
codo /cóh-doh/ *n.* elbow
coger /coh-háyr/ *v.* catch; get hold of (has vulgar

double meaning)

cojín /coh-héen/ *n.* cushion

col /cohl/ *n.* cabbage

cola /cóh-lah/ *n.* line; tail; *Arg.* glue; *Ven.* lift (in car)

colcha /cóhl-chah/ *n.* bedspread

colección /coh-layk-see-óhn/ *n.* collection

colectivo /coh-layk-tée-voh/ *n. Arg., Bol.* city bus; *adj.* collective

coles de bruselas /cóh-lays day broo-sáy-lahs/ *n.* brussels sprouts

colgador /cohl-gah-dóhr/ *n.* clothes hanger

colgar /cohl-gáhr/ *v.* hang; hang up

coliflor /coh-lee-flóhr/ *n.* cauliflower

colina /coh-lée-nah/ *n.* hill

color /coh-lóhr/ *n.* color

colorete /coh-loh-ráy-tay/ *n.* rouge; *Pan.* lipstick

columna /coh-lóom-nah/ *n.* column; pillar

combinación /cohm-bee-nah-see-óhn/ *n.* combination; *Uru.* slip (undergarment)

combustible /cohn-boos-tée-blay/ *n.* fuel

comedia /coh-máy-dee-ah/ *n.* comedy

comedor /coh-may-dóhr/ *n.* dining room

comentar /coh-mayn-táhr/ *v.* comment

comenzar /coh-mayn-sáhr/ *v.* start; begin

comer /coh-máyr/ *v.* eat

comercial /coh-mayr-see-áhl/ *adj.* commercial; business

comerciar /coh-mayr-see-áhr/ *v.* trade; deal

comercio /coh-máyr-see-oh/ *n.* business; trade

comestibles /coh-mays-tée-blays/ *n.* food; *Uru.* groceries
cómico /cóh-mee-coh/ *n.* comedian; *adj.* funny
comida /coh-mée-dah/ *n.* food; meal
comida corrida /coh-mée-dah coh-rée-dah/ *n. Mex.* restaurant special of the day
comienzo /coh-mee-áyn-soh/ *n.* beginning
comisión /coh-mee-see-óhn/ *n.* commission
como /cóh-moh/ *adv.* as; like; *conj.* as; when; if; so that
¿cómo? /cóh-moh/ *adv.* how?
comodidad /coh-moh-dee-dáhd/ *n.* comfort
cómodo /cóh-moh-doh/ *adj.* comfortable
compañero /cohm-pah-nyáy-roh/ *n.* companion; partner; *Uru.* buddy
compañía /cohm-pah-nyée-ah/ *n.* company
comparación /cohm-pah-rah-see-óhn/ *n.* comparison
comparar /cohm-pah-ráhr/ *v.* compare
compartimiento /cohm-pahr-tee-mee-áyn-toh/ *n.* compartment
compartir /cohm-pahr-téer/ *v.* share
compinche /cohm-péen-chay/ *n. Bol., RP* buddy
completar /cohm-play-táhr/ *v.* complete
completo /cohm-pláy-toh/ *adj.* complete
compra /cóhm-prah/ *n.* purchase
comprador /cohm-prah-dóhr/ *n.* buyer
comprar /cohm-práhr/ *v.* buy
comprender /cohm-prayn-dáyr/ *v.* understand
comprensión /cohm-prayn-see-óhn/ *n.* comprehen-

sion

comprobar /cohm-proh-báhr/ *v.* check; verify

computadora /cohm-poo-tah-dóh-rah/ *n.* computer

común /coh-móon/ *adj.* common

comunicación /coh-moon-ee-cah-see-óhn/ *n.* communication

con /cohn/ *prep.* with

concha /cóhn-chah/ *n.* shell; *Arg., Chi., Uru.* (has vulgar double meaning)

concierto /cohn-see-áyr-toh/ *n.* concert

concluir /cohn-cloo-éer/ *v.* conclude

conclusión /cohn-cloo-see-óhn/ *n.* conclusion

concurso /cohn-cóor-soh/ *n.* contest

condenar /cohn-day-náhr/ *v.* condemn

condición /cohn-dee-see-óhn/ *n.* condition

conducir /cohn-doo-séer/ *v.* conduct; drive

conductor /cohn-dook-tóhr/ *n.* conductor; driver

conexión /coh-nayk-see-óhn/ *n.* connection

conferencia /cohn-fay-ráyn-see-ah/ *n.* lecture

confianza /cohn-fee-áhn-sah/ *n.* confidence

confiar /cohn-fee-áhr/ *v.* trust

conflicto /cohn-fléek-toh/ *n.* conflict

confusión /cohn-foo-see-óhn/ *n.* confusion

congelar /cohn-hay-láhr/ *v.* freeze

congreso /cohn-gráy-soh/ *n.* congress; convention

conocer /coh-noh-sáyr/ *v.* know; be acquainted with

conocimiento /coh-noh-see-mee-áyn-toh/ *n.* knowledge

consecuencia /cohn-say-kwáyn-see-ah/ *n.* consequence

conseguir /cohn-say-ghéer/ *v.* get

consejo /cohn-sáy-hoh/ *n.* advice

conserje /cohn-sáyr-hay/ *n.* janitor; *Pe.* bellboy

considerable /cohn-see-day-ráh-blay/ *adj.* considerable

consideración /cohn-see-day-rah-see-óhn/ *n.* consideration

considerado /cohn-see-day-ráh-doh/ *adj.* considerate

considerar /cohn-see-day-ráhr/ *v.* consider

consignación /cohn-seeg-nah-see-óhn/ *n.* consignment

consignar /cohn-seeg-náhr/ *v.* consign; deposit in trust

consistente /cohn-sees-táyn-tay/ *adj.* consistent

consistir /cohn-sees-téer/ *v.* consist

constante /cohn-stáhn-tay/ *adj.* constant

constituir /cohn-stee-too-éer/ *v.* constitute

construcción /cohn-strook-see-óhn/ *n.* construction

cónsul /cóhn-sool/ *n.* consul

consulado /cohn-soo-láh-doh/ *n.* consulate

consultar /cohn-sool-táhr/ *v.* consult

consultorio /cohn-sool-tóh-ree-oh/ *n.* doctor's office

consumidor /cohn-soo-mee-dóhr/ *n.* consumer

consumir /cohn-soo-méer/ *v.* consume

contacto /cohn-táhk-toh/ *n.* contact; *Mex.* (elec.) outlet

contador /cohn-tah-dóhr/ *n.* accountant

contar /cohn-táhr/ *v.* count; tell

contar con /cohn-táhr cohn/ *v.* count on
contener /cohn-tay-náyr/ *v.* contain
contenido /cohn-tay-née-doh/ *n.* content
contento /cohn-táyn-toh/ *adj.* content; happy
contestación /cohn-tays-tah-see-óhn/ *n.* answer; reply
contestar /cohn-tays-táhr/ *v.* answer
continuar /cohn-tee-noo-áhr/ *v.* continue
contra /cóhn-trah/ *prep.* against
contrabando /cohn-trah-báhn-doh/ *n.* contraband; smuggling
contradictorio /cohn-trah-deek-tóh-ree-oh/ *adj.* contradictory
contrario /cohn-tráh-ree-oh/ *adj.* contrary
contraste /cohn-tráhs-tay/ *n.* contrast
contrato /cohn-tráh-toh/ *n.* contract
contribución /cohn-tree-boo-see-óhn/ *n.* contribution
contribuir /cohn-tree-boo-éer/ *v.* contribute
control /cohn-tróhl/ *n.* control
controlar /cohn-troh-láhr/ *v.* control
conveniencia /cohn-vay-nee-áyn-sée-ah/ *n.* convenience
conveniente /cohn-vay-nee-áyn-tay/ *adj.* convenient; suitable
conversación /cohn-vayr-sah-see-óhn/ *n.* conversation
conversar /cohn-vayr-sáhr/ *v.* converse; *Ec., Pe., Ven.* chat
convertir /cohn-vayr-téer/ *v.* convert
coñac /coh-nyák/ *n.* cognac; brandy

copa /cóh-pah/ *n.* wineglass; hearts (playing cards); *Mex.* drink (alcoholic)
copia /cóh-pee-ah/ *n.* copy
copiar /coh-pee-áhr/ *v.* copy
coraje /coh-ráh-hay/ *n.* courage; anger
coral /coh-ráhl/ *n.* coral
corazón /coh-rah-sóhn/ *n.* heart
corbata /cohr-báh-tah/ *n.* necktie
cordel /cohr-dáyl/ *n.* string
cordón /cohr-dóhn/ *n.* string
cordón de zapato /cohr-dóhn day sah-páh-toh/ *n.* shoestring
corona /coh-róh-nah/ *n.* crown; wreath
corporación /cohr-poh-rah-see-óhn/ *n.* corporation
corre /cóh-ray/ *imper. Ven.* hurry up
correcto /coh-ráyk-toh/ *adj.* correct
corredor /coh-ray-dóhr/ *n.* runner; corridor; *Andes, Carib.* covered porch
corredor de bolsa /coh-ray-dóhr day bóhl-sah/ *n.* stockbroker
correo /coh-ráy-oh/ *n.* mail; post office
correr /coh-ráyr/ *v.* run
correspondencia /coh-ray-spohn-dáyn-see-ah/ *n.* correspondence
corriente /coh-ree-áyn-tay/ *n.* current; *adj.* ordinary
corrupción /coh-roop-see-óhn/ *n.* corruption
corrupto /coh-róop-toh/ *adj.* corrupt
cortar /cohr-táhr/ *v.* cut
corte /cóhr-tay/ *n.* cut; *LA* court

cortés /cohr-táys/ *adj.* polite
corteza /cohr-táy-sah/ *n.* bark; crust
cortina /cohr-tée-nah/ *n.* curtain
corto /cóhr-toh/ *adj.* short
cosa /cóh-sah/ *n.* thing
coser /coh-sáyr/ *v.* sew
costa /cóh-stah/ *n.* coast
costar /coh-stáhr/ *v.* cost
costilla /coh-stée-yah/ *n.* rib; chop
costo /cóh-stoh/ *n.* cost; price
costoso /coh-stóh-soh/ *adj.* costly
costumbre /coh-stóom-bray/ *n.* custom
costura /coh-stóo-rah/ *n.* sewing; seam
costurera /coh-stoo-ráy-rah/ *n.* seamstress
cotufas /coh-tóo-fahs/ *n. Ven.* popcorn
credencial /cray-dayn-see-áhl/ *n. Mex.* ID card
crédito /cráy-dee-toh/ *n.* credit
creer /cray-áyr/ *v.* believe
crema para el cutis /cráy-mah páh-rah el cóotees/ *n.* skin cream
criada /cree-áh-dah/ *n.* maid
criado /cree-áh-doh/ *n.* servant
crimen /crée-mayn/ *n.* crime
criminal /cree-mee-náhl/ *n., adj.* criminal
criollo /cree-óh-yoh/ *n., adj.* creole; native
crisis /crée-sees/ *n.* crisis
cristal /cree-stáhl/ *n.* crystal; glass
cristalería /cree-stah-lay-rée-ah/ *n.* glassware
cristetas /crees-táy-tahs/ *n. Col.* popcorn

cruda /cróo-dah/ *n. Mex.* hangover
crudo /cróo-doh/ *adj.* raw; crude
cruel /croo-áyl/ *adj.* cruel
cruz /croos/ *n.* cross
cruzar /croo-sáhr/ *v.* cross
cuaderno /kwah-dáyr-noh/ *n.* notebook; *Mex., Ven.* pamphlet
cuadra /kwáh-drah/ *n.* city block
cuadrado /kwah-dráh-doh/ *adj.* square
cuadro /kwáh-droh/ *n.* square; picture; frame
cual /kwal/ *adv., pron.* which; such as
¿cuál? /kwal/ *adj., pron.* what? which one?
cualquiera /kwal-key-áy-rah/ *pron.* whichever; whoever; anyone
cualquier cosa /kwal-key-áyr cóh-sah/ *pron.* anything
cuando /kwán-doh/ *adv.* when
¿cuándo? /kwán-doh/ *adv.* when?
cuanto /kwán-toh/ *adj., pron.* as much as; all that which
¿cuánto? /kwán-toh/ *adj., pron.* how much?
¿Cuánto cuesta? /kwán-toh kwáys-tah/ How much does it cost?
¿Cuánto es? /kwán-toh es/ How much is it?
¿cuántos? /kwán-tohs/ *adj., pron.* how many?
¿Cuánto vale? /kwán-toh váh-lay/ How much is it?
cuarenta /kwah-ráyn-tah/ *n., adj.* forty
cuarto /kwáhr-toh/ *n.* fourth; quarter; room; *Uru.* bedroom
cuarto de dormir /kwáhr-toh day dohr méer/ *n.* bed-

room

cuate /kwáh-tay/ *n. Mex.* twin; buddy

cuatro /kwáh-troh/ *n., adj.* four

cubeta /coo-báy-tah/ *n. Mex., Uru.* bucket

cubierta /coo-bee-áyr-tah/ *n.* cover; deck

cubierto /coo-bee-áyr-toh/ *n.* place setting

cubo /cóo-boh/ *n.* cube; *Arg.* finger bowl; *Cuba, Pan.* bucket

cubrir /coo-bréer/ *v.* cover

cuchara /coo-cháh-rah/ *n.* spoon

cucharada /coo-chah-ráh-dah/ *n.* tablespoon; spoonful

cuchillito de afeitar /coo-chee-yée-toh day ah-fay--táhr/ *n. Cuba* razor blade

cuchillo /coo-chée-yoh/ *n.* knife

cuello /coo-áy-yoh/ *n.* neck; collar

cuenta /coo-áyn-tah/ *n.* account; bill

cuento /coo-áyn-toh/ *n.* story

cuerda /coo-áyr-dah/ *n.* cord; string

cuero /coo-áy-roh/ *n.* hide; leather

cuerpo /coo-áyr-poh/ *n.* body

cueva /coo-áy-vah/ *n.* cave

cuidado /coo-ee-dáh-doh/ *n.* care

cuidado /coo-ee-dáh-doh/ *imper.* be careful

cuidadoso /coo-ee-dah-dóh-soh/ *adj.* careful

cuidar /coo-ee-dáhr/ *v.* look after; take care of

culebra /coo-láy-brah/ *n.* snake

culpa /cóol-pah/ *n.* fault

culpable /cool-páh-blay/ *adj.* guilty

cultura /cool-tóo-rah/ *n.* culture
cumbre /cóom-bray/ *n.* top; summit
cumpleaños /coom-play-áh-nyohs/ *n.* birthday
cuneta /coo-náy-tah/ *n. Chi.* sidewalk
cuñada /coo-nyáh-dah/ *n.* sister-in-law
cuñado /coo-nyáh-doh/ *n.* brother-in-law
cuota /coo-óh-tah/ *n.* quota; *Mex.* toll
cuota inicial /coo-óh-tah ee-nee-see-áhl/ *Pe.* down payment
cura /cóo-rah/ *n.* cure; priest
curar /coo-ráhr/ *v.* treat; cure
curva /cóor-vah/ *n.* curve
cutis /cóo-tees/ *n.* skin
cuyo /cóo-yoh/ *adj.* whose

- D -

dama /dáh-mah/ *n.* lady
damasco /dah-máhs-coh/ *n. Chi.* apricot; *Uru.* plum
dañar /dah-nyáhr/ *v.* hurt; damage
daño /dáh-nyoh/ *n.* hurt; damage
dañoso /dah-nyóh-soh/ *adj.* harmful
dar /dahr/ *v.* give; hit
dar forma /dahr fóhr-mah/ *v.* shape
darse cuenta de /dáhr-say coo-áyn-tah day/ *v.* realize
darse por vencido /dáhr-say pohr vayn-sée-doh/ *v.* give up
darse prisa /dáhr-say prée-sah/ *v.* hurry
de /day/ *prep.* of; from; about
de antemano /day ahn-tay-máh-noh/ *adv.* beforehand
debajo /day báh-hoh/ *adv.* below; underneath
debajo de /day báh-hoh day/ *prep.* under; below
deber /day-báyr/ *n.* duty; *v.* owe; ought to; must; should
debido /day-bée-doh/ *adj.* due; proper
débil /dáy-beel/ *adj.* weak
decente /day-sáyn-tay/ *adj.* decent
de cerca /day sáyr-cah/ *adv.* at close range
décimo /dáy-see-moh/ *adj.* tenth
decir /day-séer/ *v.* say; tell
decisión /day-see-see-óhn/ *n.* decision
declaración /day-clah-rah-see-óhn/ *n.* declaration; statement

declarar /de-clah-ráhr/ *v.* declare
dedicar /day-dee-cáhr/ *v.* dedicate
dedo /dáy-doh/ *n.* finger
dedo del pie /dáy-doh del pee-áy/ *n.* toe
de edad mediana /day ay-dáhd may-dee-áh-nah/ *adj.* middle-aged
de ella /day áy-yah/ *pron.* hers
defecto /day-fáyk-toh/ *n.* defect
defectuoso /day-fayk-too-óh-soh/ *adj.* defective
definido /day-fee-née-doh/ *adj.* definite; sharp
dejar caer /day-hár cah-áyr/ *v.* drop
dejar de /day-hár day/ *v.* stop
de la clase media /day lah cláh-say máy-dee-ah/ *adj.* middle class
delgado /dayl-gáh-doh/ *adj.* thin
delicioso /day-lee-see-óh-soh/ *adj.* delicious
delito /day-lée-toh/ *n.* crime
de madera /day mah-dáy-rah/ *adj.* wooden
demanda /day-máhn-dah/ *n.* demand; lawsuit
demandar /day-mahn-dáhr/ *v.* demand; sue
demasiado /day-mah-see-áh-doh/ adj; *pron.* too much
democrático /day-moh-cráh-tee-coh/ *adj.* democratic
demora /day-móh-rah/ *n.* delay
demorar /day-moh-ráhr/ *v.* delay
demostrar /day-moh-stráhr/ *v.* demonstrate
denso /dáyn-soh/ *adj.* dense
dentista /dayn-tée-stah/ *n.* dentist
dentro /dáyn-troh/ *adv.* inside; within
dentro de /dáyn-troh day/ *prep.* inside of

departamento /day-pahr-tah-máyn-toh/ *n.* department; *Mex.* apartment
depender /day-payn-dáyr/ *v.* depend
dependiente /day-payn-dee-áyn-tay/ *n.* clerk; *adj.* dependent
deporte /day-póhr-tay/ *n.* sport
depositar /day-poh-see-táhr/ *v.* deposit
depósito /de-pós-ee-toh/ *n.* deposit; depot
de quien /day key-áyn/ *pron.* whose
¿de quién? /day key-áyn/ *pron.* whose?
derecha /day-ráy-chah/ *n.* right (direction)
derecho /day-ráy-choh/ *n.* right; law; *adj.* right; straight; *adv.* straight ahead
derecho de aduana /day-ráy-choh day ah-dwáh-nah/ *n.* custom duty
de repente /day ray-páyn-tay/ *adv.* suddenly
denamar(se) /day-rah-máhr-(say)/ *v.* spill
desafío /day-sah-fée-oh/ *n.* challenge
desafortunado /day-sah-fohr-too-náh-doh/ *adj.* unlucky
desagradable /day-sah-grah-dáh blay/ *adj.* disagreeable
desagradar /day-sah-grah-dáhr/ *v.* displease
desaparecer /day-sah-pah-ray-séhr/ *v.* disappear
desarrollar /day-sah-roh-yáhr/ *v.* develop
desarrollo /day-sah-róh-yoh/ *n.* development
desatar /day-sah-táhr/ *v.* let loose
desayuno /day-sah-yóo-noh/ *n.* breakfast
descansar /days-cahn-sáhr/ *v.* rest

descanso /days-cáhn-soh/ *n.* rest
desconfiar /days-cohn-fee-áhr/ *v.* distrust
desconocido /days-coh-noh-sée-doh/ *adj.* unknown
descontinuar /days-cohn-tee-noo-áhr/ *v.* discontinue
descortés /days-cohr-táys/ *adj.* rude
describir /days-cree-béer/ *v.* describe
descripción /days-creep-see-óhn/ *n.* description
descubrir /days-coo-bréer/ *v.* discover
descuento /days-coo-áyn-toh/ *n.* discount
desde /dáys-day/ *prep.* from; since; after
desear /day-say-áhr/ *v.* desire; wish
desempleado /days-aym-play-áh-doh/ *adj.* unemployed
desempleo /days-aym-pláy-oh/ *n.* unemployment
desenvolver /days-ayn-vohl-váyr/ *v.* unfold
deseo /day-sáy-oh/ *n.* desire
deseoso /day-say-óh-soh/ *adj.* desirous
dese prisa /dáy-say prée-sah/ *imper.* hurry up
desesperado /days-ays-pay-ráh-doh/ *adj.* desperate
desfile /days-fée-lay/ *n.* parade
desierto /day-see-áyr-toh/ *n.* desert; *adj.* deserted
desigual /day-see-gwáhl/ *adj.* unequal
desocupado /day-soh-coo-páh-doh/ *adj.* empty; unoccupied
desorden /days-óhr-dayn/ *n.* disorder
despacio /day-spáh-see-oh/ *adv.* slowly
despedida /day-spay-dée-dah/ *n.* farewell
despedir /day-spay-déer/ *v.* say good bye; fire (from job)

desperdicios /days-payr-dée-see-ohs/ *n.* waste
despertador /days-payr-tah-dóhr/ *n.* alarm clock
despertarse /days-payr-táhr/ *v.* wake; wake up
despierto /days-pee-áyr-toh/ *adj.* awake
después /days-poo-áys/ *adv.* after; afterwards
después de /days-poo-áys day/ *prep.* after
destacado /days-tah-cáh-doh/ *adj.* outstanding
destrucción /days-trook-see-óhn/ *n.* destruction
destruir /days-troo-éer/ *v.* destroy
detalle /day-táh-yay/ *n.* detail
detener /day-tay-náyr/ *v.* stop; arrest
determinar /day-tayr-mee-náhr/ *v.* determine
detrás /day-tráhs/ *adv.* behind
deuda /dáy-oo-dah/ *n.* debt
de veras /day váy-rahs/ *adv.* really
de vez en cuando /day vays ayn kwán-doh/ *adv.* once in a while
devolver /day-vohl-váyr/ *v.* return; give back
día /dée-ah/ *n.* day
diabetis /dee-ah báy-tees/ *n.* diabetes
día festivo /dée-ah fay-stée-voh/ *n.* holiday
día laborable /dée-ah lah-boh-ráh-blay/ *n.* workday
dialecto /dee-ah-láyk-toh/ *n.* dialect
diálogo /dee-áh-loh-goh/ *n.* dialogue
diamante /dee-ah-máhn-tay/ *n.* diamond
diario /dee-áh-ree-oh/ *n.* daily paper; *adj.* daily
diarrea /dee-ah-ráy-ah/ *n.* diarrhea
dibujar /dee-boo-hár/ *v.* draw
diccionario /deek-see-oh-náh-ree-oh/ *n.* dictionary

diciembre /dee-see-áym bray/ *n.* December
dicho /dée-choh/ *n.* saying
diente /dee-áyn-tay/ *n.* tooth
dieta /dee-áy-tah/ *n.* diet
diez /dee-áys/ *n., adj.* ten
diferencia /dee-fay-ráyn-see-ah/ *n.* difference
diferente /dee-fay-ráyn-tay/ *adj.* different
difícil /dee-fée-seel/ *adj.* difficult
dinero /dee-náy-roh/ *n.* money
dios /dee-óhs/ *n.* god
dirección /dee-rayk-see-óhn/ *n.* direction; address
directamente /dee-rayk-tah-máyn-tay/ *adv.* directly
directo /dee-ráyk-toh/ *adj.* straight; direct
director /dee-rayk-tóhr/ *n.* director; manager
directorio /dee-rayk-tóh-ree-oh/ *n.* directory
directorio telefónico /dee-rayk-tóh-ree-oh tay-lay--fóh-nee-coh/ *n. Mex.* phone directory
dirigente /dee-ree-háyn-tay/ *n.* leader
dirigir /dee-ree-héer/ *v.* direct; manage
disco /dées-coh/ *n.* disk; record
discotec /dees-coh-táyk/ *n. Arg.* discotheque
discoteca /dees-coh-táy-cah/ *n.* discotheque; record store
disculpa /dees-cóol-pah/ *n.* excuse; apology
disculpar /dees-cool-páhr/ *v.* apologize
discurso /dees-cóor-soh/ *n.* speech
discusión /dees-coo-see-óhn/ *n.* argument
discutir /dees-coo-téer/ *v.* argue
disentería /dee-sayn-tay-rée-ah/ *n.* dysentery

disfraz /dees-fráhs/ *n.* disguise
disfrutar /dees-froo-táhr/ *v.* enjoy
disminuir /dees-mee-noo-éer/ *v.* diminish
disolver /dee-sohl-váyr/ *v.* dissolve
disponible /dees-poh-née-blay/ *adj.* available
dispuesto /dees-pwáys-toh/ *adj.* willing
distancia /dees-táhn-see-ah/ *n.* distance
distante /dees-táhn-tay/ *adj.* distant
distinguir /dees-teen-ghéer/ *v.* distinguish
distinto /dees-téen-toh/ *adj.* different
distribuir /dees-tree-boo-éer/ *v.* distribute
distrito /dees-trée-toh/ *n.* district
disturbio /dees-tóor-bee-oh/ *n.* disturbance
diversión /dee-vayr-see-óhn/ *n.* recreation
divertido /dee-vayr-tée-doh/ *adj.* amusing
divertir /dee-vayr-téer/ *v.* amuse
divertirse /dee-vayr-téer-say/ *v.* have a good time
dividir /dee-vee-déer/ *v.* divide
división /dee-vee-see-óhn/ *n.* division
dobladillo /doh-blah-dée-yoh/ *n.* hem
doblar /doh-bláhr/ *v.* fold; turn a corner
doble /dóh-blay/ *adj.* double
doce /dóh-say/ *n., adj.* twelve
docena /doh-sáy-nah/ *n.* dozen
doctor /dohk-tóhr/ *n.* doctor
doctrina /dohk-trée-nah/ *n.* doctrine
documento /doh-coo-máyn-toh/ *n.* document
dólar /dóh-lahr/ *n.* dollar
doler /doh-láyr/ *v.* ache; hurt

dolor /doh-lóhr/ *n.* pain
dolor de cabeza /doh-lóhr day cah báy-sah/ *n.* headache
dolor de estómago /doh-lóhr day ays-tóh-mahgoh/ *n.* stomachache
dolor de muela /doh-lóhr day moo-áy-lah/ *n.* toothache
doloroso /doh-loh-róh-soh/ *adj.* painful
dominar /doh-mee-náhr/ *v.* master
domingo /doh-méen-goh/ *n.* Sunday
donde /dóhn-day/ *conj.* where
¿dónde? /¿dóhn-day?/ *adv.* where?
dondequiera /dohn-day-key-áy-rah/ *adv.* anywhere
dormir /dohr-méer/ *v.* sleep
dormitorio /dohr-mee-tóhr-ee-oh/ *n. Bol., Ec., Pe.* bedroom
dos /dohs/ *n., adj.* two
dos veces /dohs váy-says/ *adv.* twice
drama /dráh-mah/ *n.* drama; play
droga /dróh-gah/ *n.* drug; *RP* white elephant; unsaleable item
ducha /dóo-chah/ *n. Cuba, Pe., PR* shower
duchera /doo-cháy-rah/ *n. Uru.* shower
duda /dóo-dah/ *n.* doubt
dudar /doo-dáhr/ *v.* doubt
dueño /doo-áy-nyoh/ *n.* owner
dulce /dóol-say/ *adj.* sweet; *Pan.* cake
dulces /dóol-says/ *n.* candy
durante /doo-ráhn-tay/ *prep.* during

durazno /doo-ráhs-noh/ *n. Arg., CA, Mex., Pan., Pe.* peach

duro /dóo-roh/ *adj.* hard

- E -

e /ay/ *conj.* and (before i or hi)
economía /ay-coh-noh-mée-ah/ *n.* economy
económico /ay-coh-nóh-mee-coh/ *adj.* economical; economic
echar /ay-cháhr/ *v.* throw; throw away
echar al correo /ay-cháhr ahl coh-ráy-oh/ *v.* mail
echar sangre /ay-cháhr sáhn-gray/ *v.* bleed
edad /ay-dáhd/ *n.* age
edición /ay-dee-see-óhn/ *n.* edition
efectivo /ay-fayk-tée-voh/ *n.* cash; *adj.* effective; real
efecto /ay-fáyk-toh/ *n.* effect
eficiente /ay-fee-see-áyn-tay/ *adj.* efficient
ejecutar /ay-hay-coo-táhr/ *v.* execute; perform
ejemplo /ay-háym-ploh/ *n.* example
ejercicio /ay-hayr-sée-see-oh/ *n.* exercise
ejercitar /ay-hayr-see-táhr/ *v.* exercise; practice
el /ayl/ *art.* the
él /ayl/ *pron.* he
elástico /ay-láhs-tee-coh/ *n., adj.* elastic
el cual /ayl kwal/ *pron.* which; who; such
elefante /ay-lay-fáhn-tay/ *n.* elephant
elemento /ay-lay-máyn-toh/ *n.* element
elevador /ay-lay-vah-dóhr/ *n. Carib., Mex.* elevator
el mío /ayl mée-oh/ *pron.* mine
elote /ay-lóh-tay/ *n. Mex.* corn (on cob)
ella /áy-yah/ *pron.* she

ello /áy-yoh/ *pron.* it
ellos /áy-yohs/ *pron.* they
embajada /aym-bah-háh-dah/ *n.* embassy
embajador /ayn-bah-hah-dóhr/ *n.* ambassador
empacar /aym-pah-cáhr/ *v.* pack; crate
emparedado /aym-pah-ray-dáh-doh/ *n. Bol.* sandwich
empate /aym-páh-tay/ *n. Ven.* girlfriend
empezar /aym-pay-sáhr/ *v.* begin
empleada /aym-play-áh-dah/ *n. Bol., Ec., Uru., Pan.* maid
empleada doméstica /aym-play-áh-dah doh-máys--tee-cah/ *n. Pe.* maid
empleado /aym-play-áh-doh/ *n. Bol., Ec., Uru.* clerk
emplear /aym-play-áhr/ *v.* employ; use
empleo /aym-pláy-oh/ *n.* job
empresa /aym-práy-sah/ *n.* enterprise; company
empujar /aym-poo-háhr/ *v.* push
en /ayn/ *prep.* in; on
enagua /ayn-áh-gwah/ *n. Chi., PR* slip (undergarment)
en alguna parte /ayn ahl-góo-nah páhr-tay/ *adv.* somewhere
enamorada /ay-nah-moh-ráh-dah/ *n. Ec., Pe.* girlfriend
enano /ay-náh-noh/ *n.* dwarf; *Chi., Ven.* short person
encaje /ayn-cáh-hay/ *n.* lace
encantar /ayn-cahn-táhr/ *v.* charm; enchant
encarcelación /ayn-cahr-say-lah-see-óhn/ *n.* imprisonment

encarcelar /ayn-cahr-say-láhr/ *v.* imprison
en casa /ayn cáh-sah/ *adv.* at home
encender /ayn-sayn-dáyr/ *v.* light
encima de /ayn-sée-mah day/ *prep.* on top of
encoger /ayn-coh-háyr/ *v.* shrink
encontrar /ayn-cohn-tráhr/ *v.* find; meet
encrucijada /ayn-croo-see-háh-dah/ *n.* crossroads
encuentro /ayn-coo-áyn-troh/ *n.* encounter; meeting
encuesta /ayn-coo-áys-tah/ *n.* poll; survey
encurtidos /ayn-coor-tée-dohs/ *n.* pickles
enchufe /ayn-chóo-fay/ *n.* (elec.) plug
en el extranjero /ayn ayl ays-trahn-háy-roh/ *adv.* abroad
enemigo /ay-nay-mée-goh/ *n.* enemy
energía /ay-nayr-hée-ah/ *n.* energy
enero /ay-náy-roh/ *n.* January
énfasis /áyn-fah-sees/ *n.* emphasis
enfermedad /ayn-fayr-may-dáhd/ *n.* illness
enfermo /ayn-fáyr-moh/ *adj.* sick
enfocar /ayn-foh-cáhr/ *v.* focus
enganchar /ayn-gahn-cháhr/ *v.* hook
enganche /ayn-gáhn-chay/ *n. Mex.* down payment
engañar /ayn-gahn-yáhr/ *v.* deceive; cheat
engaño /ayn-gáhn-yoh/ *n.* deceit
engrasar /ayn-grah-sáhr/ *v.* grease
en ninguna parte /ayn neen-góo-nah páhr-tay/ *adv.* nowhere
enojada /ay-noh-háh-dah/ *n. Mex.* fit of anger
enojado /ay-noh-háh-doh/ *adj.* angry

enojo /ay-nóh-hoh/ *n.* anger
enorme /ay-nóhr-may/ *adj.* enormous; huge
ensalada /ayn-sah-láh-dah/ *n.* salad
en seguida /ayn say-ghée-dah/ *adv.* at once
enseñar /ayn-say-nyáhr/ *v.* show; teach
entender /ayn-tayn-dáyr/ *v.* understand
entender mal /ayn-tayn-dáyr mahl/ *v.* misunderstand
entendimiento /ayn-tayn-dee-mee-áyn-toh/ *n.* understanding
entero /ayn-táy-roh/ *adj.* entire
en todas partes /ayn tóh-dahs páhr-tays/ *adv.* everywhere
entonces /ayn-tóhn-says/ *adv.* then
entrada /ayn-tráh-dah/ *n.* entrance; *Bol.* ticket; *Col., Ec.* down payment
entrar /ayn-tráhr/ *v.* enter; come in
entre /áyn-tray/ *prep.* between; among
entregar /ayn-tray-gáhr/ *v.* deliver
entremeses /ayn-tray-máy-says/ *n.* hors d'oeuvres
entrenar /ayn-tray-náhr/ *v.* train
entusiasmo /ayn-too-see-áhs-moh/ *n.* enthusiasm
envase /ayn-váh-say/ *n.* container
en vez de /ayn vays day/ *prep.* instead of
enviar /ayn-vee-áhr/ *v.* send
envío /ayn vée-oh/ *n.* shipment
en voz alta /ayn vohs áhl-tah/ *adv.* out loud
equipaje /ay-key-páh-hay/ *n.* luggage
equipo /ay-kéy-poh/ *n.* equipment; team
equivalente /ay-key-vah-láyn-tay/ *n., adj.* equivalent

equivocado /ay-key-voh-cáh-doh/ *adj.* wrong; mistaken
equivocarse /ay-key-voh-cáhr-say/ *v.* make a mistake
error /ay-róhr/ *n.* mistake
escalera /ays-cah-láy-rah/ *n.* stairs; ladder
escalera de incendios /ays-cah-láy-rah day eensáyn--dee-ohs/ *n.* fire escape
escaparse /ays-cah-páhr-say/ *v.* escape
escasez /ays-cah-sáys/ *n.* scarcity
escaso /ays-cáh-soh/ *adj.* scarce
escena /ay-sáy-nah/ *n.* stage; scene
escoger /ays-coh-háyr/ *v.* choose
esconder /ays-cohn-dáyr/ *v.* hide
escribir /ays-cree-béer/ *v.* write
escritor /ays-cree-tóhr/ *n.* writer
escritorio /ays-cree-tóh-ree-oh/ *n.* desk
escritura /ays-cree-tóo-rah/ *n.* writing; (leg.) deed; sworn statement
escuchar /ays-coo-cháhr/ *v.* listen to
escuela /ays-kwáy-lah/ *n.* school
escuintle /ays-kwéent-lay/ *n. Mex.* small kid
escultor /ays-cool-tóhr/ *n.* sculptor
escultura /ays-cool-tóo-rah/ *n.* sculpture
esencial /ay-sayn-see-áhl/ *adj.* essential
esfuerzo /ays-foo-áyr-soh/ *n.* effort
esmalte /ays-máhl-tay/ *n.* enamel
esmalte para las uñas /ays-máhl-tay páh-rah lahs óon-yahs/ *n.* nail polish
eso /áy-soh/ *pron.* that

eso es /áy-soh ays/ *interj.* that's it
ésos /áy-sohs/ *pron.* those
espacio /ays-páh-see-oh/ *n.* space
espalda /ays-páhl-dah/ *n.* back
espárrago /ays-páh-rah-goh/ *n.* asparagus
especia /ays-páy-see-ah/ *n.* spice
eapecial /ays-pay-see-áhl/ *adj.* special
especialmente /ays-pay-see-ahl-máyn-tay/ *adv.* especially
espectáculo /ays-payk-táh-coo-loh/ *n.* spectacle; show
espejo /ays-páy-hoh/ *n.* mirror
espejuelos /ays-pay-hoo-áy-lohs/ *n.* *Cuba* eyeglasses
esperanza /ays-pay-ráhn-sah/ *n.* hope
esperar /ays-pay-ráhr/ *v.* wait for; hope for; expect
espeso /ays-páy-soh/ *adj.* thick
espina /ays-pée-nah/ *n.* thorn; spine; fish bone
espinacas /ays-pee-náh-cahs/ *n.* spinach
esposa /ays-póh-sah/ *n.* wife
esposo /ays-póh-soh/ *n.* husband
esquina /ays-kéy-nah/ *n.* corner
está bien /ays-táh bee-áyn/ *interj.* fine; OK
estable /ays-táh blay/ *adj.* stable
establecer /ays-tah-blay-sáyr/ *v.* establish
estación /ays-tah-see-óhn/ *n.* station; season
estacionamiento /ays-tah-see-oh-nah-mee-áyn-toh/ *n.* *Mex.*, *Uru.* parking; parking lot
estacionar /ays-tah-see-oh-náhr/ *v.* *Mex.*, *Uru.* park
estado /ays-táh-doh/ *n.* state
estado de cuentas /ays-táh-doh day coo-áyn-tahs/ *n.*

(com.) statement
estampilla /ays-tahm-pée-yah/ *n. Bol., Ec., Mex., PR* postage stamp
esta noche /áys-tah nóh-chay/ *adv.* tonight
estante /ays-táhn-tay/ *n.* shelf; bookcase
estaño /ays-táh-nyoh/ *n.* tin
estar /ays-táhr/ *v.* be
estar a cargo /ays-táhr ah cáhr-goh/ *v.* be in charge
estar a dieta /ays-táhr ah dee-áy-tah/ *v.* be on a diet
estar de acuerdo /ays-táhr day ah-coo-áyr-doh/ *v.* be in agreement
estar de moda /ays-táhr day móh-dah/ *v.* be in fashion
estar de pie /ays-táhr day pee-áy/ *v.* be standing
estatua /ays-táh-too-ah/ *n.* statue
este /áys-tay/ *n.* east; *adj.* this
éste /áys-tay/ *pron.* this one
estilo /ays-tée-loh/ *n.* style
estimación /ays-tee-mah-see-óhn/ *n.* esteem; estimation
estimar /ays-tee-máhr/ *v.* esteem; estimate
estimulo /ays-tée-moo-loh/ *n.* stimulus
estofado /ays-toh-fáh-doh/ *n. Pe.* stew
estómago /ays-tóh-mah-goh/ *n.* stomach
estos /áys-tohs/ *adj.* these
éstos /áys-tohs/ *pron.* these
estrecho /ays-tráy-choh/ *adj.* narrow
estrella /ays-tráy-yah/ *n.* star
estrellar /ays-tray-yáhr/ *v.* fry (eggs)

estreñimiento /ays-tray-nyee-mee-áyn-toh/ *n.* constipation
estudiante /ays-too-dee-áhn-tay/ *n.* student
estudiar /ays-too-dee-áhr/ *v.* study
estudio jurídico /ays-tóo-dee-oh hoo-rée-dee-coh/ *n.* *Ec.* law office
estufa /ays-tóo-fah/ *n.* stove
estúpido /ays-tóo-pee-doh/ *adj.* stupid
etiqueta /ay-tee-káy-tah/ *n.* tag; label
evento /ay-váyn-toh/ *n.* event
evidencia /ay-vee-dáyn-see-ah/ *n.* evidence
evidente /ay-vee-dáyn-tay/ *adj.* evident
evitar /ay-vee-táhr/ *v.* avoid
exacto /ex-áhk-toh/ *adj.* exact; *interj.* right
examen /ex-áh-mayn/ *n.* examination
examinar /ex-ah-mee-náhr/ *v.* examine
excelente /ex-say-láyn-tay/ *adj.* excellent
excepción /ex-sayp-see-óhn/ *n.* exception
excepto /ex-sáyp-toh/ *prep.* except
excesivo /ex-say-sée-voh/ *adj.* excessive
exceso /ex-sáy-soh/ *n.* excess
excluir /ex-kloo-éer/ *v.* exclude
exclusivo /ex-kloo-sée-voh/ *adj.* exclusive
excursión /ex-coor-see-óhn/ *n.* excursion
exención /ex-ayn-see-óhn/ *n.* exemption
exento /ex-áyn-toh/ *adj.* exempt
exhibición /ex-ee-bee-see-óhn/ *n.* exhibit
éxito /éx-ee-toh/ *n.* success
expansión /ex-pahn-see-óhn/ *n.* expansion

experiencia /ex-pay-ree-áyn-see-ah/ *n.* experience
experimentar /ex-pay-ree-mayn-táhr/ *v.* experience; experiment
explicación /ex-plee-cah-see-óhn/ *n.* explanation
explicar /ex-plee-cáhr/ *v.* explain
explorar /ex-ploh-ráhr/ *v.* explore
exportación /ex-pohr-tah-see-óhn/ *n.* export
exportar /ex-pohr-táhr/ *v.* export
expresar /ex-pray-sáhr/ *v.* express
expresión /ex-pray-see-óhn/ *n.* expression
expreso /ex-práy-soh/ *adj.* express; *adv.* expressly
extender /ex-tayn-dáyr/ *v.* extend
extensivo /ex-tayn-sée-voh/ *adj.* extensive
exterior /ex-tay-ree-óhr/ *adj.* exterior; foreign
externo /ex-táyr-noh/ *adj.* external
extranjero /ex-trahn-háy-roh/ *n.* foreigner; *adj.* foreign
extrañar /ex-trah-nyáhr/ *v.* miss
extraño /ex-tráh-nyoh/ *adj.* strange; foreign
extraordinario /ex-trah-ohr-dee-náh-ree-oh/ *adj.* extraordinary
extremo /ex-tráy-moh/ *adj.* extreme

- F -

fábrica /fáh-bree-cah/ *n.* factory
fabricación /fah-bree-cah-see-óhn/ *n.* manufacture
fácil /fáh-seel/ *adj.* easy
fácilmente /fáh-seel-mayn-tay/ *adv.* easily
factor /fahk-tóhr/ *n.* factor
factura /fahk-tóo-rah/ *n.* bill; invoice
faisán /fah-ee-sáhn/ *n.* pheasant
faivocló /fah-ee-voh-clóh/ *n. Arg.* snack
falda /fáhl-dah/ *n.* skirt; *Cuba* cut of beef
falso /fáhl-soh/ *adj.* false
falta /fáhl-tah/ *n.* lack
faltar /fahl-táhr/ *v.* lack; be absent
familia /fah-mée-lee-ah/ *n.* family
famoso /fah-móh-soh/ *adj.* famous
fantástico /fahn-táhs-tee-coh/ *adj.* fantastic
farmacéutico /fahr-mah-sáy-oo-tee-coh/ *n.* druggist; *adj.* pharmaceutical
farmacia /fahr-máh-see-ah/ *n.* drugstore
faro /fáh-roh/ *n.* lighthouse
fastidiar /fahs-tee-dee-áhr/ *v.* bother
febrero /fay bráy-roh/ *n.* February
febril /fay-bréel/ *adj.* feverish
fecha /fáy-chah/ *n.* date
felicitaciones /fay-lee-see-tah-see-óh-nays/ *n.* congratulations
felicitar /fay-lee-see-táhr/ *v.* congratulate

feliz /fay-lées/ *adj.* happy
femenino /fay-may-née-noh/ *adj.* feminine; female
feo /fáy-oh/ *adj.* ugly; *adv. Arg., Col., Mex.* bad
ferretería /fay-ray-tay-rée-ah/ *n.* hardware store
ferrocarril /fay-roh-cah-réel/ *n.* railroad
festejar /fay-stay-hár/ *v.* fete; honor
festivo /fay-stée-voh/ *adj.* festive
fibra /fée-brah/ *n.* fiber
ficción /feek-see-óhn/ *n.* fiction
fiebre /fee-áy-bray/ *n.* fever
fiesta /fee-áy-stah/ *n.* feast; party
figura /fee-góo-rah/ *n.* figure
figurar /fee-goo-ráhr/ *v.* depict; imagine
fila /fée-lah/ *n.* line
filmar /feel-máhr/ *v.* film
filtro /féel-troh/ *n.* filter
fin /feen/ *n.* end; aim
final /fee-náhl/ *adj.* final
financiar /fee-nahn-see-áhr/ *v.* finance
finanza /fep-náhn-sah/ *n.* finance
fin de semana /feen day say-máh-nah/ *n.* week-end
fino /fée-noh/ *adj.* fine; refined
firma /féer-mah/ *n.* signature
firmar /feer-máhr/ *v.* sign
firme /féer-may/ *adj.* firm
flaco /fláh-coh/ *adj.* thin; skinny
flete /fláy-tay/ *n.* freight; cargo; *Bol., Col., RP* race horse
flojo /flóh-hoh/ *adj.* loose; *Mex., Ven.* lazy

flor /flohr/ *n.* flower
florero /floh-ráy-roh/ *n.* vase; florist
foca /fóh-cah/ *n.* (zool.) seal
foco /fóh-coh/ *n.* focus; *Mex.* light bulb
fondo /fóhn-doh/ *n.* bottom; rear; *Mex.* slip (undergarment)
fontanero /fohn-tah-náy-roh/ *n. Mex.* plumber
forma /fóhr-mah/ *n.* form; shape
formal /fohr-máhl/ *adj.* formal; reliable; punctual
formar /fohr-máhr/ *v.* form; shape
forzar /fohr-sáhr/ *v.* force
fósforo /fóhs-foh-roh/ *n.* match
foto /fóh-toh/ *n.* photo
fotógrafo /foh-tóh-grah-foh/ *n.* photographer
fracasar /frah-cah-sáhr/ *v.* fail
fracaso /frah-cáh-soh/ *n.* failure
frase /fráh-say/ *n.* phrase; sentence
fraude /fráh-oo-day/ *n.* fraud
frazada /frah-sáh-dah/ *n.* blanket
frecuente /fray-kwáyn-tay/ *adj.* frequent
frecuentemente /fray-kwayn-tay-máyn-tay/ *adv.* frequently
fregadero /fray-gah-dáy-roh/ *n.* kitchen sink
fregar /fray-gáhr/ *v.* scrub; *LA* annoy
freír /fray-éer/ *v.* fry
fréjoles /fráy-hoh-lays/ *n. Bol., Ec.* dry beans
frente /fráyn-tay/ *n.* front; forehead
fresa /fráy-sah/ *n.* strawberry
fresco /fráys-coh/ *adj.* fresh; cool

frijoles /free-hóh-lays/ *n. Carib., Mex.* dry beans
frío /frée-oh/ *n., adj.* cold
frontera /frohn-táy-rah/ *n.* border
fruta /fróo-tah/ *n.* fruit
fuego /fwáy-goh/ *n.* fire
fuente /fwáyn-tay/ *n.* fountain; source
fuera /fwáy-rah/ *adv.* out; outside; away
fuerte /fwáyr-tay/ *adj.* strong; loud
fuerza /fwáyr-sah/ *n.* force; strength
fulo /fóo-loh/ *n. Pan.* blond
fumar /foo-máhr/ *v.* smoke
función /foon-see-óhn/ *n.* function; performance
funda /fóon-dah/ *n.* pillowcase
fundamental /foon-dah-mayn-táhl/ *adj.* fundamental
fundo /fóon-doh/ *n. Ven.* ranch
furioso /foo-ree-óh-soh/ *adj.* furious
fusil /foo-séel/ *n.* gun; rifle
fustán /foos-táhn/ *n. Pe.* slip; *Ven.* skirt
fútbol /fóot-bohl/ *n.* soccer
fútbol americano /fóot-bohl ah-may-ree-cáh-noh/ *n.* football

- G -

gabarra /gah-báh-rah/ *n. Ec.* ferry
galería /gah-lay-rée-ah/ *n.* gallery
galón /gah-lóhn/ *n.* gallon
galleta /gah-yáy-tah/ *n.* cracker; *Mex.* (also cookie)
galleticas de sal /gah-yay-tée-cahs day sahl/ *n. Cuba* soda crackers
galletita /gah-yay-tée-tah/ *n. Arg.* cracker
gallina /gah-yée-nah/ *n.* hen
gallo /gáh-yoh/ *n.* rooster
ganancias /gah-náhn-see-ahs/ *n.* profit; *Gua., Mex.* bonus
ganar /gah-náhr/ *v.* win; earn
ganchito /gahn-chée-toh/ *n. Cuba* bobby pin
gancho /gáhn-choh/ *n.* hook; *Mex.* hanger (clothes); *Pan.* bobby pin; *Ven.* hair pin
ganga /gáhn-gah/ *n.* bargain
garage /gah-rásh/ *n. Ec., Mex., Pe., Uru.* garage
garaje /gah-ráh-hay/ *n.* garage
garantía /gah-rahn-tée-ah/ *n.* guarantee; warranty
garantizar /gah-rahn-tee-sáhr/ *v.* guarantee
garganta /gahr-gáhn-tah/ *n.* throat
gas /gahs/ *n.* gas (other than gasoline)
gasa /gáh-sah/ *n.* gauze; chiffon
gaseosa /gah-say-óh-sah/ *n.* carbonated soft drink
gasfiter /gahs-fée-tayr/ *n. Chi.* plumber
gasfitero /gahs-fee-táy-roh/ *n. Ec., Pe.* plumber

gasolina /gah-soh-lée-nah/ *n.* gasoline
gastar /gah-stáhr/ *v.* spend; wear out
gasto /gáh-stoh/ *n.* expense
gatico /gah-tée-coh/ *n. Cuba* kitten
gatito /gah-tée-toh/ *n.* kitten
gato /gáh-toh/ *n.* cat
gaucho /gah-óo-choh/ *n. RP* horseman of the pampas; *adj.* sly
gelatina /hay-lah-tée-nah/ *n.* gelatine
gemelo /hay-máy-loh/ *n.* twin
general /hay-nay-ráhl/ *n., adj.* general
gente /háyn-tay/ *n.* people
genuino /hay-noo-ée-noh/ *adj.* genuine
gerencia /hay-ráyn-see-ah/ *n.* management
gerente /hay-ráyn-tay/ *n.* manager; director
germen /háyr-mayn/ *n.* germ
gesto /háy-stoh/ *n.* gesture
gigante /hee-gáhn-tay/ *n., adj.* giant
gigantesco /hee-gahn-táys-coh/ *adj.* gigantic
gimnasio /heem-náh-see-oh/ *n.* gym
ginebra /hee-náy-brah/ *n.* gin
giro /hée-roh/ *n.* money order; *adj. Gua.* drunk
globo /glóh-boh/ *n.* globe; balloon
gobernador /goh-bayr-nah-dóhr/ *n.* governor
gobierno /goh-bee-áyr-noh/ *n.* government
golf /golf/ *n.* golf
golfo /góhl-foh/ *n.* gulf
golpe /góhl-pay/ *n.* blow
golpear /gohl-pay-áhr/ *v.* hit; strike

goma /góh-mah/ *n.* gum; rubber; *Cuba* tire; eraser; *Cuba, Ec., Uru.* glue; *Pan.* hangover
gordo /góhr-doh/ *adj.* fat; *n. Mex.* (term of affection)
gota /góh-tah/ *n.* drop
gozar de /goh-sáhr day/ *n.* enjoy
grabar /grah-báhr/ *v.* record; engrave
gracias /gráh-see-ahs/ *n.* thanks
gracioso /grah-see-óh-soh/ *adj. Bol., Uru., Ven.* funny
grado /gráh-doh/ *n.* degree; grade
gramática /grah-máh-tee-cah/ *n.* grammar
gran /grahn/ *adj.* large; great
grande /gráhn-day/ *adj.* large; great
grano /gráh-noh/ *n.* grain; pimple
grasa /gráh-sah/ *n.* grease; *Mex.* shoe polish
gratificación /grah-tee-fee-cah-see-óhn/ *n.* reward
gratis /gráh-tees/ *adv.* gratis; free
grave /gráh-vay/ *adj.* serious
grifo /grée-foh/ *n. Bol.* faucet; *Pe.* gas station; *adj. Col.* conceited; *Mex.* drunk
gripa /grée-pah/ *n. Mex.* flu
gripe /grée-pay/ *n.* flu
gris /grees/ *adj.* gray
gritar /gree-táhr/ *v.* shout
grosero /groh-sáy-roh/ *adj.* rude
grupo /gróo-poh/ *n.* group
guagua /gwáh-gwah/ *n. Chi.* baby; *Cuba* bus
guajiro /gwah-hée-roh/ *n. Cuba* farmer; peasant
guajolote /gwah-hoh-lóh-tay/ *n. Mex.* turkey
guambra /gwáhm-brah/ *n. Ec.* kid

guante /gwáhn-tay/ *n.* glove
guapo /gwáh-poh/ *adj.* handsome
guardar /gwahr-dáhr/ *v.* keep; guard
guardarropa /gwahr-dah-róh-pah/ *n.* *Mex., Uru.* closet
guardia /gwáhr-dee-ah/ *n.* guard
guaso /gwáh-soh/ *n.* *Chi.* peasant
guayabo /gwah-yáh-boh/ *n.* *Col.* hangover
güero /gwáy-roh/ *n.* *Mex.* blond; fair-complected person; *adj.* blond; fair-complected
guerra /gáy-rah/ *n.* war
guía /ghée-ah/ *n.* guide
guiar /ghee-áhr/ *v.* guide
guía telefónica /ghée-ah tay-lay-fóh-nee-cah/ *n.* *Cuba, Ec., Pe., RP, Ven.* telephone directory
guineo /ghee-náy-oh/ *n.* *Pan., PR* small banana
guisado /ghee-sáh-doh/ *n.* stew
guisante /ghee-sáhn-tay/ *n.* pea
guisar /ghee-sáhr/ *v.* cook
guiso /ghée-soh/ *n.* dish; *RP* stew
guitarra /ghee-táh-rah/ *n.* guitar
gustar /goo-stáhr/ *v.* like
gusto /góo-stoh/ *n.* taste

- H -

haber /ah-báyr/ *v.* have (auxiliary)
habichuelas /ah-bee-chwáy-lahs/ *n. Mex., Pan.* green beans
hábil /áh-beel/ *adj.* capable
habilidad /ah-bee-lee-dáhd/ *n.* ability
habitación /ah-bee-tah-see-óhn/ *n.* room
hábito /áh-bee-toh/ *n.* habit
hablar /ah-bláhr/ *v.* speak
hace /áh-say/ *adv.* ago (ex. *hace un año*, a year ago)
hacer /ah-sáyr/ *v.* do; make
hacer frente /ah-sáyr fráyn-tay/ *v.* face
hacerse /ah-sáyr-say/ *v.* become
hacia /áh-see-ah/ *prep.* toward
hacia abajo /áh-see-ah ah-báh-hoh/ *adj., adv.* downward
hacia arriba /áh-see-ah ah-rée-bah/ *adj., adv.* upward
hacienda /ah-see-áyn-dah/ *n. LA* ranch; *Arg.* livestock
hallar /ah-yáhr/ *v.* find
hambre /áhm-bray/ *n.* hunger
hambriento /ahm-bree-áyn-toh/ *adj.* starving
hamburguesa /ahm-boor-gáy-sah/ *n.* hamburger
harina /ah-rée-nah/ *n.* flour
hasta /áh-stah/ *prep.* until
hasta que /áh-stah kay/ *conj.* until

hay /áh-ee/ *v.* there is; there are
hebilla /ay-bée-yah/ *n.* buckle
hecho /áy-choh/ *n.* deed; act
hecho a mano /áy-choh ah máh-noh/ *adj.* hand-made
helado /ay-láh-doh/ *n.* ice cream
hembra /áym-brah/ *n.* female
herida /ay-rée-dah/ *n.* wound
herir /ay-réer/ *v.* wound; hurt
hermana /ayr-máh-nah/ *n.* sister
hermano /ayr-máh-noh/ *n.* brother
hermoso /ayr-móh-soh/ *adj.* beautiful; handsome
hernia /áyr-nee-ah/ *n.* hernia
herramienta /ay-rah-mee-áyn-tah/ *n.* tools
hervir /ayr-véer/ *v.* boil
hielo /ee-áy-loh/ *n.* ice
hierba /ee-áyr-bah/ *n.* grass; herb
hierro /ee-áyr-oh/ *n.* iron
hígado /ée-gah-doh/ *n.* liver
higo /ée-goh/ *n.* fig
hija /ée-hah/ *n.* daughter
hijo /ée-hoh/ *n.* son
hilo /ée-loh/ *n.* thread
hinchazón /een-chah-sóhn/ *n.* swelling
histérico /ee-stáy-ree-coh/ *adj.* hysterical
hogar /oh-gáhr/ *n.* home
hoja /óh-hah/ *n.* leaf; sheet (of paper)
hoja de afeitar /óh-hah day ah-fay-táhr/ *n.* razor blade

hoja de rasurar /óh-hah day rah-soo-ráhr/ *n. Mex.* razor blade
hola /óh-lah/ *interj.* hello; hi
holgazán /ohl-gah-sáhn/ *adj. Uru.* lazy
hombre /óhm-bray/ *n.* man
hombre de negocios /óhm-bray day nay-góh-see-ohs/ *n.* businessman
hombro /óhm-broh/ *n.* shoulder
hondo /óhn-doh/ *adj.* deep
honesto /oh-náys-toh/ *adj.* honest
hongo /óhn-goh/ *n.* mushroom; fungus
honorario /oh-noh-ráh-reeoh/ *n.* fee; *adj.* honorary
hora /óh-rah/ *n.* hour; time
horario /oh-ráh-ree-oh/ *n.* schedule
horquilla /ohr-kéy-yay/ *n. Ec., Mex., Uru.* hairpin
horrible /oh-rée-blay/ *adj.* horrible
hospital /ohs-pee-táhl/ *n.* hospital
hotel /oh-táyl/ *n.* hotel
hoy /oy/ *n., adv.* today
hueco /wáy-coh/ *n.* hole; *adj.* hollow; *n. Ven.* pothole
huelga /wáyl-gah/ *n.* strike (labor)
hueso /wáy-soh/ *n.* bone
huésped /wáys-payd/ *n.* guest
huevo /wáy-voh/ *n.* egg
huir /oo-éer/ *v.* flee; run away
humanidad /oo-mah-nee-dáhd/ *n.* humanity
humano /oo-máh-noh/ *adj.* human; humane
humilde /oo-méel-day/ *adj.* humble

humo /óo-moh/ *n.* smoke
hundir /oon-déer/ *v.* sink

- I -

idea /ee-dáy-ah/ *n.* idea
ideal /ee-day-áhl/ *n., adj.* ideal
idioma /ee-dee-óh-mah/ *n.* language
idiota /ee-dee-óh-tah/ *n.* idiot
ídolo /ée-doh-loh/ *n.* idol
iglesia /ee-gláy-see-ah/ *n.* church
igual /ee-gwáhl/ *adj.* equal
igualdad /ee-gwahl-dáhd/ *n.* equality
ilegal /ee-lay-gáhl/ *adj.* illegal
ilimitado /ee-lee-mee-táh-doh/ *adj.* unlimited
imagen /ee-máh-hen/ *n.* image
imaginar /ee-mah-hee-náhr/ *v.* imagine
imitación /ee-mee-tah-see-óhn/ *n.* imitation
impaciente /eem-pah-see-áyn-tay/ *adj.* impatient
impacto /eem-páhk-toh/ *n.* impact
impedir /eem-pay-déer/ *v.* impede; prevent
impermeable /eem-payr-may-áh-blay/ *n.* raincoat; *adj.* waterproof
importaciones /eem-pohr-tah-see-óh-nays/ *n.* imports
importador /eem-pohr-tah-dóhr/ *n.* importer
importancia /eem-pohr-táhn-see-ah/ *n.* importance
importante /eem-pohr-táhn-tay/ *adj.* important
importar /eem-pohr-táhr/ *v.* import; matter
imposible /eem-poh-sée-blay/ *adj.* impossible
impotente /eem-poh-táyn-tay/ *adj.* impotent

impresión /eem-pray-see-óhn/ *n.* impression; printing
impresionante /eem-pray-see-oh-náhn-tay/ *adj.* impressive
impresionar /eem-pray-see-oh-náhr/ *v.* make an impression
impresor /eem-pray-sóhr/ *n.* printer
imprevisto /eem-pray-vées-toh/ *adj.* unexpected
impuesto /eem-pwáys-toh/ *n.* tax
impuesto de utilidades /eem-pwáys-toh day oo-tee--lee-dáh-days/ *n.* income tax
impuesto sobre la renta /eem-pwáys-toh sóh-bray lah ráyn-tah/ *n. Mex.* income tax
impulsar /eem-pool-sáhr/ *v.* impel; drive
inadecuado /een-ah-day-kwáh-doh/ *adj.* inadequate
inauguración /een-ah-oo-goo-rah-see-óhn/ *n.* inauguration
incapacidad /een-cah-pah-see-dáhd/ *n.* incapacity
incapaz /een-cah-páhs/ *adj.* incapable; incompetent
incentivo /een-sayn-tée-voh/ *n.* incentive
incesante /een-say-sáhn-tay/ *adj.* unceasing
incidente /een-see-dáyn-tay/ *n.* incident; *adj.* incidental
incierto /een-see-áyr-toh/ *adj.* uncertain
incluir /een-cloo-éer/ *v.* include
incluso /een-clóo-soh/ *v.* form including
incomodidad /een-coh-moh-dee-dáhd/ *n.* discomfort;inconvenience
incómodo /een-cóh-moh-doh/ *adj.* uncomfortable

incompleto /een-cohm-pláy-toh/ *adj.* incomplete
inconsciente /een-cohn-see-áyn-tay/ *adj.* unconscious
inconveniente /een-cohn-vay-nee-áyn-tay/ *adj.* inconvenient
increíble /een-cray-ée-blay/ *adj.* incredible
inculto /een-cóol-toh/ *adj.* uncultured
indefinido /een-day-fee-née-doh/ *adj.* indefinite
independencia /een-day-payn-dáyn-see-ah/ *n.* independence
independiente /een-day-payn-dee-áyn-tay/ *adj.* independent
indicación /een-dee-cah-see-óhn/ *n.* indication
indicar /een-dee-cáhr/ *v.* indicate
indígena /een-dée-hay-nah/ *n.* native; *adj.* indigenous
individual /een-dee-vee-doo-áhl/ *n., adj.* individual
industria /een-dóo-stree-ah/ *n.* industry
ineficaz /een-ay-fee-cáhs/ *adj.* ineffectual
inesperado /een-ays-pay-ráh-doh/ *adj.* unexpected
infectar /een-fayk-táhr/ *v.* infect
infeliz /een-fay-lées/ *adj.* unhappy
inferior /een-fay-ree-óhr/ *n.* subordinate; *adj.* inferior; lower
infiel /een-fee-áyl/ *adj.* unfaithful
infierno /een-fee-áyr-noh/ *n.* hell
infinito /een-fee-née-toh/ *n., adj.* infinite
influencia /een-floo-áyn-see-ah/ *n.* influence
influenza /een-floo-ayn-sah/ *n.* *PR* flu
informar /een-fohr-máhr/ *v.* inform

informe /een-fóhr-may/ *n.* report
ingreso /een-gráy-soh/ *n.* admission
ingresos /een-gráy-sohs/ *n.* income
injusto /een-jóo-stoh/ *adj.* unjust
inmediatamente /een-may-dee-ah-tah-máyn-tay/ *adv.* immediately
inmediato /een-may-dee-áh-toh/ *adj.* immediate
inmigrante /een-mee-gráhn-tay/ *n.* immigrant
inmigrar /een-mee-gráhr/ *v.* immigrate
inmune /een-móo-nay/ *adj.* immune
innecesario /een-nay-say-sáh-ree-oh/ *adj.* unnecessary
innocuo /een-nóh-coo-oh/ *adj.* harmless
innumerable /een-noo-may-ráh blay/ *adj.* innumerable
inocente /een-oh-sáyn-tay/ *adj.* innocent
inodoro /een-oh-dóh-roh/ *n.* toilet; *adj.* odorless
inscribir /een-skree-béer/ *v.* inscribe
inscripción /een-skreep-see-óhn/ *n.* inscription; registration
insecto /een-sáyk-toh/ *n.* insect
inseguro /een-say-góo-roh/ *adj.* unsure; unsafe
insignificante /een-seeg-nee-fee-cáhn-tay/ *adj.* insignificant
insistir /een-see-stéer/ *v.* insist
insolación /een-soh-lah-see-óhn/ *n.* sunstroke
inspeccionar /een-spayk-see-oh-náhr/ *v.* inspect
instante /een-stáhn-tay/ *n.* instant

instituir /een-stee-too-éer/ *v.* institute
instituto /een-stee-tóo-toh/ *n.* institute
instrucción /een-strook-see-óhn/ *n.* instruction
instruir /een-stroo-éer/ *v.* instruct
instrumento /een-stroo-máyn-toh/ *n.* instrument
insuficiente /een-soo-fee-see-áyn-tay/ *adj.* insufficient
insultar /een-sool-táhr/ *v.* insult
insulto /een-sóol-toh/ *n.* insult
inteligente /een-tay lee-háyn-tay/ *adj.* intelligent
intendente /een-tayn-dáyn-tay/ *n. Arg.* mayor
intentar /een-tayn-táhr/ *v.* try; attempt
interior /een-tay-ree-óhr/ *n., adj.* interior; inside; *adj.* inner
interno /een-táyr-noh/ *adj.* internal; inner
intérprete /een-táyr-pray-tay/ *n.* interpreter
interruptor /een-tay-roop-tóhr/ *n.* switch
inválido /een-váh-lee-doh/ *n., adj.* invalid
investigación /een-vay-stee-gah-see-óhn/ *n.* investigation; research
invierno /een-vee-áyr-noh/ *n.* winter; *LA* rainy season
invisible /een-vee-sée-blay/ *n. Ec.* hairpin; *adj.* invisible
invitación /een-vee-tah-see-óhn/ *n.* invitation
invitado /een-vee-táh-doh/ *n.* guest
invitar /een-vee-táhr/ *v.* invite
involucrar /een voh-loo-cráhr/ *v.* involve

ir /eer/ *v.* go
ir a caballo /eer ah cah-báh-yoh/ *v.* ride horseback
ir de compras /eer day cóhm-prahs/ *v.* go shopping
ir en coche /eer ayn cóh-chay/ *v.* go by car; drive
irrazonable /ee-rah-sohn áh blay/ *adj.* unreasonable
irrompible /ee-rohm-pée-blay/ *adj.* unbreakable
irse /éer say/ *v.* go away
isla /ées-lah/ *n.* island
izquierdo /ees-key-áyr-doh/ *adj.* left

- J -

jaba /háh bah/ *n. Cuba* shopping bag
jabón /hah bóhn/ *n.* soap
jacal /hah-cáhl/ *n. Gua., Mex., Ven.* hut; shack
jalada /hah-láh-dah/ *n. Pe.* ride; lift
jalar /hah-láhr/ *v.* pull
jalea /hah-láy-ah/ *n.* jelly
jamás /hah-máhs/ *adv.* never; ever
jamón /hah-móhn/ *n.* ham
jarabe /hah-ráh-bay/ *n.* syrup
jardín /hahr-déen/ *n.* garden
jardín zoológico /har-déen soh-lóh-hee-coh/ *n.* zoo
jarra /háh-rah/ *n.* jar
jarro /háh-roh/ *n.* pitcher
jefe /háy-fay/ *n.* chief; boss
jerga /háyr-gah/ *n.* slang
jíbaro /hée-bah-roh/ *n. PR* farmer; peasant
jicotea /hee-coh-táy-ah/ *n.* turtle
jimagua /hee-máh-goo-ah/ *n. Cuba* twin
jitomate /hee-toh-máh-tay/ *n. Mex.* tomato
jojoto /hoh-hóh-toh/ *n. Ven.* corn
jolote /hoh-lóh-tay/ *n. CA* turkey
joven /hóh-vayn/ *n.* young person; *adj.* young
joya /hóh-yah/ *n.* jewel
joyería /hoh-yay-rée-ah/ *n.* jewelry store
joyero /hoh-yáy-roh/ *n.* jeweler
juego /hwáy-goh/ *n.* game; gambling; set (articles

used together)

juez /hways/ *n.* judge

jugador /hoo-gah-dóhr/ *n.* player; gambler

jugar /hoo-gáhr/ *v.* play; gamble

jugar a las bochas /hoo-gáhr ah lahs bóh-chahs/ *v.* bowl

jugar al boliche /hoo-gahr ahl boh-lée-chay/ *v.* bowl

jugo /hóo-goh/ *n.* juice

jugo de china /hóo-goh day chée-nah/ *n. PR* orange juice

jugo de naranja /hóo-goh day nah-ráhn-hah/ *n.* orange juice

juguete /hoo-gáy-tay/ *n.* toy

jungla /hóon-glah/ *n.* jungle

junta /hóon-tah/ *n.* board; *Mex., Ven.* meeting

juntar /hoon-táhr/ *v.* join

junto /hóon-toh/ *adj.* joined

junto a /hóon-toh ah/ *prep.* close to

juntos /hóon-tohs/ *adv.* together

jurado /hoo-ráh-doh/ *n.* jury

justicia /hoo-stée-see-ah/ *n.* justice

justificación /hoo-stee-fee-cah see-óhn/ *n.* justification

justificar /hoo-stee-fee-cáhr/ *v.* justify

justo /hóo-stoh/ *adj.* just; right

juventud /hoo-vayn-tóod/ *n.* youth; young people

juzgar /hoas-gáhr/ *v.* judge

- K -

kilogramo /key-loh-gráh-moh/ *n.* kilogram
kilómetro /key-lóh-may-troh/ *n.* kilometer (approx. 5/8 mile)
kilovatio /key-loh váh-tee-oh/ *n.* kilowatt

- L -

la /lah/ *art.* the
labio /láh-bee-oh/ *n.* lip
labrador /lah-brah-dóhr/ *n. Bol.* peasant
lado /láh-doh/ *n.* side
ladrón /lah-dróhn/ *n.* thief
lago /láh goh/ *n.* lake
la mayor parte /lah may-yóhr páhr-tay/ *n.* majority
lámpara /láhm-pah-rah/ *n.* lamp
lamparita /lahm-pah-rée-tah/ *n. Arg.* light bulb
lana /láh-nah/ *n.* wool; *Mex.* money (slang)
langosta /lahn-góh-stah/ *n.* lobster
langostino /lahn-goh-stée-noh/ *n.* prawn
lápiz /láh-pees/ *n.* pencil
lápiz de labios /láh pees day láh bee-ohs/ *n.* lipstick
largo /láhr-goh/ *adj.* long
las /lahs/ *art.* the
las onces /lahs óhn-says/ *n. Chi.* snack
lastimar /lah stee-máhr/ *v.* hurt
lata /láh-tah/ *n.* can
látigo /láh-tee-goh/ *n.* whip
latitud /lah-tee-tóod/ *n.* latitude
latón /lah-tóhn/ *n.* brass
lavabo /lah-váh-boh/ *n. Mex.* bathroom sink
lavadero /lah-vah-dáy-roh/ *n. Bol., Chi., Pe., Ven.* kitchen sink

lavamanos /lah-vah-máh-nohs/ *n. Bol., Chi., Ven.* bathroom sink
lavaplatos /lah-vah-pláh-tohs/ *n. Bol., Chil., Ven.* kitchen sink
lavatorio /lah-vah-tóh-ree-oh/ *n.* washroom; *Pe.* bathroom sink
lavandería /lah-vahn-day-rée-ah/ *n.* laundry
lavar /lah-váhr/ *v.* wash
lazo /láh-soh/ *n.* bow
le /lay/ *pron.* to him; to her; to it; to you
leal /lay-áhl/ *adj.* loyal
lector /layk-tóhr/ *n.* reader
lectura /layk-tóo-rah/ *n.* reading
leche /láy-chay/ *n.* milk
lechuga /lay-chóo-gah/ *n.* lettuce
lechuza /lay-chóo-sah/ *n.* owl
leer /lay-áyr/ *v.* read
legal /lay-gáhl/ *adj.* legal
legalizar /lay-gah-lee-sáhr/ *v.* legalize
lejano /lay-háhn-noh/ *adj.* distant
lejos /láy-hohs/ *adv.* far
lengua /láyn-gwah/ *n.* language; tongue
lenguado /layn-gwáh-doh/ *n.* sole (fish)
lenguaje /layn-gwáh-hay/ *n.* language
lente /láyn-tay/ *n.* lens
lentejas /layn-táy-hahs/ *n.* lentils
lentes /láyn-tays/ *n. Mex.* eyeglasses

lento /láyn-toh/ *adj.* slow
letra /láy-trah/ *n.* letter (alphabet)
letras /láy-trahs/ *n.* lyrics
letrero /lay-tráy-roh/ *n.* sign
levantar /lay vahn-táhr/ *v.* raise; lift
levantarse /lay-vahn-táhr-say/ *v.* get up
ley /lay/ *n.* law
libertad /lee-bayr-táhd/ *n.* freedom
libra /lée-brah/ *n.* pound
libre /lée-bray/ *adj.* free
librería /lee-bray-rée-ah/ *n.* bookstore
libreta de conductor /lee-bráy-tah day cohn-dook--tóhr/ *n. Uru.* driver's license
libro /lée-broh/ *n.* book
licencia /lee-sáyn see-ah/ *n.* license
licencia de conducir /lee-sáyn-see-ah day cohndoo-sé-er/ *n. Mex.* driver's license
licenciar /lee-sayn-see-áhr/ *v.* license
licor /lee-cóhr/ *n.* liquor; liqueur
líder /lée-dayr/ *n.* leader
lima /lée-mah/ *n.* lime; file
lima para las uñas /lée-mah páh-rah lahs óonyahs/ *n.* nailfile
limar /lep-máhr/ *v.* file
limitar /lee-mee-táhr/ *v.* limit
límite /lée-mee-tay/ *n.* limit
limón /lee-móhn/ *n.* lemon; lime

limonada /lee-moh-náh-dah/ *n.* lemonade
limpiabotas /leem-pee-ah-bóh-tahs/ *n. Carib., Ven.* shoeshine boy
limpiar /leem-pee-áhr/ *v.* clean
limpieza /leem-pee-áy-sah/ *n.* cleanliness
limpio /léem-pee-oh/ *adj.* clean
linea /lée-nay-ah/ *n.* line
lino /lée-noh/ *n.* linen
líquido /lée-key-doh/ *n.* liquid
liso /lée-soh/ *adj.* smooth; plain
lista /lée-stah/ *n.* list; *Cuba* menu
listo /lée-stoh/ *adj.* ready; clever
living /léev-ing/ *n. Chi.* living room
llama /yáh-ma/ *n.* flame; *Andes* (zool.) llama
llamada /yah-máh-dah/ *n.* call
llamar por teléfono /yah-máhr pohr tay-láy-fohnoh/ *v.* phone
llanta /yáhn-tah/ *n. Mex., Uru.* tire
llanura /yah-nóo-rah/ *n.* plain
llave /yáh-vay/ *n.* key; *Mex., Pe.* faucet
llegada /yay-gáh-dah/ *n.* arrival
llegar /yay-gáhr/ *v.* arrive
llenar /yay-náhr/ *v.* fill
lleno /yáy-noh/ *adj.* full
llevar /yay-váhr/ *v.* take; carry
llorar /yoh-ráhr/ *v.* cry
llover /yoh-váyr/ *v.* rain

lluvia /yóo-vee-ah/ *n.* rain
lobo /lóh-boh/ *n.* wolf
local /loh-cáhl/ *n.* place; *adj.* local
loco /lóh-coh/ *adj.* crazy
locura /loh-cóo-rah/ *n.* madness
lo mismo /loh mées-moh/ *pron.* the same
lomo /lóh-moh/ *n.* back; loin
lomo de burro /lóh-moh day bóo-roh/ *n.* *Uru.* speed bumps
lo que /loh kay/ *pron.* that which
longaniza /lohn-gah-née-sah/ *n.* sausage
loro /lóh-roh/ *n.* parrot
los /lohs/ *art.* the
los dos /lohs dohs/ *pron., adj.* both
lotería /loh-tay-rée-ah/ *n.* lottery
loza /lóh-sah/ *n.* crockery; china
loza de barro /lóh-sah day báh-roh/ *n.* clay pottery
lucir /loo-séer/ *v.* shine; *Mex.* show off
lucrativo /loo-crah-tée-voh/ *adj.* lucrative
lucha /lóo-chah/ *n.* fight; struggle
luchar /loo-cháhr/ *v.* fight; struggle
lugar /loo-gáhr/ *n.* place
lujo /lóo-hoh/ *n.* luxury
luna /lóo-nah/ *n.* moon
luna de miel /lóo-nah day mee-áyl/ *n.* honeymoon
lunfardo /loon-fáhr-doh/ *n.* *Arg.* underworld slang
lustrabotas /loos-trah-bóh-tahs/ *n.* *Chi., Ec., Pe.*

shoeshine boy
lustrador /loos-trah-dóhr/ *n. Uru.* shoeshine boy
luz /loos/ *n.* light

- M -

macarrones /mah-cah-róh-nays/ *n.* macaroni
macho /máh-choh/ *n., adj.* male
madera /mah-dáy-rah/ *n.* wood
madrastra /mah-dráh-strah/ *n.* stepmother
madre /máh-dray/ *n.* mother; *Mex.* has vulgar meaning
madrina /mah-drée-nah/ *n.* godmother
maduro /mah-dóo-roh/ *adj.* mature; ripe
maíz /mah-ées/ *Cuba, Mex., Pe., Uru. n.* corn
mal /mahl/ *n.* evil; sickness; *adj.* bad
malagua /mah-láh-goo-ah/ *n.* Pe jelly fish
mala hierba /máh-lah ee-áyr-bah/ *n.* weed
maldad /mahl-dáhd/ *n.* evil; wickedness
malentendido /mahl-ayn-tayn-dée-doh/ *n.* misunderstanding
maleta /mah-láy-tah/ *n.* suitcase
malgastar /mahl-gah-stáhr/ *v.* waste
malo /máh-loh/ *adj.* bad; sick
mamá /mah-máh/ *n. Mex.* mother
manantial /mah-nahn-tee-áhl/ *n.* spring (water)
mancha /máhn-chah/ *n.* stain
manchar /mahn-cháhr/ *v.* stain
mandar /mahn-dáhr/ *v.* send; order
mandarina /mahn-dah-rée-nah/ *n.* tangerine
mando /máhn-doh/ *n.* command
manejar /mah-nay-háhr/ *v.* manage; drive

manera /mah-náy-rah/ *n.* manner; way
manga /máhn-gah/ *n.* sleeve
mango /máhn-goh/ *n.* mango
maní /mah-née/ *n.* peanuts (except in Mex.)
manicura /mah-nee-cóo-rah/ *n.* manicure
manija /mah-née-hah/ *n.* handle
manilla /mah-née-yah/ *n.* *Ven.* door handle
mano /máh-noh/ *n.* hand
manta /máhn-tah/ *n.* blanket
manteca /mahn-táy-cah/ *n.* *RP* butter
mantecado /mahn-tay-cáh-doh/ *n.* *PR* ice cream
mantel /mahn-táyl/ *n.* tablecloth
mantener /mahn-tay-náyr/ *v.* maintain; keep
mantequilla /mahn-tay-kéy-yah/ *n.* butter (except *RP*)
manual /mah-noo-áhl/ *n., adj.* manual
manzana /mahn-sáh-nah/ *n.* apple; square block
mañana /mah-nyáh-nah/ *n.* morning; *adv.* tomorrow
mapa /máh-pah/ *n.* map
máquina /máh-key-nah/ *n.* machine; *Cuba* taxi
máquina de afeitar /máh-key-nah day ah-fay-táhr/ *n.* razor
máquina de escribir /máh-key-nah day es-cree-béer/ *n.* typewriter
mar /mahr/ *n.* sea
maravilloso /mah-rah-vee-yóh-soh/ *adj.* marvelous
marca /máhr-cah/ *n.* brand
marea /mah-ráy-ah/ *n.* tide

mareado /mah-ray-áh-doh/ *adj.* dizzy
marfil /mahr-féel/ *n.* ivory
margarina /mahr-gah-rée-nah/ *n.* margarine
marido /mah-rée-doh/ *n.* husband
marina de guerra /mah-rée-nah day gáy-rah/ *n.* navy
marinero /mah-ree-náy-roh/ *n.* sailor
marioneta /mah-ree-oh-náy-tah/ *n. Uru.* puppet
mariposa /mah-ree-póh-sah/ *n.* butterfly
marisco /mah-rées-coh/ *n.* shellfish
marítimo /mah-rée-tee-moh/ *adj.* maritime
mármol /máhr-mohl/ *n.* marble
marrano /mah-ráh-noh/ *n.* pig
martes /máhr-tays/ *n.* Tuesday
marzo /máhr-soh/ *n.* March
más /mahs/ *adv.* more; most
masa /máh-sah/ *n.* mass; dough
más allá /mahs ah-yáh/ *adv.* farther on
más bien /mahs bee-áyn/ *adv.* rather
mascota /mahs-cóh-tah/ *n.* mascot; *Mex.* pet
masculino /mahs-coo-lée-noh/ *adj.* masculine
matar /mah-táhr/ *v.* kill
materia /mah-táy-ree-ah/ *n.* matter; subject (in school)
material /mah-tay-ree-áhl/ *n., adj.* material
maternidad /mah-tayr-nee-dáhd/ *n.* maternity
matrícula /mah-trée-coo-lah/ *n.* registration; *Uru.* license plate
matrimonio /mah-tree-móh-nee-oh/ *n.* marriage; mar-

ried couple

mayo /máh-yoh/ *n.* May

mayor /mah-yóhr/ *adj.* larger; older

mayoría /mah-yoh-rée-ah/ *n.* majority

me /may/ *pron.* me; to me

mecánico /may-cáh-nee-coh/ *n.* mechanic; *adj.* mechanical

mediano /may-dee-áh-noh/ *adj.* medium; middle

medianoche /may-dee-ah-nóh-chay/ *n.* midnight

medias /máy-dee-ahs/ *n.* socks

medibacha /may-dee-báh-chah/ *n. Arg.* panty

medicamento /may-dee-cah-máyn-toh/ *n.* medication

medicina /may-dee-sée-nah/ *n.* medicine

médico /máy-dee-coh/ *n.* doctor; *adj.* medical

medida /may-dée-dah/ *n.* measurement

medidor /may-dee-dóhr/ *n.* meter

medio /máy-dee-oh/ *n., adj.* half; middle

medio crudo /máy-dee-oh cróo-doh/ *adj.* rare (meat)

mediodía /may-dee-oh-dée-ah/ *n.* noon

medir /may-déer/ *v.* measure

medusa /may-dóo-sah/ *n. Bol., Uru.* jelly fish

mejor /may-hóhr/ *adj.* better; best

mejoramiento /may-hoh-rah-mee-áyn-toh/ *n.* improvement

mejorar /may-hoh-ráhr/ *v.* improve

melocotón /may-loh-coh-tóhn/ *n.* Carib., Pe. peach

melón /may-lóhn/ *n.* melon; *Cuba* watermelon

mellizo /may-yée-soh/ *n.* twin

mendigo /mayn-dée-goh/ *n.* beggar
menor /may-nóhr/ *n.* minor (age); *adj.* less; least; smaller; younger
menos /máy-nohs/ *adj., adv.* minus; less
menta /máyn-tah/ *n.* mint
mente /máyn-tay/ *n.* mind
mentira /mayn-tée-rah/ *n.* lie
menú /may-nóo/ *n.* menu
mercado /mayr-cáh-doh/ *n.* market
mercancía /mayr-cahn-sée-ah/ *n.* merchandise; goods
mercante /mayr-cáhn-tay/ *adj.* merchant
merecer /may-ray-sáyr/ *v.* deserve
merienda /may-ree-áyn-dah/ *n.* snack
mermelada /mayr-may-láh-dah/ *n.* jam; marmalade
mero /máy-roh/ *n.* halibut like fish; *adj. Mex.* very; very own
mes /mays/ *n.* month
mesa /máy-sah/ *n.* table
mesera /may-sáy-rah/ *n. Mex.* waitress
mesero /may-sáy-roh/ *n. Mex.* waiter
mesonera /may-soh-náy-rah/ *n. Ven.* waitress
mesonero /may-soh-náy-roh/ *n. Ven.* waiter
metal /may-táhl/ *n.* metal
método /máy-toh-doh/ *n.* method
metro /máy-troh/ *n.* meter (measurement); *Mex.* subway
mezcla /máys-clah/ *n.* mixture
mezclar /mays-cláhr/ *v.* mix

mi /mee/ *adj.* my
mico /mée-coh/ *n.* monkey
miedo /mee-áy-doh/ *n.* fear
miedoso /mee-ay-dóh-soh/ *adj.* fearful
miel /mee-áyl/ *n.* honey; *Mex.* honey; syrup
mientras que /mee-áyn-trahs kay/ *conj.* while
miércoles /mee-áyr-coh-lays/ *n.* Wednesday
mil /meel/ *n., adj.* thousand
milla /mée-yah/ *n.* mile
millón /mee-yóhn/ *n.* million
millonario /mee-yoh-náh-ree-oh/ *n.* millionaire
mina /mée-nah/ *n.* mine
mineral /mee-nay-ráhl/ *n., adj.* mineral
mínimo /mée-nee-moh/ *n., adj.* minimum
minuto /mee-nóo-toh/ *n.* minute
mío /mée-oh/ *adj.* my; *pron.* mine
mirada /mee-ráh-dah/ *n.* look
mirar /mee-ráhr/ *v.* look at
misa /mée-sah/ *n.* (rel.) mass
mismo /mées-moh/ *adj., pron.* same
mitad /mee-táhd/ *n.* half; middle
moción /moh-see-óhn/ *n.* motion
moda /móh-dah/ *n.* fashion
modales /moh-dáh-lays/ *n.* manners
moderno /moh-dáyr noh/ *adj.* modern
modismo /moh-dées-moh/ *n.* idiom
modista /moh-dée-stah/ *n.* dressmaker
mofeta /moh-fáy-tah/ *n.* skunk

mojado /moh-háh-doh/ *n. Mex.* wetback; *adj.* wet
mojar /moh-háhr/ *v.* wet
molestar /moh-lays-táhr/ *v.* bother
molestia /moh-láys-tee-ah/ *n.* bother
momento /moh-máyn-toh/ *n.* moment
monasterio /moh-nah-stáy-ree-oh/ *n.* monastery
mondadientes /mohn-dah-dee-áyn-tays/ *n. Bol.* toothpicks
mondongo /mohn-dóhn-goh/ *n. Mex., Pe., RP* tripe
moneda /moh-náy-dah/ *n.* coin
mono /móh-noh/ *n.* monkey; *adj.* cute
montaña /mohn-táh-nyah/ *n.* mountain
montañoso /mohn-tah-nyóh-soh/ *adj.* mountainous
monte /móhn-tay/ *n.* woodlands; wilds
monumento /moh-noo-máyn-toh/ *n.* monument
morado /moh-ráh-doh/ *adj.* purple
moral /moh-ráhl/ *n.* morality; *adj.* moral
moreno /moh-ráy-noh/ *adj.* dark
morfi /móhr-fee/ *n. Arg.* lunch
morir /moh-réer/ *v.* die
morocho /moh-róh-choh/ *n. Ven.* twin
morral /moh-ráhl/ *n. Mex.* shopping bag
mosca /móhs-cah/ *n.* fly
mosquito /mohs-kéy-toh/ *n.* mosquito
mostrar /mohs-tráhr/ *v.* show
mota /móh-tah/ *n.* powder puff; *Mex.* marijuana
motocicleta /moh-toh-see-cláy-tah/ *n.* motorcycle
motor /moh-tóhr/ *n.* motor; engine

mover /moh-váyr/ *v.* move
mozo /móh-soh/ *n. Ec., Pe., RP* waiter
muchacha /moo-cháh-chah/ *n.* girl
muchacho /moo-cháh-choh/ *n.* boy
mucho /móo-choh/ *adj., adv.* much
muchos /móo-chohs/ *adj., pron.* many
muebles /moo-áy blays/ *n.* furniture
muela /moo-áy-lah/ *n.* back tooth; molar
muerte /moo-áyr-tay/ *n.* death
muerto /moo-áyr-toh/ *adj.* dead
muertos /moo-áyr-tohs/ *n. CR* speed bumps
muestra /moo-áys-trah/ *n.* sample
mugre /móo-gray/ *n.* dirt; filth
mujer /moo-háyr/ *n.* woman
mujer de negocios /moo-háyr day nay-góh-see-ohs/ *n.* businesswoman
mundo /móon-doh/ *n.* world
municipal /moo-nee-see-páhl/ *adj.* municipal
muñeca /moo-nyáy-cah/ *n.* doll; wrist
museo /moo-sáy-oh/ *n.* museum
música /móo-see-cah/ *n.* music
músico /móo-see-coh/ *n.* musician
muy /móo-ee/ *adv.* very
muy bien /móo-ee bee-áyn/ *interj.* very well; fine

- N -

nacer /nah-sáyr/ *v.* be born
nacido /nah-sée-doh/ *adj.* born
nacimiento /nah-see-mee-áyn-toh/ *n.* birth
nación /nah-see-óhn/ *n.* nation
nacional /nah-see-oh-náhl/ *adj.* national
naco /náh-coh/ *n.* *Arg.* fear; scare; *Col.* stewed corn; *adj.* *Mex.* scruffy; lower class
nada /náh-dah/ *pron.* nothing
nadador /nah-dah-dóhr/ *n.* swimmer
nadar /nah-dáhr/ *v.* swim
nadie /náh-dee-ay/ *pron.* nobody; no one
nafta /náhf-tah/ *n.* *Arg.* gas
naipes /náh-ee-pays/ *n.* *Ec.*, *Pe.* playing cards
naranja /nah-ráhn-hah/ *n.* orange
nariz /nah-rées/ *n.* nose
nativo /nah-tée-voh/ *n.*, *adj.* native
natural /nah-too-ráhl/ *adj.* natural
naturaleza /nah-too-rah-láy-sah/ *n.* nature
navaja /nah-váh-hah/ *n.* razor
navegar /nah-vay-gáhr/ *v.* navigate; sail
Navidad /nah-vee-dáhd/ *n.* Christmas
necesidad /nay-say-see-dáhd/ *n.* necessity
necesario /nay-say-sáh-ree-oh/ *adj.* necessary
necesitar /nay-say-see-táhr/ *v.* need
negar /nay-gáhr/ *v.* deny
negociación /nay-goh-see-ah-see-óhn/ *n.* negotiation

negocio /nay-góh-see-oh/ *n.* business
negro /náy-groh/ *n., adj.* black
nene /náy-nay/ *n.* child
nervioso /nayr-vee-óh-soh/ *adj.* nervous
neumático /nay-oo-máh-tee-coh/ *n. Chi., Uru.* tire
nevar /nay-váhr/ *v.* snow
ni /nee/ *conj.* neither
nieta /nee-áy-tah/ *n.* granddaughter
nieto /nee-áy-toh/ *n.* grandson
nieve /nee-áy-vay/ *n.* snow; *Mex.* sherbet
ninguno /neen-góo-noh/ *adj.* no; not any; *pron.* none
niña /née-nyah/ *n.* girl
niño /née-nyoh/ *n.* boy
no /noh/ *adv.* no; not
nocivo /noh-sée-voh/ *adj.* harmful
noche /nóh-chay/ *n.* night
nogal /noh-gáhl/ *n.* walnut
no hacer caso de /noh ah-sáyr cáh-soh day/ *v.* pay no attention to; ignore
nombrar /nohm-bráhr/ *v.* name
nombre /nóhm-bray/ *n.* name
norma /nóhr-mah/ *n.* norm
normal /nohr-máhl/ *adj.* normal
norte /nóhr-tay/ *n.* north
nos /nohs/ *pron.* us
nosotros /noh-sóh-trohs/ *pron.* we
nosotros mismos /noh-sóh-trohs mées-mohs/ *pron.* ourselves
nota /nóh-tah/ *n.* note

notar /noh-táhr/ *v.* note
noticias /noh-tée-see-ahs/ *n.* news
novela /noh-váy-lah/ *n.* novel
noveno /noh-váy-noh/ *adj.* ninth
noventa /noh-váyn-tah/ *n., adj.* ninety
novia /nóh-vee-ah/ *n.* girl friend; bride
novio /nóh-vee-oh/ *n.* boyfriend; groom
nuera /noo-áy-rah/ *n.* daughter-in-law
nuestro /noo-áys-troh/ *adj.* our
nueve /noo-áy-vay/ *n., adj.* nine
nuevo /noo-áy-voh/ *adj.* new
nuez /noo-áys/ *n.* nut; walnut; *Mex.* pecan
nulo /nóo-loh/ *adj.* null
número /nóo-may-roh/ *n.* number
numeroso /noo-may-róh-soh/ *adj.* numerous
nunca /nóon-cah/ *adv.* never
nutrición /noo-tree-see-óhn/ *n.* nutrition

- O -

o /oh/ *conj.* or; either
obedecer /oh-bay-day-sáyr/ *v.* obey
objetar /ohb-hay-táhr/ *v.* object
objeto /ohb-háy-toh/ *n.* object
objectos de valor /ohb-háy-tohs day vah-lóhr/ *v.* valuables
obra maestra /óh-brah mah-áys-trah/ *n.* masterpiece
observación /ohb-sayr-vah-see-óhn/ *n.* observation
observar /ohb-sayr-váhr/ *v.* observe
observatorio /ohb-sayr-vah-tóh-ree-oh/ *n.* observatory
obstáculo /ohb-stáh-coo-loh/ *n.* obstacle
obstrucción /ohb-strook-see-óhn/ *n.* obstruction
obtener /ohb-tay-náyr/ *v.* obtain; get
obvio /óhn-vee-oh/ *adj.* obvious
ocasión /oh-cah-see-óhn/ *n.* occasion
ocasional /oh-cah-see-ohn-náhl/ *adj.* occasional
océano /oh-sáy-ah-noh/ *n.* ocean
octavo /ohk-táh-voh/ *adj.* eighth
octubre /ok-tóo-bray/ *n.* October
oculista /oh-coo-lées-tah/ *n.* oculist
ocupación /oh-coo-pah-see-óhn/ *n.* occupation
ocupar /oh-coo-páhr/ *v.* occupy
ocurrir /oh-coo-réer/ *v.* occur; happen
ochenta /oh-cháyn-tah/ *n., adj.* eighty
ocho /óh-choh/ *n., adj.* eight

odiar /oh-dee-áhr/ *v.* hate
oeste /oh-áy-stay/ *n.* west
ofender /oh-fayn-dáyr/ *v.* offend
ofensa /oh-fáyn-sah/ *n.* offense
ofensivo /oh-fayn-sée-voh/ *n., adj.* offensive
oferta /oh-fáyr-tah/ *n. Mex.* sale; sale item
oficial /oh-fee-see-áhl/ *n.* official; officer; *adj.* official
oficina /oh-fee-sée-nah/ *n.* office
oficina de correos /oh-fee-sée-nah day coh-ráy-ohs/ *n. Mex.* post office
ofrecer /oh-fray-sáyr/ *v.* offer
ofrecimiento /oh-fray-see-mée-ayn-toh/ *n.* offer
oído /oh-ée-doh/ *n.* ear
oír /oh-éer/ *v.* hear
ojo /óh-hoh/ *n.* eye
ojotas /oh-hóh-tahs/ *n. Andes, RP* sandals
ola /óh-lah/ *n.* wave
oler /oh-láyr/ *v.* smell
olor /oh-lóhr/ *n.* smell
olvidadizo /ohl-vee-dah-dée-soh/ *adj.* forgetful
olvidar /ohl-vee-dáhr/ *v.* forget
olla /óh-yah/ *n.* pot; kettle
omitir /oh-mee-ter/ *v.* omit
omoto /oh-móh-toh/ *adj. Ec.* short (person)
once /óhn-say/ *n., adj.* eleven
ondulación /ohn-doo-lah-see-óhn/ *n. Bol.* curl
ónix /óh-neeks/ *n.* onyx
onza /óhn-sah/ *n.* ounce
ópera /óh-pay-rah/ *n.* opera

opinión /oh-pee-nee-óhn/ *n.* opinion
oponer /oh-poh-náyr/ *v.* oppose
oportunidad /oh-pohr-too-nee-dáhd/ *n.* opportunity; chance
opuesto /oh-pwáys-toh/ *adj.* opposite
orden /óhr-dayn/ *n.* order
orden de arresto /óhr-dayn day ah-ráys-toh/ *n.* warrant for arrest
orden de pago /óhr-dayn day páh-goh/ *n.* money order
oreja /oh-ráy-hah/ *n.* ear
organización /ohr-gah-nee-sah-see-óhn/ *n.* organization
organizar /ohr-gah-nee-sáhr/ *v.* organize
orgullo /ohr-góo-yoh/ *n.* pride
orgulloso /ohr-goo-yóh-soh/ *adj.* proud
oro /óh-roh/ *n.* gold
orquesta /ohr-káy-stah/ *n.* orchestra
orquídea /ohr-kéy-day-ah/ *n.* orchid
oscuro /ohs-cóo-roh/ *adj.* dark
otoño /oh-tóh-nyoh/ *n.* autumn; fall
otra vez /óh-trah vays/ *adv.* again
otro /óh-troh/ *adj.* other; another
oveja /oh-váy-hah/ *n.* sheep

- P -

paciente /pah-see-áyn-tay/ *n., adj.* patient
padrastro /pah-dráh-stroh/ *n.* stepfather
padre /páh-dray/ *n.* father; *adj. Mex., Pe.* terrific
padres /páh-drays/ *n.* parents
padrino /pah-drée-noh/ *n.* godfather
pagar /pah-gáhr/ *v.* pay; pay for
página /páh-hee-nah/ *n.* page
pago /páh-goh/ *n.* payment
país /pah-ées/ *n.* country; nation
paisaje /pah-ee-sáh-hay/ *n.* landscape
pájaro /páh-hah-roh/ *n.* bird
pajita /pa-hée-tah/ *n. Chi., Uru.* drinking straw
palabra /pah-láh brah/ *n.* word
palco /páhl-coh/ *n.* box (theater)
pálido /páh-lee-doh/ *adj.* pale
palillo /pah-lée-yoh/ *n. Mex.* toothpick
palma /páhl-mah/ *n.* palm
palo de dientes /páh-loh day dee-áyn-tays/ *n. Pe.* toothpick
paloma /pah-lóh-mah/ *n.* pigeon; dove
palomitas /pah-loh-mée-tahs/ *n. Mex.* popcorn
palta /páhl-tah/ *n. SA* avocado
pan /pahn/ *n.* bread
panadería /pah-nah-day-rée-ah/ *n.* bakery
panchos /páhn-chohs/ *n. Arg.* hot dogs
panga /páhn-gah/ *n. Mex.* ferry

panqué /pahn-káy/ *n. Col., Ven.* pancakes
panqueque /pahn-káy-kay/ *n. Bol., Pe., RP* pancakes
pantaleta /pahn-tah-láy-tah/ *n. Mex.* panty
pantalón /pahn-tah-lóhn/ *n.* trousers; pants
pantalla /pahn-táh-yah/ *n.* movie or TV screen
pantallas /pahn-táh-yahs/ *n. PR* earrings
pantimedia /pahn-tee-máy-dee-ah/ *n. Mex.* pantyhose
pan tostado /pahn tohs-táh-doh/ *n. Mex.* toast
panty /páhn-tee/ *n. Chi.* panty
panza /páhn-sah/ *n. Bol., Cuba* tripe
paño /páh-nyoh/ *n.* cloth
pañuelo /pah-nyoo-áy-loh/ *n.* scarf; handkerchief
papa /páh-pah/ *n.* potato; pope
papá /pah-páh/ *n.* daddy
papagayo /pah-pah-gáh-yoh/ *n.* parrot
papaya /pah-páh-yah/ *n.* papaya
papel /pah-páyl/ *n.* paper; role
papelera /pah-pay-láy-rah/ *n.* wastebasket
papelería /pah-pay-lay-rée-ah/ *n.* stationery store
papel higiénico /pah-páyl ee-hee-áyn-ee-coh/ *n.* toilet paper
paquete /pah-káy-tay/ *n.* package
par /pahr/ *n.* pair
para /páh-rah/ *prep.* to; for
paracaídas /pah-rah-kah-ée-dahs/ *n.* parachute
parada /pah-ráh-dah/ *n.* bus stop
paradero /pah-rah-dáy-roh/ *n. Chi., Col.* bus stop
paraguas /pah-ráh-gwahs/ *n.* umbrella
paraíso /pah-rah-ée-soh/ *n.* paradise

parar /pah-ráhr/ *v.* stop
parásito /pah-ráh-see-toh/ *n.* parasite
pardo /páhr-doh/ *adj.* brown
parecer /pah-ray-sáyr/ *v.* seem; appear
parecido /pah-ray-sée-doh/ *adj.* similar to
pared /pah-ráyd/ *n.* wall
pareja /pah-ráy-hah/ *n.* couple; pair
pariente /pah-ree-áyn-tay/ *n.* relative
parque /páhr-kay/ *n.* park; ammunition
parqueadero /pahr-kay-ah-dáy-roh/ *n. Col., Ec.* parking lot
parquear /pahr-kay-áhr/ *v. Bol., Cuba* park
parqueo /pahr káy-oh/ *n. Bol., Cuba* parking lot
parrilla /pah-rée-yah/ *n.* grill; broiler
parte /páhr-tay/ *n.* part
participar /pahr-tee-see-páhr/ *v.* participate
particular /pahr-tee-coo-láhr/ *adj.* private
partido /pahr-tée-doh/ *n.* (pol.) party; game
partir /pahr-téer/ *v.* divide; leave
pasado /pah-sáh-doh/ *n., adj.* past
pasaje /pah-sáh-hay/ *n.* passage; fare
pasajero /pah-sah-háy-roh/ *n.* passenger
pasamano /pah-sah-máh-noh/ *n.* handrail
pasapalos /pah-sah-páh-lohs/ *n. Ven.* snacks
pasaporte /pah-sah-póhr-tay/ *n.* passport
pasar /pah-sáhr/ *v.* pass; *Arg., Ven.* pass (in car)
pasar por alto /pah-sáhr pohr áhl toh/ *v.* pass over; skip
pase(n) /páh-say(n)/ *imper.* come in

paseo /pah-sáy-oh/ *n.* walk; ride; boulevard
pasiero /pah-see-áy roh/ *n. Pan.* buddy
pasita /pah-sée-tah/ *n.* raisin
paso /páh-soh/ *n.* step
pasta /páh-stah/ *n.* pasta
pasta de dientes /páh-stah day dee-áyn tays/ *n.* toothpaste
pastel /pah-stáyl/ *n.* pie; *Mex.* cake
pastelería /pah-stay-lay rée-ah/ *n.* bakery
pastilla /pah-stée-yah/ *n.* pill; tablet
pasto /páh-stoh/ *n.* grass; *Mex., RP* lawn
patear /pah-tay áhr/ *v.* kick
patente /pah táyn-tay/ *n. Arg., Chi.* licenae plate; *adj.* evident
patilla /pah-téa-yah/ *n. Col. Ven.* watermelon
patio /páh-tee-oh/ *n.* patio
patria /páh-tree-ah/ *n.* homeland
patrón /pah-tróhn/ *n.* boss
pavimento /pah vee-máyn-toh/ *n.* pavement
pavo /páh voh/ *n.* turkey; *Arg.* kid
pay /páh-ee/ *n. Mex.* pie
payuca /pah-yóo-cah/ *n. Arg.* peasant
paz /pahs/ *n.* peace
peaje /pay-áh-hay/ *n. Ec., Uru., Ven.* toll
peatón /pay ah-tóhn/ *n.* pedestrian
pecado /pay-cáh-doh/ *n.* sin
pecar /pay-cáhr/ *v.* sin
pedazo /pay-dáh-soh/ *n.* piece
pedir /pay-déer/ *v.* ask for; order

pedir prestado /pay-déer pray-stáh-doh/ *v.* ask for a loan; borrow
pega /páy-gah/ *n. Ven.* glue
pegamento /pay-gah-máyn-toh/ *n. Mex., Uru.* glue
pegar /pay-gáhr/ *v.* hit; stick
pelao /pay-láh-oh/ *n. Pan.* kid
pelar /pay-láhr/ *v.* peel
pelea /pay-láy-ah/ *n.* fight
pelear /pay-lay-áhr/ *v.* fight
pelear el precio /pay-lay-áhr ayl práy-see-oh/ *v. Chi.* bargain
película /pay-lée-coo-lah/ *n.* film
peligro /pay-lée-groh/ *n.* danger
peligroso /pay-lee-gróh-soh/ *adj.* dangerous
pelo /páy-loh/ *n.* hair
peluquería /pay-loo-kay-rée-ah/ *n.* beauty shop; barbershop (except *Cuba*)
peluquero /pay-loo-káy-roh/ *n.* hairdresser; barber (except *Cuba*)
pendientes /payn-dee-áyn-tays/ *n. Cuba* dangling earrings
península /pay-néen-soo-lah/ *n.* peninsula
pensamiento /payn-sah-mee-áyn-toh/ *n.* thought
pensar /payn-sáhr/ *v.* think
pensión /payn-see-óhn/ *n.* boarding house
peor /pay-óhr/ *adj., adv.* worse; worst
pepino /pay-pée-noh/ *n.* cucumber
pequeño /pay-káy-nyoh/ *adj.* small; *Ven.* short (person)

pera /páy-rah/ *n.* pear
perchero /payr-cháy-roh/ *n. Cuba* clothes hanger
perder /payr-dáyr/ *v.* lose
pérdida /páyr-dee-dah/ n.loss
perdido /payr-dée-doh/ *adj.* lost
perdón /payr-dóhn/ *n.* pardon
perdonar /payr-doh-náhr/ *v.* pardon; forgive
perejil /pay-ray-héel/ *n.* parsley
perezoso /pay-ray-sóh-soh/ *adj.* lazy
perfecto /payr-fáyk-toh/ *adj.* perfect
perfume /payr-fóo-may/ *n.* perfume
perilla /pay-rée-yah/ *n.* doorknob
periódico /pay-ree-óh-dee-coh/ *n.* newspaper
periodista /pay-ree-oh-dée-stah/ *n.* journalist
período /pay-rée-oh-doh/ *n.* period
perla /páyr-lah/ *n.* pearl
permanente /payr-mah-náyn-tay/ *n., adj.* permanent
permiso /payr-mée-soh/ *n.* permission; permit
permiso de conducir /payr-mée-soh day cohn-doo-sé-er/ *n. Mex.* driver's license
permiso de manejo /payr-mée-soh day mah-náy-hoh/ *n. Arg.* driver's license
permitir /payr-mee-téer/ *v.* permit
pero /páy-roh/ *conj.* but
perro /páy-roh/ *n.* dog
perro caliente /páy-roh cah-lee-áyn-tay/ *n. Cuba, Mex.* hot dog
perseguidora /payr-say-ghee-dóh-rah/ *n. Pe.* hang-over

perseguir /payr-say-ghéer/ *v.* pursue
persona /payr-sóh-nah/ *n.* person
personal /payr-soh-náhl/ *n.* personnel; *adj.* personal
personalidad /payr-soh-nah-lee-dáhd/ *n.* personality
pertenecer /payr-tay-nay-sáyr/ *v.* belong
pertenencias /payr-tay-náyn-see-ahs/ *n.* belongings
pesadilla /pay-sah-dée-yah/ *n.* nightmare
pesado /pay-sáh-doh/ *adj.* heavy; insufferable
pesar /pay-sáhr/ *v.* weigh
pesca /páys-cah/ *n.* fishing
pescado /pays-cáh-doh/ *n.* fish (as food)
pescador /pays-cah-dóhr/ *v.* fisherman
pesero /pay-sáy-roh/ *n. Mex.* jitney
peso /páy-soh/ *n.* weight; peso (currency)
pestaña /pays-táh-nyah/ *n.* eyelash
petaca /pay-táh-cah/ *n. Mex.* valise
petición /pay-tee-see-óhn/ *n.* petition
petizo /pay-tée-soh/ *n. Bol., RP* short person
petróleo /pay-tróh-lay-oh/ *n.* petroleum; gas
pez /pays/ *n.* fish (line)
piano /pee-áh-noh/ *n.* piano
pibe /pée-bay/ *n. Arg.* kid
picante /pee-cáhn-tay/ *adj.* hot (spicy)
picaporte /pee-cah-póhr-tay/ *n. Arg., Cuba* door handle
picar /pee-cáhr/ *v.* prick; sting
picazón /pee-cah-sóhn/ *n.* itch
pico /pée-coh/ *n.* beak
pichincha /pee-chéen-chah/ *n. Arg.* sale

pie /pee-áy/ *n.* foot; *Chi.* down payment
piedra /pee-áy-drah/ *n.* rock; stone
piel /pee-áyl/ *n.* skin
pierna /pee-áyr-nah/ *n.* leg
pieza /pee-áy-sah/ *n.* piece; *Arg., Chi.* room
pieza de repuesto /pee-áy-sah day ray-pwáys-toh/ *n.* spare part
pijamas /pee-cháh-mahs/ *n.* pajamas
pila /pée-lah/ *n.* battery; pile
píldora /péel-doh-rah/ *n.* pill
pileta /pee-láy-tah/ *n. Arg.* swimming pool; bathroom sink; *Uru.* sink (in general)
piloto /pee-lóh-toh/ *n.* pilot
pimienta /pee-mee-áyn-tah/ *n.* black pepper
pinche /péen-chay/ *n. Chi.* bobby pin; *adj.* (vulgar in Mex.)
pintar /peen-táhr/ *v.* paint
pintor /peen-tóhr/ *n.* painter
pintoresco /peen-toh-ráys-coh/ *adj.* picturesque
pintura /peen-tóo-rah/ *n.* paint
pintura de labios /peen-tóo-rah day láh-bee-ohs/ *n. Mex.* lipstick
piña /pée-nyah/ *n.* pineapple (except Arg.)
pipocas /pee-póh-cahs/ *n. Bol.* popcorn
pipote de basura /pee-póh-tay day bah-sóo-rah/ *n. Ven.* wastebasket
pirámide /pee-ráh-mee-day/ *n.* pyramid
pisar /pee-sáhr/ *v.* step on
piscina /pee-sée-nah/ *n.* swimming pool (except *Arg.*

and *Mex.*)
pisco /pées-coh/ *n. Col., Pe.* local brandy
piso /pée-soh/ *n.* floor
piso bajo /pée-soh báh-hoh/ *n.* ground floor
pitillo /pee-tée-yoh/ *n.* cigarette; *Ven.* drinking straw
pito /pée-toh/ *n.* whistle; *Ec., Pan.* car horn
placa /pláh-cah/ *n. Mex.* license plate
placard /plah-cáhrd/ *n. RP* closet
plan /plahn/ *n.* plan
plancha /pláhn-chah/ *n.* iron
planchar /plahn-cháhr/ *v.* iron
planear /plahn-nay-áhr/ *v.* plan
plano /pláhn-noh/ *n.* plan; *adj.* flat
planta /pláhn-tah/ *n.* plant
planta baja /pláhn-tah báh-hah/ *n. Mex.* ground floor
plantar /plahn-táhr/ *v.* plant
plata /pláh-tah/ *n.* silver; money
plataforma /plah-tah-fóhr-mah/ *n.* platform
plátano /pláh-tah-noh/ *n.* plantain; banana
plática /pláh-tee-cah/ *n.* chat
platicar /plah-tee-cáhr/ *v.* chat
platillo /plah-tée-yoh/ *n.* saucer
plato /pláh-toh/ *n.* plate; dish
playa /pláh-yah/ *n.* beach
playa de estacionamiento /pláh-yah day es-tah--see-oh-nah-mee-áyn-toh/ *n. Chi., RP* parking lot
plaza mayor /pláh-sah mah-yóhr/ *n.* main square
plazo /pláh-soh/ *n.* term
pleito /pláy-toh/ *n.* dispute; law suit

plomero /ploh-máy-roh/ *n.* plumber
pluma /plóo-mah/ *n.* pen
población /poh-blah-see-óhn/ *n.* population
pobre /póh-bray/ *adj.* poor
poco /póh-coh/ *adj., pron.* little
poco común /póh-coh coh-móon/ *adj.* unusual
poco importante /póh-coh eem-pohr-táhn-tay/ *adj.* unimportant
pocos /póh-cohs/ *adj., pron.* few
poco satisfactorio /póh-coh sah-tees-fahk-tóh--ree-oh/ *adj.* unsatisfactory
pocho /póh-choh/ *n. Chi.* short, fat person; *Mex.* Americanized Mexican
pochoclo /poh-chóh-cloh/ *n. Arg.* popcorn
poder /poh-dáyr/ *n.* power; *v.* be able to
poderoso /poh-day-róh-soh/ *adj.* powerful
policía /poh-lee-sée-ah/ *n.* police
policía acostado /poh-lee-sée-ah ah-cohs-táh-doh/ *n. Ec.* speed bumps
política /poh-lée-tee-cah/ *n.* policy; politics
político /poh-lée-tee-coh/ *n.* politician; *adj.* political
polola /poh-lóh-lah/ *n. Chi.* girl friend
pololo /poh-lóh-loh/ *n. Chi.* boyfriend
pollera /poh-yáy-rah/ *n. RP* skirt
pollo /póh-yoh/ *n.* chicken
polvera /pohl-váy-rah/ *n.* powder puff
polvo /póhl-voh/ *n.* powder
pomelo /poh-máy-loh/ *n. Arg.* grapefruit
pon /pohn/ *n. PR* lift (in car)

ponche /póhn-chay/ *n.* punch
poner /poh-náyr/ *v.* put; place
ponerse /poh-náyr-say/ *v.* put on
ponerse en contacto con /poh-náyr-say ayn cohn--táhk-toh cohn/ *v.* get in touch with
popotes /poh-póh-tays/ *n. Mex.* drinking straws
popular /poh-poo-láhr/ *adj.* popular
por /pohr/ *prep.* by; through; by way of
porcelana /pohr-say-láh-nah/ *n.* porcelain
porcentaje /pohr-sayn-táh-hay/ *n.* percentage
por ciento /pohr see-áyn-toh/ *n.* percent
porción /pohr-see-óhn/ *n.* portion
por consiguiente /pohr cohn-see-ghee-áyn-tay/ *adv.* consequently; therefore
pordiosero /pohr-dee-oh-sáy-roh/ *n.* beggar
por eso /pohr áy-soh/ *adv.* therefore
por favor /pohrfah-vóhr/ *adv.* please
por la noche /pohr lah nóh-chay/ at night
pororó /poh-roh-róh/ *n. RP* popcorn
porotos /poh-róh-tohs/ *n. Chi.* dry beans
porotos verdes /poh-róh-tohs váyr-days/ *n. Chi.* green beans
por persona /pohr payr-sóh-nah/ *adj., adv.* per capita
porque /póhr-kay/ *conj.* because
¿por qué? /pohr kay/ *interr.* why?
porte /póhr-tay/ *n.* postage; carrying charge; *Chi.* birthday present
poseedor /poh-say-ay-dóhr/ *n.* owner
poseer /poh-say-áyr/ *v.* possess

posibilidad /poh-see-bee-lee-dáhd/ *n.* possibility
posible /poh-sée-blay/ *adj.* possible
posiblemente /poh-see-blay-máyn-tay/ *adv.* possibly
posición /poh-see-see-óhn/ *n.* position
positivo /poh-see-tée-voh/ *adj.* positive
posponer /pohs-poh-náyr/ *v.* postpone
postal /pohs-táhl/ *n. Arg., Ec.* postcard; *adj.* postal
posterior /pohs-tay-ree-óhr/ *adj.* back; later
postre /póh-stray/ *n.* dessert
pote /póh-tay/ *n. Ven.* can
pozo /póh-soh/ *n.* well (water); *Chi., Col.* puddle; *Ec.* spring
práctica /práhk-tee-cah/ *n.* practice
practicar /prahk-tee-cáhr/ *v.* practice
práctico /práhk-tee-coh/ *adj.* practical
prado /práh-doh/ *n.* meadow; promenade
precio /práy-see-oh/ *n.* price
precipitar /pray-see-pee-táhr/ *v.* rush
precisión /pray-see-see-óhn/ *n.* precision; *Chi.* haste
preciso /pray-sée-soh/ *adj.* necessary; precise
preferencia /pray-fay-ráyn-see-ah/ *n.* preference
preferible /pray-fay-rée-blay/ *adj.* preferible
preferir /pray-fay-réer/ *v.* prefer
pregunta /pray-góon-tah/ *n.* question
preguntar /pray-goon-táhr/ *v.* ask a question
preguntarse /pray-goon-táhr-say/ *v.* wonder
prenda de vestir /práyn-dah day vays-téer/ *n.* article of clothing
prensa /práyn-sah/ *n.* press

preocupación /pray-oh-coo-pah-see-óhn/ *n.* worry
preocuparse /pray-oh-coo-páhr-say/ *v.* be worried
preparación /pray-pah-rah-see-óhn/ *n.* preparation
preparar /pray-pah-ráhr/ *v.* prepare
presencia /pray-sáyn-see-ah/ *n.* presence
presentación /pray-sayn-tah-see-óhn/ *n.* presentation; appearance
presentar /pray-sayn-táhr/ *v.* present
presente /pray-sáyn-tay/ *n.* present; gift; *adj.* present
presidente /pray-see-dáyn-tay/ *n.* president
presidente municipal /pray-see-dáyn-tay moo-nee--see-páhl/ *n. Mex.* mayor
presión /pray-see-óhn/ *n.* pressure
prestar /pray-stáhr/ *v.* lend
presupuesto /pray-soo-pwáy-stoh/ *n.* budget
primario /pree-máh-ree-oh/ *adj.* primary
primavera /pree-mah-váy-rah/ *n.* spring
primero /pree-máy-roh/ *adj.* first
primer piso /pree-máyr pée-soh/ *n. Pe.* ground floor
primitivo /pree-mee-tée-voh/ *adj.* primitive
primo /prée-moh/ *n.* cousin
principal /preen-see-páhl/ *adj.* principal; main
principio /preen-sée-pee-oh/ *n.* beginning; principle
prioridad /pree-oh-ree-dáhd/ *n.* priority
prisa /prée-sah/ *n.* hurry; *Ven.* speed bumps
prisión /pree-see-óhn/ *n.* prison
prisionero /pree-see-oh-náy-roh/ *n.* prisoner
privado /pree-váh-doh/ *adj.* private
privilegio /pree-vee-láy-hee-oh/ *n.* privilege

proa /próh-ah/ *n.* prow (boat)
probable /proh báh-blay/ *adj.* probable
probar /proh-báhr/ *v.* prove; try
probarse /proh-báhr-say/ *v.* try on
problema /proh bláy-mah/ *n.* problem
procedimiento /proh-say-dee-mee-áyn-toh/ *n.* procedure
procesar /proh-say-sáhr/ *v.* sue
proceso /proh-sáy-soh/ *n.* process; lawsuit
producir /proh-doo-séer/ *v.* produce
producto /proh-dóok-toh/ *n.* product
profesor /proh-fay-sóhr/ *n.* professor; teacher
profundidad /proh-foon-dee-dáhd/ *n.* depth
profundo /proh-fóon-doh/ *adj.* deep
progresar /proh-gray-sáhr/ *v.* progress
progreso /proh-gráy-soh/ *n.* progress
prohibir /proh-ee-béer/ *v.* prohibit
promedio /proh-máy-dee-oh/ *n.* average
promesa /proh-máy-sah/ *n.* promise
prometer /proh-may-táyr/ *v.* promise
pronto /próhn-toh/ *adv.* quick; *Uru.* right now
pronunciación /proh-noon-see-ah-see-óhn/ *n.* pronunciation
pronunciar /proh-noon-see-áhr/ *v.* pronounce
propiedad /proh-pee-ay-dáhd/ *n.* property
propina /proh-pée-nah/ *n.* tip
propio /próh-pee-oh/ *adj.* proper; same
proponer /proh-poh-náyr/ *v.* propose
propósito /proh-póh-see-toh/ *n.* purpose; intention

prosecución /proh-say-coo-seẹ-óhn/ *n.* prosecution
prostituta /proh-stee-tóo-tah/ *n.* prostitute
protección /proh-tayk-see-óhn/ *n.* protection
proteger /proh-tay-háyr/ *v.* protect
protestar /proh-tays-táhr/ *v.* protest
proveer /proh-vay-áyr/ *v.* provide; supply
proverbio /proh-váyr-bee-oh/ *n.* proverb
provincia /proh-véen-see-ah/ *n.* province
provisiones /proh-vee-see-óh-nays/ *n. Uru.* groceries
proyecto /proh-yáyk-toh/ *n.* project
prueba /proo-áy-bah/ *n.* test; proof
publicación /poo-blee-cah-see-óhn/ *n.* publication
publicar /poo-blee-cáhr/ *v.* publish
público /póo-blee-coh/ *n.* public; audience; *adj.* public
pudín /poo-déen/ *n. Cuba, Ven.* pudding
pueblo /pwáy-bloh/ *n.* people; town
puente /pwáyn-tay/ *n.* bridge
puerco /pwáyr-coh/ *n.* pig; pork
puerta /pwáyr-tah/ *n.* door
puerto /pwáyr-toh/ *n.* port
puesta de sol /pwáys-tah dayl sohl/ *n.* sunset
puesto que /pwáys-toh kay/ *conj.* since
pulgada /pool-gáh-dah/ *n.* inch
pulmonía /pool-moh-née-ah/ *n.* pneumonia
pulpería /pool-pay-rée-ah/ *n. LA* grocery store (except *Carib.* and Mex.)
pulpero /pool-páy-roh/ *n. LA* grocer (except *Carib.* and Mex.)

pulsera /pool-sáy-rah/ *n.* bracelet
punto /póon-toh/ *n.* point; period; stitch
puntual /poon-too-áhl/ *adj.* punctual
puñado /poo-nyáh-doh/ *n.* handful
pureza /poo-ráy-sah/ *n.* purity
purificar /poo-ree-fee-cáhr/ *v.* purify
puro /póo-roh/ *n. Mex., Pe.* cigar; *adj.* pure

- Q -

que /kay/ *pron.* that; which; who; whom
¿qué? /kay/ *adj., pron.* What? Which?
quebrado /kay-bráh-doh/ *adj.* broken
quedarse /key-dáhr-say/ *v.* remain
queja /káy-hah/ *n.* complain
quejar /kay-háhr/ *v.* complain
que le aproveche /kay lay ah-proh-váy-chay/ *interj.* bon appétit
quemar /kay-máhr/ *v.* burn
querer /kay-ráyr/ *v.* wish; want; love
querido /kay-rée-doh/ *adj.* dear; beloved
queso /káy-soh/ *n.* cheese
¿Qué tal? /kaytahl/ How's everything?
quiebra /key-áy-brah/ *n.* bankruptcy
quien /key-áyn/ *interr.* who; whom
¿quién? /key-áyn/ *interr.* Who?, Whom?
quienquiera /key-ayn-key-áy-rah/ *pron.* anyone, anybody
quienquiera que /key-ayn-key-áy-rah kay/ *pron.* whoever
quincalla /keyn-cáh-yah/ *n.* hardware store
quince /kéyn-say/ *n., adj.* fifteen
quinto /kéyn-toh/ *adj.* fifth
quitar /key-táhr/ *v.* take away

quitarse /key-táhr-say/ *v.* take off
quizás /key-sáhs/ *adv.* perhaps

- R -

rábano /ráh-bah-noh/ *n.* radish
radio /ráh-dee-oh/ *n.* radio
rama /ráh-mah/ *n.* branch
rancio /ráhn-see-oh/ *adj.* rancid
ranchero /rahn-cháy-roh/ *n. Mex.* owner of ranch; worker on ranch
rancho /ráhn-choh/ *n.* ranch; *Ven.* shack
rango /ráhn-goh/ *n.* range; rank
rapidez /rah-pee-dáys/ *n.* speed
rápido /ráh-pee-doh/ *adj.* fast
raqueta /rah-káy-tah/ *n.* racket
raramente /rah-rah-máyn-tay/ *adv.* rarely; seldom
raro /ráh-roh/ *adj.* rare; strange
rascar /rahs-cáhr/ *v.* scratch
rasguño /rahs-góo-nyoh/ *n.* scratch
raso /ráh-soh/ *adj.* smooth; common
raspar /rahs-páhr/ *v.* scrape; *Ven.* go away; die
raspón /rahs-póhn/ *n. Col.* straw hat; *Mex.* scrape
rasurar /rah-soo-ráhr/ *v.* shave
ratero /rah-táy-roh/ *n.* thief
ratón /rah-tóhn/ *n.* mouse; *Ven.* hangover
rayos X /ráh-yohs áyk-ees/ *n.* X-rays
raza /ráh-sah/ *n.* race; breed
razón /rah-sóhn/ *n.* reason; right
razonable /rah-soh-náh-blay/ *adj.* reasonable
real /ray-áhl/ *adj.* real

realmente /ray-ahl-máyn-tay/ *adv.* really
rebanada /ray-bah-náh-dah/ *n.* slice
rebanar /ray-bah-náhr/ *v.* slice
rebasar /ray-bah-sáhr/ *v. Mex., Uru.* pass (in car)
recado /ray-cáh-doh/ *n.* message
recargar /ray-cahr-gáhr/ *v.* reload; recharge
recámara /ray-cáh-mah-rah/ *n. Mex.* bedroom
receta /ray-sáy-tah/ *n.* prescription; recipe
recetar /ray-say-táhr/ *v.* prescribe
rechazar /ray-chah-sáhr/ *v.* reject
recibir /ray-see-béer/ *v.* receive
recibo /ray-sée-boh/ *n.* receipt
reciente /ray-see-áyn-tay/ *adj.* recent
recientemente /ray-see-ayn-tay-máyn-tay/ *adv.* recently
recipientes /ray-see-pee-áyn-tays/ *n. Ven.* empties
reclamación /ray-clah-mah-see-óhn/ *n.* claim
reclamar /ray-clah-máhr/ *v.* claim; demand
recobrar /ray-coh-bráhr/ *v.* recover
recoger /ray-coh-háyr/ *v.* pick up
recomendar /ray-coh-mayn-dáhr/ *v.* recommend
recompensa /ray-cohm-páyn-sah/ *n.* reward
reconocer /ray-coh-noh-sáyr/ *v.* recognize
reconocimiento /ray-coh-noh-see-mee-áyn-toh/ *n.* recognition
recordar /ray-cohr-dáhr/ *v.* remember
recuerdo /ray-kwáyr-doh/ *n.* memory; souvenir
recurso /ray-cóor-soh/ *n.* resource
red /rayd/ *n.* net; network

redondo /ray-dóhn-doh/ *adj.* round
reducción /ray-dook-see-óhn/ *n.* reduction
reducir /ray-doo-séer/ *v.* reduce
reemplazar /ray-aym-plah-sáhr/ *v.* replace
refacciones /ray-fahk-see-óh-nays/ *n.* *Mex.* spare parts
referencia /ray-fay-ráyn-see-ah/ *n.* reference
referir /ray-fay-réer/ *v.* refer
refrán /ray-fráhn/ *n.* saying; proverb
refrescar /ray-frays-cáhr/ *v.* refresh; cool
refresco /ray-fráys-coh/ *n.* soft drink
refrigerador /ray-free-hay-rah-dóhr/ *n.* refrigerator
regadera /ray-gah-dáy-rah/ *n.* *Mex.* shower (bath)
regalar /ray-gah-láhr/ *v.* give
regalo /ray-gáh-loh/ *n.* gift
regatear /ray-gah-tay-áhr/ *v.* bargain
regateo /ray-gah-táy-oh/ *n.* bargaining
región /ray-hee-óhn/ *n.* region
registro /ray-hée-stroh/ *n.* registration; registry
regla /ráy-glah/ *n.* rule; menstrual period
regresar /ray-gray-sáhr/ *v.* return
regreso /ray-gráy-soh/ *n.* return
rehusar /ray-oo-sáhr/ *v.* refuse
reír /ray éer/ *v.* laugh
relacionar /ray-lah-see-oh-náhr/ *v.* relate
relajar /ray-lah-háhr/ *v.* relax
relativo /ray-lah-tée-voh/ *adj.* relative
relicario /ray-lee-cáh-ree-oh/ *n.* shrine; *LA* locket
religión /ray-lee-hee-óhn/ *n.* religion

religioso /ray-lee-hee-óh-soh/ *adj.* religious
reloj /ray-lóh/ *n.* clock; watch
remendar /ray-mayn-dáhr/ *v.* mend
remitente /ray-mee-táyn-tay/ *n.* sender
remitir /ray-mee-téer/ *v.* forward
remo /ráy-moh/ *n.* oar
remolacha /ray-moh-láh-chah/ *n.* beet (except Mex.)
rendir /rayn-déer/ *v.* surrender
renovar /ray-noh-váhr/ *v.* renew
rentar /rayn-táhr/ *v.* rent
renunciar /ray-noon-see-áhr/ *v.* renounce; resign
reparación /ray-pah-rah-see-óhn/ *n.* repair
reparaciones /ray-pah-rah-see-óh-nays/ *n. Arg., Ven.* spare parts
reparar /ray-pah-ráhr/ *v.* repair
repentino /ray-payn-tée-noh/ *adj.* sudden
repetición /ray-pay-tee-see-óhn/ *n.* repetition
repetir /ray-pay-téer/ *v.* repeat
repollo /ray-póh-yoh/ *n.* cabbage
representar /ray-pray-sayn-táhr/ *v.* represent
reproducir /ray-proh-doo-séer/ *v.* reproduce
reptil /rayp-téel/ *n.* reptile
repuestos /ray-pwáys-tohs/ *n. Pe., Uru.* spare parts
requerir /ray-kay-réer/ *v.* require
requisito /ray-key-sée-toh/ *n.* requirement
resaco /ray-sáh-cah/ *n. Bol., Uru.* hangover
resbalar /rays-bah-láhr/ *v.* slip; slide
reservación /ray-sayr-vah-see-óhn/ *n.* reservation
reservar /ray-sayr-váhr/ *v.* reserve

resfriado /rays-free-áh-doh/ *n.* head cold
residente /ray-see-dáyn-tay/ *n.* resident
resolver /ray-sohl-váyr/ *v.* resolve
respetar /rays-pay-táhr/ *n.* respect
respeto /rays-páy-toh/ *n.* respect
responder /rays-pohn-dáyr/ *v.* respond
responsable /rays-pohn-sáh-blay/ *n.* director; *adj.* responsible
respuesta /rays-pwáy-stah/ *n.* reply
restar /ray-stáhr/ *v.* substract
resto /ráy-stoh/ *n.* rest
restos /ráy-stohs/ *n.* remains
restaurante /rays-tah-oo-ráhn-tay/ *n.* restaurant
resultado /ray-sool-táh-doh/ *n.* result
retiro /ray-tée-roh/ *n.* retirement
retraso /ray-tráh-soh/ *n.* delay
reumatismo /ray-oo-mah-tées-moh/ *n.* rheumatism
reunión /ray-oo-nee-óhn/ *n.* meeting
revelar /ray-vay-láhr/ *v.* develop
revista /ray-vée-stah/ *n.* review; magazine
ribera /ree-báy-rah/ *n.* bank (of river)
rico /rée-coh/ *adj.* rich; delicious
riel /ree-áyl/ *n.* rail
riesgo /ree-áys-goh/ *n.* risk
rifle /rée-flay/ *n.* rifle
rincón /reen-cóhn/ *n.* corner
riñón /ree-nyóhn/ *n.* kidney
río /rée-oh/ *n.* river
riqueza /ree-káy-sah/ *n.* wealth

risa /rée-sah/ *n.* laughter
rizado /ree-sáh-doh/ *adj.* curly
rizar /ree-sáhr/ *v.* curl
rizo /rée-soh/ *n.* curl
robar /roh-báhr/ *v.* rob; steal
robo /róh-boh/ *n.* robbery
roca /róh-cah/ *n.* rock
rodilla /roh-dée-yah/ *n.* knee
rojo /róh-hoh/ *n., adj.* red
romance /roh-máhn-say/ *n.* romance
rompemuelles /rohm-pay-moo-áy-yays/ *n. Pe.* speed bumps
romper /rohm-páyr/ *v.* break
ron /rohn/ *n.* rum
roña /róh-nah/ *n.* scab; *Arg.* dirt
ropa /róh-pah/ *n.* clothes
ropa interior /róh-paheen-tay-ree-óhr/ *n.* underwear
ropero /roh-páy-roh/ *n.* closet
rosa /róh-sah/ *n.* rose
rosado /roh-sáh-doh/ *n., adj.* pink
rosetas de maíz /roh-sáy-tahs day mah-ées/ *n.* popcorn
rosita /roh-sée-tah/ *n. Chi.* earring
rositas de maíz /roh-sée-tahs day mah-ées/ *n. Cuba* popcorn
roto /róh-toh/ *adj.* broken
rubí /roo-bée/ *n.* ruby
rubio /róo-bee-oh/ *n., adj.* blond
rueda /roo-áy-dah/ *n.* wheel

ruido /roo-ée-doh/ *n.* noise
ruidoso /roo-ee-dóh-soh/ *adj.* noisy
ruta /róo-tah/ *n.* route
rutina /roo-tée-nah/ *n.* routine

- S -

sábado /sáh-bah-doh/ *n.* Saturday
sábana /sáh-bah-nah/ *n.* sheet
saber /sah-báyr/ *v.* know; know how to
sabiduría /sah-bee-doo-rée-ah/ *n.* wisdom
sabio /sáh-bee-oh/ *adj.* wise
sabor /sah-bóhr/ *n.* flavor; taste
saborear /sah-boh-ray-áhr/ *v.* savor; taste
sabroso /sah-bróh-soh/ *adj.* delicious
sacar foto /sah-cáhr fóh-toh/ *v.* take a picture
sacerdote /sah-sayr-dóh-tay/ *n.* priest
saco /sáh-coh/ *n.* sack; jacket
sacudir /sah-coo-déer/ *v.* shake; dust
sal /sahl/ *n.* salt; *CA, Mex., Uru.* misfortune
sala /sáh-lah/ *n. Cuba, Mex., Uru.* living room
salario /sah-láh-ree-oh/ *n.* wages
salchicha /sahl-chée-chah/ *n.* sausage; *Mex.* frankfurter
salida /sah-lée-dah/ *n.* exit; departure
salida del sol /sah-lee-dah dayl sohl/ *n.* sunrise
salir /sah-léer/ *v.* come out; leave
salmón /sahl-móhn/ *n.* salmon
salón /sah-lóhn/ *n.* salon; *Pe.* living room
salón de belleza /sah-lóhn day bay-yáy-sah/ *n.* beauty shop
salonero /sah-loh-náy-roh/ *n. Ec.* waiter
salpullido /sahl-poo-yée-doh/ *n.* rash

salsa /sáhl-sah/ *n.* sauce; gravy; dressing; *Carib.* tropical dance music
salsa picante /sáhl-sah pee-cáhn-tay/ *n.* chilli sauce
saltar /sahl-táhr/ *v.* jump
salud /sah-lóod/ *n.* health
saludable /sah-loo-dáh-blay/ *adj.* healthy
saludar /sah-loo-dáhr/ *v.* greet
saludo /sah-lóo-doh/ *n.* greeting
salvaje /sahl-váh-hay/ *adj.* wild
salvamento /sahl-vah-máyn-toh/ *n.* salvage; rescue
salvar /sahl-váhr/ *v.* save
sanar /sah-náhr/ *v.* heal; cure
sanción /sahn-see-óhn/ *n.* sanction; penalty
sancionar /sahn-see-oh-náhr/ *v.* sanction; penalize
sandalias /sahn-dáh-lee-ahs/ *n.* sandals
sandía /sahn-dée-ah/ *n.* watermelon
sánduche /sáhn-doo-chay/ *n. Ec.* sandwich
sandwich /sáhnd-oo-eech/ *n.* sandwich
sangrar /sahn-gráhr/ *v.* bleed
sangre /sáhn-gray/ *n.* blood
sanguche /sahn-góo-chay/ *n. Arg.* sandwich
sanitario /sah-nee-táh-ree-oh/ *n. Mex.* restroom; *adj.* sanitary
sano /sáh-noh/ *adj.* healthy
santo /sáhn-toh/ *n.* saint; *adj.* holy
santuario /sahn-too-áh-ree-oh/ *n.* sanctuary; shrine
sardina /sahr-dée-nah/ *n.* sardine
sastre /sáh-stray/ *n.* tailor
satisfacción /sah-tees-fahk-see-óhn/ *n.* satisfaction

satisfacer /sah-tees-fah-sáyr/ *v.* satisfy
satisfactorio /sah-tees-fahk-tóh-ree-oh/ *adj.* satisfactory
satisfecho /sah-tees-fáy-choh/ *adj.* satisfied
saya /sáh-yah/ *n. Cuba* skirt
sayuela /sah-yoo-áy-lah/ *n. Cuba* slip
sazón /sah-sóhn/ *n.* seasoning
secar /sáy-cáhr/ *v.* dry
sección /sayk-see-óhn/ *n.* section
seco /sáy-coh/ *adj.* dry
secretaria /say-cray-táh-ree-ah/ *n.* secretary (female)
secretario /say-cray-táh-ree-oh/ *n.* secretary (male)
secreto /say-cráy-toh/ *n.* secret
sed /sayd/ *n.* thirst
seda /sáy-dah/ *n.* silk
seguir /say-ghéer/ *v.* follow; continue
según /say-góon/ *prep.* according to
segundo /say-góon-doh/ *adj.* second
seguramente /say-goo-rah-máyn-tay/ *adv.* surely
seguridad /say-goo-ree-dáhd/ *n.* security
seguro /say-góo-roh/ *adj.* sure; safe
seguro de vida /say-góo-roh day vée-dah/ *n.* life insurance
seis /says/ *n., adj.* six
selección /say-layk-see-óhn/ *n.* selection
selva /sáyl-vah/ *n.* jungle; woods
sellar /say-yáhr/ *v.* stamp; seal
sello /sáy-yoh/ *n.* stamp; seal
semana /say-máh-nah/ *n.* week

semanal /say-mah-náhl/ *adj.* weekly
semana santa /say-máh-nah sáhn-tah/ *n.* Holy Week
semilla /say-mée-yah/ *n.* seed
senado /say-náh-doh/ *n.* senate
sencillo /sayn-sée-yoh/ *adj.* simple; single
sendero /sayn-dáy-roh/ *n.* path
sensación /sayn-sah-see-óhn/ *n.* sensation
sensible /sayn-sée-blay/ *adj.* sensitive
sensual /sayn-soo-áhl/ *adj.* sensual
sentimiento /sayn-tee-mee-áyn-toh/ *n.* feeling
sentar /sayn-táhr/ *v.* seat
sentarse /sayn-táhr-say/ *v.* sit down
sentencia /sayn-táyn-see-ah/ *n.* (leg.) sentence
sentido /sayn-tée-doh/ *n.* sense
señal /say-nyál/ *n.* signal; sign
señor /say-nyóhr/ *n.* sir; mister
señora /say-nyóh-rah/ *n.* missus
señorita /say-nyoh-rée-tah/ *n.* miss; young lady
separación /say-pah-rah-see-óhn/ *n.* separation
separado /say-pah-ráh-doh/ *adj.* separate
separar /say-pah-ráhr/ *v.* separate
septiembre /sayp-tee-áym-bray/ *n.* September
séptimo /sáyp-tee-moh/ *adj.* seventh
sequedad /say-kay-dáhd/ *n.* dryness; drought
ser /sayr/ *n.* being; essence; *v.* be
serenata /say-ray-náh-tah/ *n.* serenade
ser humano /sayr oo-máh-noh/ *n.* human being
serie /sáy-ree-ay/ *n.* series
serpiente /sayr-pee-áyn-tay/ *n.* serpent; snake

servicio /sayr-vée-see-oh/ *n.* service; restroom
servilleta /sayr-vee-yáy-táh/ *n.* napkin
servir /sayr-véer/ *v.* serve
sesión /say-see-óhn/ *n.* session
sesenta /say-sáyn-tah/ *n., adj.* sixty
setenta /say-táyn-tah/ *n., adj.* seventy
severo /say-váy-roh/ *adj.* severe; strict
sexo /sáyk-soh/ *n.* sex
sexto /sáyks-toh/ *adj.* sixth
si /see/ *conj.* if; whether
si /see/ *adv.* yes; indeed
siempre /see-áym-pray/ *adv.* always
siempre que /see-áym-pray kay/ *adv., conj.* whenever
sierra /see-áy-rah/ *n.* mountain range; saw
sierva /see-áyr-vah/ *n. Arg.* maid
siesta /see-áy-stah/ *n.* midday rest
siete /see-áy-tay/ *n., adj.* seven
siglo /séeg-loh/ *n.* century
significado /seeg-nee-fee-cáh-doh/ *n.* meaning
silbar /seel-báhr/ *v.* whistle
silbato /seel-báh-toh/ *n.* whistle
silencioso /see-layn-see-óh-soh/ *adj.* silent; quiet
silla /sée-yah/ *n.* chair
silla de montar /sée-yah day mohn-táhr/ *n.* saddle
sillón /see-yóhn/ *n.* easy chair
sí mismo /see mées-moh/ *pron.* oneself
símbolo /séem boh-loh/ *n.* symbol
similar /see-mee-láhr/ *adj.* similar
simpático /seem-páh-tee-coh/ *adj.* nice; charming

simplificar /seem-plee-fee-cáhr/ *v.* simplify
sin /seen/ *prep.* without
sincero /seen-sáy-roh/ *adj.* sincere
sindicato /seen-dee-cáh-toh/ *n.* labor union
sin embargo /seen aym-báhr-goh/ *adv.* nevertheless
sin falta /seen fáhl-tah/ *adv.* without fail
singular /seen-goo-láhr/ *adj.* singular
sin mancha /seen máhn-chah/ *adj.* unblemished
sino /sée-noh/ *conj.* but rather
síntoma /séen-toh-mah/ *n.* symptom
sirope /see-róh-pay/ *n. Cuba* syrup
sirvienta /seer-vee-áyn-tah/ *n.* servant; maid
sirviente /seer-vee-áyn-tay/ *n.* servant
sistema /sees-táy-mah/ *n.* system
situación /see-too-ah-see-óhn/ *n.* situation; position
situado /see-too-áh-doh/ *adj.* located
sobre /sóh-bray/ *n.* envelope; *prep.* on; upon
sobrepasar /soh-bray-pah-sáhr/ *v.* exceed; *Pe.* pass (in car)
sobrepeso /soh-bray-páy-soh/ *n.* overweight
sobrina /soh-brée-nah/ *n.* niece
sobrino /soh-brée-noh/ *n.* nephew
social /soh-see-áhl/ *adj.* social
sociedad /soh-see-ay-dáhd/ *n.* society; company
socio /sóh-see-oh/ *n.* partner; *Cuba* buddy
socorro /soh-cóh-roh/ *n.* help; *imper.* help
soda /sóh-dah/ *n.* club soda
sol /sohl/ *n.* sun
solamente /soh-lah-máyn-tay/ *adv.* only

soldado /sohl-dáh-doh/ *n.* soldier
solicitar /soh-lee-see-táhr/ *v.* seek
sólido /sóh-lee-doh/ *n., adj.* solid
solo /sóh-loh/ *adj.* only; alone
soltar /sohl-táhr/ *v.* let go; release
soltera /sohl-táy-rah/ *n., adj.* single (woman)
soltero /sohl-táy-roh/ *n., adj.* single (bachelor)
solución /soh-loo-see-óhn/ *n.* solution
sombra /sóhm-brah/ *n.* shade
sombrero /sohm bráy-roh/ *n.* hat
someter /soh-may-táyr/ *v.* submit
sonar /soh-náhr/ *v.* sound
sonido /soh-née-doh/ *n.* sound
sonreír /sohn-ray-éer/ *v.* smile
sonrisa /sohn-rée-sah/ *n.* smile
soñar /soh-nyár/ *v.* dream
sopa /sóh-pah/ *n.* soup
sorbente /sohr-báyn-tay/ *n. Cuba* drinking straw
sorbete /sohr-báy-tay/ *n. Ec.* drinking straw
sordo /sóhr-doh/ *adj.* deaf
sorprender /sohr-prayn-dáyr/ *v.* surprise
sorpresa /sohr-práy-sah/ *n.* surprise
sospechar /sohs-pay-cháhr/ *v.* suspect
sótano /sóh-tah-noh/ *n.* basement
su /soo/ *adj.* his; her; its; their; your; one's
suave /soo-áh-vay/ *adj.* smooth; soft
subir /soo-béer/ *v.* go up
subscribir /soos-cree-béer/ *v.* subscribe
subscripción /soos-creep-see-óhn/ *n.* subscription

substituir /soob-stee-too-éer/ *v.* substitute; replace
subterráneo /soob-tay-ráh-nay-oh/ *n. Arg., Bol.* subway
suburbio /soo-bóor-bee-oh/ *n.* suburb
suceder /soo-say-dáyr/ *v.* happen
suciedad /soo-see-ay-dáhd/ *n.* dirt; filth
sucio /sóo-see-oh/ *adj.* dirty
sucursal /soo-coor-sáhl/ *n.* (com.) branch
sudamericano /sood-ah-may-ree-cáh-noh/ *n., adj.* South American
sudar /soo-dáhr/ *v.* sweat
sudor /soo-dóhr/ *n.* sweat
suegra /swáy-grah/ *n.* mother-in-law
suegro /swáy-groh/ *n.* father-in-law
suela /swáy-lah/ *n.* sole of shoe
sueldo /swáyl-doh/ *n.* salary
suelo /swáy-loh/ *n.* ground
suelto /swáyl-toh/ *adj.* loose
sueño /swáy-nyo/ *n.* dream; sleep
suerte /swáyr-tay/ *n.* luck
suéter /swáy-tayr/ *n.* sweater
suficiente /soo-fee-see-áyn-tay/ *adj.* sufficient; enough
sufrir /soo-fréer/ *v.* suffer
sugerir /soo-hay-réer/ *v.* suggest
sugestión /soo-hays-tee-óhn/ *n.* suggestion
sumamente /soo-mah-máyn-tay/ *adv.* extremely
sumar /soo-máhr/ *v.* add
suministro /soo-mee-nées-troh/ *n.* supply

sumisión /soo-mee-see-óhn/ *n.* submission
superficial /soo-payr-fee-see-áhl/ *adj.* superficial
superficie /soo-payr-fée-see-ay/ *n.* surface
superintendente /soo-pay-reen-tayn-dáyn-tay/ *n.* superintendent; supervisor
superior /soo-pay-ree-óhr/ *adj.* superior; upper
supersticioso /soo-payr-stee-see-óh-soh/ *adj.* superstitious
supervisar /soo-payr-vee-sáhr/ *v.* supervise
suplemento /soo-play-máyn-toh/ *n.* supplement
suponer /soo-poh-náyr/ *v.* suppose
sur /soor/ *n.* south
surtido /soor-tée-doh/ *n.* selection; supply
suspirar /sos-pee-ráhr/ *v.* sigh
susto /sóos-toh/ *n.* scare
susurrar /soo-soo-ráhr/ *v.* whisper
susurro /soo-sóo-roh/ *n.* whisper

- T -

tabaco /tah-báh-coh/ *n.* tobacco; *CA, Cuba, Ven.* cigar
tableta /tah-bláy-tah/ *n.* tablet
taburete /tah-boo-ráy-tay/ *n.* stool
tacón /tah-cóhn/ *n.* heel
tacho /táh-choh/ *n.* *Arg.* garbage can; taxi
tal /tahl/ *adj.* such; such a
talón /tah-lóhn/ *n.* heel; stub (check)
tal vez /tahl vays/ *adv.* perhaps
tamaño /tah-máh-nyoh/ *n.* size
también /tahm-bee-áyn/ *adv.* too; also
tampoco /tahm-póh-coh/ *adv.* neither; not either
tangerina /tahn-hay-rée-nah/ *n.* tangerine
tan pronto como /tahn próhn-toh cóh-moh/ as soon as
tapa /táh-pah/ *n.* cover; lid
tapera /tah-páy-rah/ *n.* *SA* shack
tapete /tah-páy-tay/ *n.* *Mex.* throw rug
tapón /tah-póhn/ *n.* stopper; plug
taquilla /tah-kéy-yah/ *n.* box office; *CR* tavern
tardar /tahr-dáhr/ *v.* delay; be late
tarde /táhr-day/ *n.* afternoon; *adv.* late
tarifa /tah-rée-fah/ *n.* tariff; fare
tarjeta /tahr-háy-tah/ *n.* card
tarjeta de presentación /tahr-háy-tah day pray-sayn--tah-see-óhn/ *n.* business card

tarjeta postal /tahr-háy-tah pohs-táhl/ *n.* postcard
tarta /táhr-tah/ *n. Bol., Uru.* pie
tarro /táh-roh/ *n.* jar; *LA* beer mug
tasa /táh-sah/ *n.* rate
taxi /táhk-see/ *n.* taxi
taxímetro /tahk-sée-may-troh/ *n.* taxi meter; *Uru.* taxi
taza /táh-sah/ *n.* cup; bowl; toilet bowl
tazón /tah-sóhn/ *n.* bowl
té /tay/ *n.* tea
teatro /tay-áh-troh/ *n.* theater
teclado /tay-cláh-doh/ *n.* keyboard
técnico /táyk-nee-coh/ *n.* technician; *adj.* technical
tela /táy-lah/ *n.* cloth; fabric
teléfono /tay-láy-foh-noh/ *n.* telephone
telegrama /tay-lay-gráh-mah/ *n.* telegram
tema /táy-mah/ *n.* theme; subject
temblor /taym-blóhr/ *n.* tremor; earthquake
temer /tay-máyr/ *v.* fear
temperatura /taym-pay-rah-tóo-rah/ *n.* temperature
temporada /taym-poh-ráh-dah/ *n.* season
temporal /taym-poh-ráhl/ *adj.* temporary
temprano /taym-práh-noh/ *adj., adv.* early
tendero /tayn-dáy-roh/ *n.* grocer; shopkeeper
tenedor /tay-nay-dóhr/ *n.* fork
tener /tay-náyr/ *v.* have; own
tener cuidado /tay-náyr coo-ee-dáh-doh/ *v.* be careful
tener éxito /tay-náyr áyk-see-toh/ *v.* be successful
tener hambre /tay-náyr áhm-bray/ *v.* be hungry
tener miedo /tay-náyr mee-áy-doh/ *v.* be afraid

tener que /tay-náyr kay/ *v.* have to; must
tener razón /tay-náyr rah-sóhn/ *v.* be right
tener recursos para /tay-náyr ray-cóor-sohs páh-rah/ *v.* afford
tener sed /tay-náyr sayd/ *v.* be thirsty
tenis /táy-nees/ *n.* tennis
teñir /tay-nyéer/ *v.* dye
tequila /tay-kéy-lah/ *n. Mex.* liquor distilled from maguey plant
tercer(o) /tayr-sáyr-(oh)/ *adj.* third
tercera parte /tayr-sáy-rah páhr-tay/ *n.* third
terminar /tayr-mee-náhr/ *v.* finish; end
término /táyr-mee-noh/ *n.* term
ternera /tayr-náy-rah/ *n.* veal
terremoto /tay-ray-móh-toh/ *n.* earthquake
terrible /tay-rée-blay/ *adj.* terrible
territorio /tay-ree-tóh-ree-oh/ *n.* territory
testamento /tays-tah-máyn-toh/ *n.* (leg.) will
testigo /tays-tée-goh/ *n.* witness
tiburón /tee-boo-róhn/ *n.* shark
tiempo /tee-áym-poh/ *n.* time; weather
tienda /tee-áyn-dah/ *n.* store; tent; *Pe.* department store
tienda de abarrotes /tee-áyn-dah day ah-bah-róh--tays/ *n. Mex.* grocery store
tienda de campaña /tee-áyn-dah day cahm-páh-nyah/ *n.* tent
tienda de departamentos /tee-áyn-dah day day-pahr--tah-máyn-tohs/ *n.* department store

tienda de segunda mano /tee-áyn-dah day say-góon--dah máh-noh/ *n.* secondhand store
tierra /tee-áy-rah/ *n.* land; earth
tijeras /tee-háy-rahs/ *n.* scissors
timbre /téem-bray/ *n.* bell; *Mex.* postage stamp
tímido /tée-mee-doh/ *adj.* shy; timid
tina /tée-nah/ *n. Mex.* bathtub
tinta /téen-tah/ *n.* ink
tinte /téen-tay/ *n.* dye
tía /tée-ah/ *n.* aunt
tío /tée-oh/ *n.* uncle
típico /tée-pee-coh/ *adj.* typical; regional
tipo de cambio /tée-poh day cáhm-bee-oh/ *n.* rate of exchange
tirar /tee-ráhr/ *v.* pull
tiro /tée-roh/ *n.* shot
títere /tée-tay-ray/ *n.* puppet
título /tée-too-loh/ *n.* title; degree
toalla /toh-áh-yah/ *n.* towel
tobillo /toh-bée-yoh/ *n.* ankle
tocar /toh-cáhr/ *v.* touch; knock; play (instrument)
tocino /toh-sée-noh/ *n.* bacon
todavía /toh-dah-vée-ah/ *adv.* still; yet
todo /tóh-doh/ *adj.* all; every
todo el mundo /tóh-doh ayl móon-doh/ *pron.* everybody
toma-corriente /tóh-mah-coh-ree-áyn-tay/ *n.* (elect.) outlet
tomate /toh-máh-tay/ *n.* tomato

tomar /toh-máhr/ *v.* take; eat; drink
tonelada /toh-nay-láh-dah/ *n.* ton
tontería /tohn-tay-rée-ah/ *n.* nonsense
tonto /tóhn-toh/ *adj.* dumb; silly
topes /tóh-pays/ *n. Mex.* speed bumps
tormenta /tohr-máyn-tah/ *n.* storm
tornillo /tohr-née-yoh/ *n.* screw
toronja /toh-róhn-hah/ *n.* grapefruit
torre /tóh-ray/ *n.* tower
torta /tóhr-tah/ *n. Arg.* pie; *Ec.* cake; *Mex.* sandwich on roll; *Uru.* pancake; cake
tortilla /tohr-tée-yah/ *n.* tortilla; *Cuba* omelet
tortuga /tohr-tóo-gah/ *n.* turtle
tos /tohs/ *n.* cough
toscano /tohs-cáh-noh/ *n. Arg.* cigar
tosco /tóhs-coh/ *adj. Ven.* rude
total /toh-táhl/ *n., adj.* total
trabajar /trah-bah-háhr/ *v.* work
trabajo /trah-báh-hoh/ *n.* work; trouble
traducción /trah-dook-see-óhn/ *n.* translation
traducir /trah-doo-séer/ *v.* translate
traer /trah-áyr/ *v.* bring
tráfico /tráh-fee-coh/ *n.* traffic
tragar /trah-gáhr/ *v.* swallow
trago /tráh-goh/ *n.* swallow; *Carib., Mex.* drink (alcoholic)
traje /tráh-hay/ *n.* suit; costume
trampa /tráhm-pah/ *n.* trap; trick
tranquilo /trahn-kéy-loh/ *adj.* calm; peaceful

transbordador /trahns-bohr-dah-dóhr/ *n.* ferry
transferencia /trahns-fay-ráyn-see-ah/ *n.* transfer
transmitir /trahns-mee-téer/ *v.* transmit
transportar /trahns-pohr táhr/ *v.* transport
transporte /trahns-póhr-tay/ *n.* transportation
trapeador /trah-pay-ah-dóhr/ *n. Ec.* slang
tratado /trah-táh-doh/ *n.* treaty
tratamiento /trah-tah-mee-áyn-toh/ *n.* (med.) treatment
trato /tráh-toh/ *n.* treatment; deal
trece /tráy-say/ *n., adj.* thirteen
treinta /tráyn-tah/ *n., adj.* thirty
tremendo /tray-máyn-doh/ *adj.* tremendous
tren /trayn/ *n.* train
trenza /tráyn-sah/ *n.* braid
tres /trays/ *n., adj.* three
tribu /trée-boo/ *n.* tribe
trigo /trée-goh/ *n.* wheat
trinche /tréen-chay/ *n. Andes, Mex.* fork
tripa /trée-pah/ *n.* tripe
tripulación /tree-poo-lah-see-óhn/ *n.* crew
triste /trée-stay/ *adj.* sad
tristeza /tree-stáy-sah/ *n.* sadness
tropical /troh-pee-cáhl/ *adj.* tropical
trópico /tróh-pee-coh/ *n.* tropic
trucha /tróo-chah/ *n.* trout
truco /tróo-coh/ *n.* trick
tu /too/ *adj.* your (familiar)
tú /too/ *pron.* you (familiar)

tumba /tóom-bah/ *n.* tomb
túnel /tóo-nayl/ *n.* tunnel
turno /tóor-noh/ *n.* turn

- U -

último /óol-tee-moh/ *adj.* last
un /oon/ *art.* a; an
una /óon-ah/ *art.* a; an
una vez /óon-ah vays/ *adv.* once
único /óo-nee-coh/ *adj.* only
unidad /oo-nee-dáhd/ *n.* unit; unity
uniforme /oo-nee-fóhr-may/ *n., adj.* uniform
unión /oo-nee-óhn/ *n.* union
universidad /oo-nee-vayr-see-dáhd/ *n.* university
un (o) /óo-noh/ *adj., pron.* one
unos /óo-nohs/ *adj., pron.* some
uno u otro /óo-noh oo óh-troh/ *pron.* one or the other
uña /óo-nya/ *n.* fingernail
urbano /oor-báh-noh/ *adj.* urban
urgente /oor-háyn-tay/ *adj.* urgent
usar /oo-sáhr/ *v.* use
uso /óo-soh/ *n.* use
usted /oo-stáy/ *pron.* you
ustedes /oo-stáy-days/ *pron.* (plural) you
usual /oo-soo-áhl/ *adj.* usual
útil /óo-teel/ *adj.* useful
uva /óo-vah/ *n.* grape

- V -

vacancia /vah-cáhn-see-ah/ *n.* vacancy
vacante /vah-cáhn-tay/ *adj.* vacant
vacilar /vah-see-láhr/ *v.* vacillate
vacío /vah-sée-oh/ *adj.* empty
vacíos /vah-sée-ohs/ *n. Pe.* (plural) empties
vacunar /vah-coo-náhr/ *n.* vaccinate
vago /váh-goh/ *adj. Cuba* lazy
vagón /vah-góhn/ *n. Ec.* sleeping car (train)
vagón comedor /vah-góhn coh-may-dóhr/ *n. Uru.* dining car
vainilla /vah-ee-née-yah/ *n.* vanilla
valer /vah-láyr/ *v.* be worth
válido /váh-leedoh/ *adj.* valid
valiente /vah-lee-áyn-tay/ *adj.* brave
valioso /vah-lee-óh-soh/ *adj.* valuable
valle /váh-yay/ *n.* valley
valor /vah-lóhr/ *n.* value; courage
valores /vah-lóh-rays/ *n.* valuables
vals /vahls/ *n.* waltz
valuar /vah-loo-áhr/ *v.* value
vapor /vah-póhr/ *n.* steam
variable /vah-ree-áh-blay/ *adj.* variable
variado /vah-ree-áh-doh/ *adj.* varied
variedad /vah-ree-ay-dáhd/ *n.* variety
varios /váh-ree-ohs/ *adj.* various
vaso /váh-soh/ *n.* drinking glass

vaya /váh-yah/ *imper. Arg.* hurry up
vecindad /vay-seen-dáhd/ *n.* neighborhood
vecino /vay-sée-noh/ *n.* neighbor
vegetal /vay-hay-táhl/ *n., adj.* vegetable
vegetariano /vay-hay-tah-ree-áh-noh/ *n., adj.* vegetarian
vehículo /vay-ée-coo-loh/ *n.* vehicle
veinte /váyn-tay/ *n., adj.* twenty
vela /váy-lah/ *n.* candle; sail
velocidad /vay-loh-see-dáhd/ *n.* speed
venado /vay-náh-doh/ *n.* deer
vencido /vayn-sée-doh/ *adj.* conquered; expired
vendedor /vayn-day-dóhr/ *n.* salesman; *Arg.* clerk
vender /vayn-dáyr/ *v.* sell
venir /vay-néer/ *v.* come
venta /váyn-tah/ *n.* sale; SD grocery store
venta al mayoreo /váyn-tah ahl mah-yoh-ráy-oh/ *n.* wholesale
venta al menudeo /váyn-tah ahl may-noo-dáy-oh/ *n.* retail
ventaja /vayn-táh-hah/ *n.* advantage
ventana /vay-táh-nah/ *n.* window
ventilador /vayn-tee-lah-dóhr/ *n.* electric fan
ver /vayr/ *v.* see
verano /vay-ráh-noh/ *n.* summer
verbal /vayr báhl/ *adj.* verbal
verbo /váyr-boh/ *n.* verb
verdad /vayr-dáhd/ *n.* truth
¿Verdad? /vayr-dáhd/ *interr.* Right?

verdadero /vayr-dah-dáy-roh/ *adj.* true; real
verde /váyr-day/ *adj.* green
vereda /vay-ráy-dah/ *n.* path; *Ec., Pe., Uru.* sidewalk
vergüenza /vayr-gwáyn-sah/ *n.* shame
verruga /vay-róo-gah/ *n.* wart
versátil /vayr-sáh-teel/ *adj.* versatile
vestido /vay-stée-doh/ *n.* dress
vestir /vay-stéer/ *v.* dress
vía /vée-ah/ *n.* way; route
viaducto /vee-ah-dóok-toh/ *n.* viaduct
viajar /vee-ah-háhr/ *v.* travel
viaje /vee-áh-hay/ *n.* trip
víbora /vée-boh-rah/ *n.* snake
víctima /véek-tee-mah/ *n.* victim
vida /vée-dah/ *n.* life
vidrio /vée-dree-oh/ *n.* glass
viejo /vee-áy-hoh/ *n.* old man; *adj.* old
viento /vee-áyn-toh/ *n.* wind
viernes /vee-ayr-nays/ *n.* Friday
vigilar /vee-hee-láhr/ *v.* watch; guard
villa /vée-yah/ *n.* town; *Arg.* slum
vinagre /vee-náh-gray/ *n.* vinegar
vino /vée-noh/ *n.* wine
vino de Jerez /vée-noh day hay-ráys/ *n.* sherry
violación /vee-oh-lah-see-óhn/ *n.* violation; rape
violar /vee-oh-láhr/ *v.* violate; rape
violencia /vee-oh-láyn-see-ah/ *n.* violence
violento /vee-oh-lóyn-toh/ *adj.* violent
viruela /vee-roo-áy-lah/ *n.* smallpox

visa /vée-sah/ *n.* visa
visita /vee-sée-tah/ *n.* visit
visitante /vee-see-táhn-tay/ *n.* visitor
visitar /vee-see-táhr/ *v.* visit
viso /vée-soh/ *n. Uru.* slip
vista /vée-stah/ *n.* view
viuda /vee-óo-dah/ *n.* widow
viudo /vee-óo-doh/ *n.* widower
víveres /vée-vay-rays/ *n.* groceries
vivir /vee-véer/ *v.* live
vivo /vée-voh/ *adj.* alive; clever
volar /voh-láhr/ *v.* fly
voltio /vóhl-tee-oh/ *n.* volt
volumen /voh-lóo-mayn/ *n.* volume
voluntad /voh-loon-táhd/ *n.* will
volver /vohl-váyr/ *v.* return
volverse /vohl-váyr-say/ *v.* become
vomitar /voh-mee-táhr/ *v.* vomit
vómito /vóh-mee-toh/ *n.* vomit
votar /voh-táhr/ *v.* vote
voto /vóh-toh/ *n.* vote
vos /vohs/ *pron. SA* used instead of familiar *tú* you
voz /vohs/ *n.* voice
vuelo /vwáy-loh/ *n.* flight

- X -

xilófono /see-lóh-foh-noh/ *n.* xylophone

- Y -

y /ee/ *conj.* and
ya /yah/ *adv.* already; now
yate /yáh-tay/ *n.* yacht
yerno /ee-áyr-noh/ *n.* son-in-law
yo /yoh/ *pron.* I

- Z -

zacate /sah-cáh-tay/ *n. CA, Mex.* grass
zafacón /sah-fah-cóhn/ *n. PR* wastebasket
zafiro /sah-fée-roh/ *n.* sapphire
zanahoria /sah-nah-óh-ree-ah/ *n.* carrot
zancudo /sahn-cóo-doh/ *n.* mosquito
zapallo /sah-páh-yoh/ *n. Andes, RP* pumpkin
zapato /sah-páh-toh/ *n.* shoe
zarcillos /sahr-sée-yohs/ *n. Ven.* earrings
zócalo /sóh-cah-loh/ *n. Mex.* main square
zona /sóh-nah/ *n.* zone
zopilote /soh-pee-lóh-tay/ *n. CA, Mex.* buzzard
zorrillo /soh-rée-yoh/ *n. Arg., Bol., CA, Mex.* skunk
zorro /sóh-roh/ *n.* fox
zumo /sóo-moh/ *n. CR* juice

Other Spanish Interest Titles from Hippocrene

SPANISH GRAMMAR
224 pages - 5 ½ x 8 ½ - ISBN 0-87052-893-9 - W - $12.95pb - (273)

SPANISH-ENGLISH/ ENGLISH-SPANISH PRACTICAL DICTIONARY
338 pages - 5 ½ x 8 ¼ - 35,000 entries - ISBN 0-7818-0179-6 - NA - $9.95pb - (211)

SPANISH-ENGLISH/ ENGLISH-SPANISH CONCISE DICTIONARY (Latin America)
310 pages - 4 x 6 - 8,000 entries - ISBN 0-7818-0261-x - W - $11.95pb - (258)

MASTERING SPANISH
338 pages - 5 ½ X 8 ½ - ISBN 0-87052-059-8 - USA - $11.95 - (527)
2 cassettes: ISBN 0-87052-067-9 - USA - $12.95 - (426)

MASTERING ADVANCED SPANISH
326 pages - 5 ½ x 8 ½ - ISBN 0-7818-0081-1 - W - $14.95pb - (413)
2 cassettes: ISBN 0-7818-0089-7 - W - $12.95 - (426)

SPANISH HANDY DICTIONARY
120 pages - 5 x 7 ¾ - ISBN 0-7818-0012-9 - W - $8.95pb - (189)

SPANISH-ENGLISH/ ENGLISH-SPANISH DICTIONARY OF COMPUTER TERMS
120 pages - 5 ½ x 8 ½ - 5,700 entries - ISBN 0-7818-0148-6 - W - $16.95hc - (36)